REPRESENTATIVE

AMERICAN SPEECHES

1984–1985

edited by OWEN PETERSON
Professor, Department of Speech Communication
Louisiana State University

THE REFERENCE SHELF

Volume 57 Number 3

THE H. W. WILSON COMPANY

New York   1985

THE REFERENCE SHELF

The books in this series contain reprints of articles, excerpts from books, and addresses on current issues and social trends in the United States and other countries. There are six separately bound numbers in each volume, all of which are generally published in the same calendar year. One number is a collection of recent speeches; each of the others is devoted to a single subject and gives background information and discussion from various points of view, concluding with a comprehensive bibliography. Books in the series may be purchased individually or on subscription.

Library of Congress Cataloging this serial as follows:

Representative American speeches. 1937/38–
    New York, H. W. Wilson Co.
    v. 21 cm. (The Reference Shelf)
    Annual.
    Indexes:
    Author index: 1937/38–1959/60, with 1959/60;
    1960/61–1969/70, with 1969/70; 1970/71–1979/80,
with 1979/80.
    Editors: 1937/38–1958/59, A.C. Baird.—1959/60–69/70, L.
Thonssen.—1970/71–1979/80, W.W. Braden.—1980/81– O.
Peterson
    Key title: Representative American speeches, ISSN 0197–6923.
    1. American orations—20th century. 2. Speeches, addresses, etc.
1. Baird, Albert Craig, 1883– ed. II. Thonsen,
Lester, 1904– ed. III. Braden, Waldo Warder, 1911– ed.
IV. Peterson, Owen, 1924– ed. V. Series.
PS668.B3   815.5082   38–27962
                                                  MARC-S

    Library of Congress   [8402r61]rev3

Printed in the United States of America

CONTENTS

DETERMINING FOREIGN POLICY

A TIME TO REMEMBER

NATIONAL CHALLENGES AND PRIORITIES

PREFACE

Following the Chinese custom of naming years, if one had named 1983 the "Year of the Secondary Schools," then 1984 was surely the "Year of the Presidential Election." Of the many rhetorical events commanding attention during the years, most were related to the election.

As early as May, the Democratic primaries in various states had already produced a dozen debates which, in the opinion of one political analyst, would have more to do with how people voted than all the political commercials seen on television (H. Raines, *New York Times,* June 27, 1984, p. 10). Although the nominees had already been determined, the national conventions provided each party with an opportunity to influence the electorate. To counter the effect of the Democrats' selection of Geraldine Ferraro as the first woman vice-presidential candidate by a major party, the Republicans featured speeches by several prominent GOP women at their convention. The Democrats, after their discordant primary campaign, attempted to turn their convention into a display of unity with major addresses by those who had been the main challengers to nominee Walter Mondale.

The presidential campaign itself was lackluster. Both parties relied heavily on spot commercial messages to influence the electorate. A positive feature of the election was two debates between the major parties' presidential nominees and one exchange between the vice-presidential candidates. The debates were not without problems, however. Critics complained about format, while and the media and viewing public too often tended to focus on trivial matters—the speakers' use of notes, eye contact, hesitation—and apparently judged the participants' performances more on personality than their handling of issues. Still, the debates presented the voters with their only opportunity to see and compare the candidates together.

While the various televised debates may have contributed somewhat to voters' understanding of the candidates and their positions in both the primaries and the general election, among impartial, veteran political observers, there was almost universal agreement that image and symbols were far more crucial than substance in the outcome of the 1984 elections.

In any case, the 1984 campaign was the longest and most expensive in United States history. Because of the high cost of television advertising, candidates for national office were increasingly dependent on financial support from political action committees and pressure groups. Critics of the influence of special interest groups suffered a major setback on March 18, 1985, when the United States Supreme Court ruled that the First Amendment protected unlimited independent campaign expenditures by political action groups.

After the political scene, the quality of American education, highlighted by a series of reports and conferences in 1983, continued to be a main concern of public speakers in 1984–85. Other topics of major address during the year were foreign policy and the need for corporate and civic responsibility.

Some of the most important speeches each year are given by speakers who call attention to significant problems that have been generally overlooked, ignored, or neglected. This year's volume includes several addresses reminding the country of ethical and more commitments that must be met.

Remembrances are important. Speeches which inspire us by recalling the accomplishments, contributions, and sacrifices of others help to pass on our heritage from one generation to the next. Three such inspirational addresses appear in this volume.

Many have contributed to the preparation of this volume. I particularly want to thank Anne-Marie Ecuyer for the valuable assistance. I also wish to express appreciation to Dennis Cali, Virginia Conrad, Eugenie Haik, and Jean Jackson for their contributions.

As usual, my colleagues at Louisiana State University have provided me with support and useful advice. I especially thank Waldo W. Braden, Dan Brown, Stephen L. Cooper, Gresdna Doty, Mary Frances HopKins, Francine Merritt, Harold Mixon, and James Traynham.

I appreciate the assistance of the many persons who have supplied me with information about the speeches, speakers, audiences, and occasions for the addresses in this year's collection. I particularly want to thank David P. Bryden, Betsy Freeman, Bob Haakenson, Julie T. Hoover, Randy Huwa, Robert C. Jeffrey, Ray Johnsen, Kay Kahler, Beverly Whitaker Long, U.S. Representative Tom Lantos, Susan Lendkering, Rev. Robert N. Lynch, John Patton, Jackie Rider, Virginia Sassaman, Stephen C. Schlesinger, Professor Robert Schmuhl, Russell Shaw, Senator Paul Simon, Barbara Vandegrift, and U.S. Representative Sidney Yates.

Owen Peterson

Baton Rouge, Louisiana
May 18, 1985

DEMOCRACY'S MOST IMPORTANT RIGHT:
TO VOTE[1]

Leonard Goldenson[2]

"Why don't more Americans vote?" asked veteran political commentator Richard L. Strout in the *Christian Science Monitor* on January 11, 1985. Citing the latest figures from the Committee for the Study of the American Elector, he noted that only 53.3% of eligible voters cast their ballots in the 1984 presidential election, the smallest percentage of any democracy. In contrast, in most recent elections in their countries the number of eligible voters casting ballots in Belgium was 94%, West Germany and Italy 89%, France 85%, Spain 79%, and Britain 72%. Strout also noted that in the past 28 years, United States voter turnout in presidential elections has dropped from 62.8 to 53.3%.

In the middle of the 1984 presidential campaign, Leonard H. Goldenson, chairman of the board and chief executive officer of the American Broadcasting Companies, Inc., addressed this question in a speech to members of the International Radio and Television Society on September 25, 1984. For many years Mr. Goldenson had been active in his concern over the decline in American voting and had worked to solve it through a series of public service activities carried out by ABC. These included the Symposium on American Voter Participation, cosponsored by ABC and Harvard University, the formation of an Advisory Committee on Voter Education to carry out recommendations of the symposium, and the initiation of a broad public affairs program at ABC designed to educate and inform potential voters.

Mr. Goldenson's speech was given at the first Newsmaker Luncheon of the International Radio and Television Society (IRTS) of the 1984–85 season. The organization holds nine such luncheon meetings a year. The IRTS is an organization of individuals professionally engaged in management, sales, or executive production in the radio, television, and cable industries and their allied fields. It sponsors annual seminars, college conferences, and summer internships for college students majoring in communications.

Following the noon luncheon, in the Grand Ballroom of the Waldorf-

---

[1]Delivered to the International Radio and Television Society at its first monthly luncheon lecture in the Grand Ballroom of the Waldorf-Astoria in New York City at 1:30 P.M. on September 25, 1984.

[2]For biographical note, see Appendix.

Astoria Hotel in New York City, Goldenson began his address at approximately 1:30 P.M. He spoke to an audience of 925 people in the communications industry, members of the IRTS and their guests, the press, and others.

Leonard Goldenson's speech: I remember back in 1960 discussing the possibility of election-year debates with Frank Stanton and others. Later that year, television and radio for the first time brought presidential debates into living rooms across America, and I was very excited about prospects for the republic and the contribution that we could make to its welfare. After all, voting turnout in that election hit nearly 63%, the highest in years. It struck me that with the help of modern broadcasting, America could restore the extraordinary voting patterns we enjoyed in the late 19th century and create an even more vibrant democracy.

But what has happened since has been a national embarrassment. Voting turnouts have steadily declined, falling by over 10 percentage points to a low of under 53% in 1980. Our current President came into office with the votes of only one-fourth of our citizenry. For every voter who pulled the lever in his favor, two stayed home. Among the 24 major industrial democracies in the world, the United States sank next to the bottom in voter participation.

People ask: what difference does it make? And indeed, some studies indicate that if all of our eligible voters had come out in 1980, most of the same men and women would have been elected. But that's not the point.

The point is that the right to vote represents one of our most cherished institutions, "the crown jewel of our democracy," as President Reagan has said. A vote cast freely and in private is an expression of the people's will—a covenant between the governed and those who exercise power in their name. When a person casts a ballot, he makes an investment of faith and trust in a candidate; in return, he expects the candidate to live up to a high standard of responsibility. A bond is formed that can sustain those who govern through bad times as well as good. Moreover, voting is a part of the discipline—the responsibility, if you will—of maintaining a democracy. As much as anything else we do, it symbolizes our commitment to our system of government.

But when people refuse to vote—when they refuse to make that pledge of support—our candidates enter public office with little more than a victory built on a house of cards. They have neither a bond nor a mandate for governing. It is no coincidence that during this past quarter century, when voting sharply declined, there was a marked increase in people's dissatisfaction with their government.

The mystery that surrounds these past 25 years is why voter turnout has dropped so much. Logic would say it should have increased. The higher the income and education, for example, the more likely a person is to vote. Both have gone up, but it hasn't affected the number of people who vote. The nation has also dismantled many of the highest legal barriers to voting identified by a presidential commission two decades ago. Literacy tests and poll taxes, for example, have become relics of the past. And during this same time, the commercial networks have more than doubled their time for public affairs programming, while the number of all-news and talk shows has exploded on radio and television. So, where have all the voters gone?

In December, 1982, I made a trip to the John F. Kennedy School of Government at Harvard to pose that question and to talk about ways to address it. I proposed that in order to ensure "gavel-to-gavel" coverage of party conventions, the three commercial networks each pay for a third of the cost for Public Broadcasting Service to carry the full proceedings. We would each continue our coverage of major convention news, but PBS would keep its camera rolling from beginning to end. Though that idea did not come to fruition, I'm happy to say that both Cable News Network and C-Span did carry the full convention schedules. What concerns me, however, is that full proceedings were still not available to the 60% of American viewers who did not have cable or cannot afford it. I think the three networks need to reassess the situation in 1988, and reconsider the idea of funding full coverage by PBS.

Another proposition we discussed at Harvard was for ABC and Harvard to sponsor jointly a conference on the subject of voting. That symposium was held in Washington a year ago, attended by a distinguished panel of statesman, public leaders, political experts, scholars and journalists. Among the most active participants were Gerald Ford and Jimmy Carter.

Our symposium identified two major causes of nonvoting and agreed that action should promptly be taken on both. The second is of particular relevance to broadcasting, but for a moment, let me describe the first—something we called "structural" barriers to voting.

In examining voting patterns across the world, it turns out that despite recent reforms, the United States continues to make voting registration significantly more difficult than any other democratic country. In Canada, for example, special registrars periodically go door-to-door signing up eligible voters. In the United Kingdom, registration forms are mailed every year to households. And once people are registered, they stay on the rolls, even though they may move somewhere else.

The United States is the only nation where the entire burden of registration is placed on the individual and not shared by the state. Our hodgepodge of voting laws makes it difficult for many people, especially the poor and uneducated, to understand what they must do to become properly qualified. Registration books usually close 30 days before elections, long before campaigns reach their peak in the media. Hours of registration can be inconvenient. And the myriad of registration deadlines is confusing, as well. For example, how many of us here today know our specific registration deadlines? For most of us, it falls on October 9 or 16. (And incidently, we'll make it easy for you—you can do it just outside these doors.)

And we've also found that those who change addresses are especially likely to fall out of the voting net. Professor Raymond Wolfinger of Berkeley has discovered that about a third of all Americans move during every two-year cycle—and on average, their registration rate takes about five years to catch up with those who haven't moved.

What would happen if registration laws were simplified and reformed? The best answer probably comes from the five states in the country that now allow election-day registration or require no registration at all: Minnesota, Wisconsin, North Dakota, Maine and Oregon. In those states, the turnout in 1980 ranged from nearly 10 to 20 points above the national average.

It is abundantly clear from experience that when Americans are registered, they are much more likely to vote. In 1980, fully 86% of those who were registered in this country then voted for President. That's a higher turnout, I might add, than in countries like the United Kingdom, Japan, Canada and Israel. The answer is clear: We must lower every conceivable barrier between the potential voter and the ballot box.

Personally, I favor an overhaul of registration laws, the adoption of Sunday voting, keeping polls open for 24 hours, and closing all the polls at the same hour. There is no good reason why polls can't open on a Sunday after church services. It's simply a better day for most of our citizens to vote, and especially our young married couples, where both partners frequently work and juggle babysitting responsibilities. Just look at the Sunday voting experience in France, Spain, and West Germany—turnouts there are well over 80%.

Now let me turn to the second problem we identified in our symposium last year, and this one, as I said, is more directly tied to the concerns of this audience: the problem of motivating our voters.

The evidence here is not as hard, but there seems little doubt that interest in voting had been dulled in recent years. As most presidential candidates acknowledge, our campaigns have become so long and tedious that boredom is a national disease. One need look no further than the ratings from the conventions this summer: viewing during the conventions set two new records—record lows. For the commercial networks, the convention weeks this summer were the two lowest-rated weeks of the year, and the conventions themselves drew the lowest ratings of any conventions in television history.

Many citizens apparently believe it doesn't make any difference whether they go to the polls. They feel neither an obligation to vote nor a stake in the outcome. And many of those who would like to vote wake up near election day and realize for the first time that they haven't cleared the registration hurdles.

Clearly, there is much to be done. The candidates bear an obligation to run more inspiring campaigns than we have seen in the past. There's too much packaging and not enough substance to ex-cite many voters. Viewing campaign ads as a whole, it's hard to tell whether you're supposed to go out and vote or buy diet soda.

Our political parties also bear responsibility for the time devoted to campaigns: they are insufferably long.

Our schools must also instill in young people the belief that voting is the first obligation of citizenship. High schools now teach driver's education; why shouldn't they teach voter education, too?

But surely, we in the broadcasting industry have a towering responsibility as well. Part of that lies in our news divisions. I have been pleased to learn in recent days that initial surveys of 1984 campaign coverage find the networks are devoting a good deal more attention this year to the issues—to substance—and less to what is called "horserace" stories. One of our foremost jobs is to clarify the issues and the choices before the country. Never has the thorough and objective reporting been more important, or the recognition that we serve a broad and pluralistic society.

In my judgement, the networks have also taken a responsible approach to the touchy question of exit polls. At ABC, we will not project the winner in any state until the voting booths in that state have been closed. I understand that CBS and NBC are following a similar course.

Beyond that, the networks offered to host debates between the candidates, feeling the debates could be free-wheeling exchanges that would greatly benefit voters. I want to congratulate the League of Women Voters and its president Dorothy Ridings, who is with us today, for once again taking on the responsibility of organizing the debates. The league, as you know, has long contributed to voter awareness, and we look forward to working with our friends there in the coming weeks.

The other part of our responsibility as broadcasters lies in our sense of civic obligation—the degree to which we voluntarily take it upon ourselves to impress upon people the importance of voting and how to register. In my view, we should spare no effort in this regard. Nothing we do will ever be too much.

This kind of programming does not fit easily into a newscast, of course, because it falls outside the realm of day-to-day news coverage.

NBC, for example, has produced an excellent half-hour educational program on the electoral process. CBS is running a very effective series of public service announcements. And Group W and many other broadcasters represented here today are pursuing their own public service efforts, which, I am happy to say, are too numerous to mention individually.

At my own company, drawing on the recommendations of the ABC/Harvard Symposium, we are undertaking the most ambitious voter education project in our history.

ABC's public affairs effort encompasses our radio, television, and publishing operations, as well as our owned and affiliated stations. It includes public service announcements by celebrities like Dinah Shore and Reggie Jackson urging all Americans to register and vote, and spots with the same message by prominent Americans like Coretta Scott King and Henry Kissinger. We are also highlighting this issue with special segments on "Good Morning America" editorials, public affairs programs, a community relations campaign, a rebroadcast of our documentary on the symposium, and special PSA's [public service announcements] for children on Saturday mornings.

I tell you all this not only because I am proud—and I am—but because those of us who have had the privilege of serving in this industry for so long—men like Dr. Stanton, Bill Paley, Grant Tinker, the distinguished leaders of the broadcasting groups, and many others—all believe so deeply that broadcasting should serve large and noble purposes. It is especially important that as we emerge from an age of government regulation, we set new standards of excellence and accept broadened responsibilities.

Ladies and gentlemen, let me close on this note. There will always be those, of course, who scoff and insist we can't turn around anything so fundamental as voting. They think we're embarked on Mission Impossible. But let me say that I can't imagine any of them followed the Olympic games this summer in Los Angeles.

What we saw there almost defied gravity. A city unwilling to accept liability for the games suddenly caught the Olympic spirit, and the games became a runaway success. Over 50,000 citizens transformed themselves into hard-working volunteers. Businesses large and small pitched in. Fans flocked into the stadiums. And just a few days ago, the Los Angeles Organizing Committee announced that contrary to all expectations, the first private Olympics in history had made a stunning provit of $150 million—money that can be plowed back into athletic competition. Peter Ueberroth, a man who deserves a lot of credit, put it well: "The organizing committee is just part of an outpouring of the Americcan spirit."

Surely that is what we have seen emerge in these past months across the land—an Olympic spirit, a new patriotism, a new American spirit. Call it what you will, but it is there, it is real, it is powerful. And in the days ahead, we ought to hitch it to some important goals in our national life.

One of the highest of these goals, I submit, is a vigorous democracy where every American takes pride in casting a vote. I ask you, leaders in the communications field, to take it upon yourselves to do all you can to help us fulfill that dream.

Thank you very much.

POLITICAL ACTION COMMITTEES: .
A THREAT TO REPRESENTATIVE GOVERNMENT[1]
FRED WERTHEIMER[2]

Following the 1984 election, Brooks Jackson of the *Wall Street Journal* (December 24, 1984, p. 26) reported: "New figures show money from political action committees is talking more loudly than ever." In the election, more than 3,800 political action committees [PACs]—groups organized to support specific candidates or issues—were prepared to spend as much as $120 million to influence the outcome.

Following the election, a computer-aided tabulation of the campaign finance reports showed PAC contributions to winning House candidates had increased from 35% in 1982 to 44%. Senate winners got 23% of their funds from PACs compared to 14% when the same seats were contested in 1976. Although Federal Election Commission figures were not available, Jackson concluded " . . . [It] is clear that many powerful PACs

[1]Delivered at 1:00 P.M. on September 19, 1984, in the ballroom of the National Press Club, Washington, D. C.

[2]For biographical note, see Appendix.

continued to grow in this latest election year and that lawmakers have become even more reliant on them for campaign funds."

Fred Wertheimer, President of Common Cause, an independent, non-partisan lobby organized to represent the general public rather than any special interest, addressed the issue of the influence of PACs before the National Press Club in Washington, D. C. The National Press Club is one of the capitol's, and indirectly, the nation's best forums for the discussion of major public issues. It provides its 4,300 members, including 2,250 journalists, with a variety of educational and cultural programs, speakers' luncheons, newsmakers' breakfasts, and evening "rap sessions". Frank Aukofer of the *Milwaukee Journal,* a past president, says that, "It is, without doubt, the most active club in the world" (Martin Tolchin, *New York Times,* April 4, 1984, p. 12).

Wertheimer delivered his address at one of the club's regular series of speakers' luncheons on September 19, 1984, in the ballroom of the National Press Club. His audience of approximately 200 included journalists, Common Cause staff, and PAC representatives. The speech was broadcast live on National Public Radio and taped for showing on C-SPAN. Wertheimer spoke following a luncheon which began at 12:30. He was followed by Herbert Schmertz, Vice President for Public Affairs for the Mobil Oil corporation, who defended PACs. Within six months of Wertheimer's speech, the United States Supreme Court on March 18, 1985, decided that the First Amendment protects unlimited independent campaign expenditures by political action committees. Overturning Federal Election Commission restrictions, the court decided that

> . . . direct spending to communicate ideas and opinions are not the same thing as a campaign contribution and should not be treated in the same way. Nothing is more fundamental to the freedom of speech and association than letting people get together to spend their own money to broadcast or publish what they think about politics and public policy. (Michael J. Malbin, *Christian Science Monitor,* March 26, 1985, p. 17)

Fred Wertheimer's speech: I appreciate the opportunity to return to the National Press Club to address the issue of political action committees or PACs. When I spoke to the Press Club on this subject in February of 1983, I opened my remarks by saying, "Our system of representative government is under siege because of the destructive role that PACs are now playing in the political process. It's time for us to do something about this extraordinary threat."

Today, as we head into a congressional election where a record number of PACs—some 3,800—are about to give a record amount of PAC money—as much as $120 million—the PAC problem has only become more dangerous and the need to deal with it only more obvious.

The PAC system is a system in which interest groups are using campaign contributions to buy influence, access, and ultimately results in the United States Congress. It is a system that is making our elected officials obligated to the groups financing their elections at the expense of the constituents who are electing them to Congress. It is a system that is undermining the integrity of Congress and threatening our whole concept of representative government.

The concerns of Common Cause about campaign contributions in general and PAC money in particlular are not new.

In 1973, at a time when labor was playing the dominant role in the PAC arena, Common Cause Chairman John Gardner told the Senate Commerce Committee that "there is nothig in our political system today that creates more mischief, more corruption, and more alienation and distrust on the part of the public than does our system of financing elections."

In 1974 Common Cause fought hard against an amendment proposed by labor and business groups to expand the ability of unions and corporations to have PACs. We lost that fight, and it was the attachment of this pro-PAC amendment to the 1974 campaign finance reform bill—along with the rejection by Congress of public financing for their own races—that paved the way for the PAC explosion of the past decade.

Some people talk about the growth of PACs as an unintended consequence of the 1974 reforms. But the fact is that the pro-PAC amendment that passed was never a reform. The consequences were not only intended, they were engineered by PAC forces.

Today we have two very different systems for financing presidential and congressional elections. And nothing more strongly demonstrates the difference than the role of PAC contributions in these two systems. Under the presidential public financing system PACs will make approxiamtely $1 million in campaign contributions to the 1984 presidential candidates. Under the congressional system PAC contributions are expected to reach as high as $120 million.

PAC contributions play a minimal role in the presidential system and a dominant role in the congressional one.

This is not to say the presidential system is without problems
today. There are some obvious and significant problems with
presidential public financing that have arisen as people have
sought out and found ways of evading the law. But these problems
are solvable and they are also dwarfed by the problems caused by
PACs in the financing of congressional races.

As we predicted a decade ago, PACs now play a far more important part in congressional campaign fundraising. Candidates
now raise far more of their campaign warchests from PACs than
they did in 1974. In 1982, for example, House winners got more
than one-third of their campaign funds from PACs, and more
than 100 members raised over half of their funds from PACs.
Members who serve as committee chairs and in leadership positions in the House got an average of 54 percent of their campaign
funds from PACs in their 1982 reelection campaigns. At the same
time the role of PAC funds has been growing, the role of small
contributions from individuals has been declining, according to
Democratic Study Group report issued this month. This study
concludes that in 1982 House and Senate incumbents—for the
first time—raised more of their campaign funds from PACs than
they raised in small contributions from individual donors.

In the last few years, however, something very important has
happened in this country, and that is the development of a growing
awareness and recognition of the fact that the PAC system is a rot-
ten system, a system that is undermining our democracy, a system
that must be changed. We know the debate has shifted when Senator Barry Goldwater, in testimony before the Senate Rules Committee entitled "Unlimited Campaign Financing: A Crisis of
Liberty", says, "Unlimited campaign spending eats at the heart
of the democratic process. It feeds the growth of special interest
groups created solely to channel money into political campaigns.
It creates an impression that every candidate is bought and owned
by the biggest givers."

We know that public concern is rising when Irving Shapiro,
former chairman and chief executive officer of DuPont and the
former chairman of the Business Roundtable, describes the cur-

rent system of financing congressional campaigns as "an invidious thing, it's corrupting, it does pollute the system."

We know that concern about PACs is reaching new audiences when last month we read an editorial in the industry trade journal *Chemical Week,* which warned:

[A] new force has intruded into our system of representative democracy that, if unchecked, could topple it or seriously hurt it. We refer to the phenomenon of Political Action Committees. . . . The plain truth of the matter, no matter what gloss is put on it, is that PAC money aims at influencing congressional action. The other side of the coin is that new candidates and incumbents alike become beholden to their PAC benefactors. That's the whole point, isn't it?

We know that PAC money is becoming a political liability when all canadiates in the race for the Senate seat from Massachusetts pledge not to take PAC money; other candidates around the country—in Florida, in Maine, in Nebraska, in North Carolina—have taken a no-PAC pledge.

These developments reflect the fact that a chorus of opposition to the role of PACs in financing elections is growing across the political spectrum. In recent years PACs have attempted to portray themselves as the new, improved form of citizen participation. But the American people know what's going on, and they aren't buying it. The results of a Harris poll conducted earlier this year showed 70 percent of the American people oppose candidates for high federal office taking PAC funds.

PAC contributions have two very profound effects on our political system. First, they provide an enormous advantage for incumbents over challengers in the financing of their campaigns.

In 1982, incumbents raised $54 million from PACs compared with $16 million given to their challengers. This is a ratio of 3.4 to 1 in favor of incumbents. When we look at the fact that all the rest of the campaign money only favored incumbents by 1.3 to 1, it becomes crystal clear that PACs are investing in incumbents.

When it comes to women challengers, furthermore, the bias of PACs in favor of incumbents appears to be far more pronounced. A Common Cause study of fundraising by Senate candidates in the '84 election (through June 30th of this year) showed PACs favoring incumbents over women challengers by nearly 12 to 1, compared with the general 4 to 1 incumbent-to-challenger PAC ratio we're seeing in all Senate races this election.

The tremendous imbalance in funds between incumbents and challengers has apparently played a key role in persuading one of the nation's leading political observers, David Broder of *The Washington Post*, to rethink his position and recently call for "a system of public financing for Senate and House races that gives challengers some kind of fair break in going up against incumbents."

Second, PAC contributions are improperly affecting public policy decisions by improperly influencing our congressional representatives.

Here's how *Business Week*, in coming out in favor of new PAC limits and congressional public financing, has described the role of PACs:

It would be hard to find a PAC that gives solely to support good government. Most see their contributions as an investment in promoting laws favoring their interests. Breaking the link between contributions and expected favors would help officeholders resist the demands of special interests.

Interest groups are lobbying with one hand and giving candidates substantial sums of money with the other. As Representative Jim Leach from Iowa has said:

A government of the people, by the people and for the people cannot be a government where influence is purchasable through substantial campaign contributions. It is simply a fact of life that when big money in the form of group contributions enter the political arena, big obligations are entertained.

PAC money doesn't guarantee victory but it does provide unfair and inappropriate influence for PACs over our elected officials and over legislative decisions.

It used to be that PAC advocates would vehemently deny that they were getting anything in return for their contributions. Now, even the staunchest defenders of PACs, such as Dick Armstrong of the Public Affairs Council, have admitted that political money will buy some access.

Most political observers know that PACs are getting far more than access for their political money. But even if that were all they were getting it would be dead wrong. We cannot have a political system where certain groups, because they give large campaign contributions, can gain more access and have a greater opportunity to influence elected leaders than the constituents who voted them into office in the first place.

Buying access is no more acceptable in our democracy than buying influence or buying political results.

We are told by some that the efforts to enact limits on campaign contributions by PACs violate our constitutional guarantees of free speech and the right of association. But the Supreme Court squarely faced and rejected that argument in the 1976 case of *Buckley* v. *Valeo*. The court understood that at stake here is not freedom of speech but the very integrity of our representative system of government. The court recognized, as the Constitution does, that there is no constitutional right to buy political influence and political results.

In reaching this conclusion, the Supreme Court clearly recognized that there is a fundamental difference between spending money to advocate the merits of one's point of view—as Mobil Oil does, for example, with its issue advertising campaigns—and giving money to a public official who is making government decisions that can benefit or harm the contributor of those funds.

We are reaching a consensus in this country that PACs are absolutely inimical to the system of representative government envisioned in our constitution. But the big question remaining is whether that public concensus can be translated into a congressional consensus and congressional action.

One of the most critical developments along these lines is the rapidly growing number of members of Congress who are now publicly calling for a change in the PAC system. During 1984, the number of cosponsors of H.R. 4428, a new campaign finance reform bill, has grown from 100 to 147. This means that at the very time when members of Congress have to go to PACs for campaign money, they are also choosing publicly to identify themselves with the need to change this system. This legislation would limit the role of PACs and increase the importance of small private contributions in financing congressional races.

We are headed for a showdown on this issue in Congress. We hope the battle will take place next year. It will be extremely difficult. The PACs have an enormous stake in using all their clout to maintain the current system.

But it may be that the toughest part of this battle has already been won. The PAC system is discredited in the country today. It is rejected by the pubic and is becoming an ever-widening stain on the standing of the Congress and the integrity of its members.

At stake here is the very essence of our form of representative government. And the public is going to insist, I believe, on a government whose obligations are first and foremost to the people of this country, not the PACs.

A CASE FOR THE DEMOCRATS 1984:
A TALE OF TWO CITIES[1]
MARIO M. CUOMO[2]

On the eve of the Democratic National Convention in July, 1984, party delegates conceded that their national ticket faced an uphill fight against President Ronald Reagan in November. A *New York Times* poll of delegates indicated that only 35% believed that a tickt headed by Walter F. Mondale could carry their home states. Another 35% rated the Republicans as favorites while the remainder called the contest a tossup. (*New York Times,* July 16, 1984, p. Y13). Among the obstacles that the Democrats faced were Reagan's personal popularity, the perception of him as a national spirit of patriotism and optimism in part engendered by the incumbent, and improved economic conditions. The Democrats' chances were made even slimmer by the internal strife resulting from the challenges of Senator Gary Hart and the Reverend Jesse Jackson to Mondale's nomination.

What was needed at the convention was someone who could unify the party, inspire the delegates, and offer an alternative to the Republicans. Traditionally, this is the role of the convention keynote speaker. Tapped to deliver the speech at the 1984 convention was Mario M. Cuomo, the Governor of New York, elected only two years before. Although relatively

[1]Delivered as the keynote address at the Democratic National Convention in the Moscone Center, San Francisco, California, on July 16, 1984.
[2]For biographical note, see Appendix.

unknown nationally before the convention, Mario Cuomo emerged after this speech as a political star and potential standard bearer of his party.

Preceding Governor Cuomo's address, former President Jimmy Carter had spoken briefly and a film tribute to Harry S. Truman had been shown. Cuomo's immediate audience consisted of the 3,944 delegates, press representatives and spectators in San Francisco's Moscone Center. His larger audience consisted of more than 20 million households who viewed the speech on television at prime time on the evening of July 16, 1984.

Cuomo, who takes a very active part in the preparation of his speeches, was reported to have "worked on the speech for more than a week, sitting around talking it out with aides and then writing the words himself on a yellow legal pad." (Michael Oreskenes, *New York Times,* July 24, 1984, p. 13).

The response to the keynote address must have been more than satisfying to the Governor and the Democratic Party. Godfrey Sperling, Jr., wrote in the *Christian Science Monitor* that the delegates "were enthralled with him. . . . Cuomo's performance was electrifying." (July 31, 1984, p. 11). Terry Coleman of *The Guardian* (U.K.) called it "the speech of a master. . . . He changed the whole tone of the convention. He had something to say. He was the only speaker all day who had the confidence to speak quietly. He was the only one whose presence commanded silence" (July 18, 1984, p. 21). Also writing for *The Guardian,* Harold Jackson observed, "The general mood of the convention had been tangibly changed—even electrified. . . . [His] delivery to the packed convention hall showed that there is at least one effective rival to the great communicator in the White House"(July 18, 1984, p. 6). Howell Raines of the *New York Times* (July 22, 1984, p. 1) said that "from Mr. Cuomo . . . flowed language so fine as to amount, some said, to the making of literature."

The reviews on television and in the press were unstinting. "As for skill and delivery, effective delivery, I think it's the best I've ever heard," David Brinkley told the ABC audience in the minute after the speech ended, with pandemonium still reigning in the convention hall. Immediately after the speeches, the governor's aides who had remained in Albany while the convention was going on reported a surprising and unparalleled response. According to Michael Oreskes, writing in the *New York Times*:

> It started with the phone calls, some of them in the middle of the night. Then came the letters, hundreds of them a day, from every corner of the state and virtually every state of the union. People wanted Governor Cuomo to know how inspired they were by his keynote address at the Democratic National Convention. . . . State officials who have worked here for a long time say they have never seen anything quite like the response . . . that has followed the address delivered to the convention last week (July 24, 1984, p. 13).

Governor Cuomo's speech: On behalf of the Empire State and the family of New York, I thank you for the great privilege of being allowed to address this convention. Please allow me to skip the stories and the poetry and the temptation to deal in nice but vague rhetoric. Let me instead use this valuable opportunity to deal with the questions that should determine this election and that are vital to the American people.

Ten days ago, President Reagan admitted that although some people in this country seemed to be doing well nowadays, others were unhappy, and even worried, about themselves, their families and their futures. The President said he didn't understand that fear. He said, "Why, this country is a shining city on a hill." The President is right. In many ways we are "a shining city on a hill." But the hard truth is that not everyone is sharing in this city's splendor and glory.

A shining city is perhaps all the President sees from the portico of the White House and the veranda of his ranch, where everyone seems to be doing well. But there's another part of the city, the part where some people can't pay their mortgages and most young people can't afford one, where students can't afford the education they need and middle-class parents watch dreams they hold for their children evaporate.

In this part of the city there are more poor than ever, more families in trouble. More and more people who need help but can't find it. Even worse: there are elderly people who tremble in the basements of the houses there. There are people who sleep in the city's streets, in the gutter, where the glitter doesn't show. There are ghettos where thousands of young people, without an education or a job, give their lives away to drug dealers every day. There is despair, Mr. President, in faces you never see, in places you never visit in your shining city.

In fact, Mr. President, this nation is more a "Tale of Two Cities" than it is a "Shining City on a Hill." Maybe if you visited more places, Mr. President, you'd understand.

Maybe if you went to Appalachia where some people still live in sheds and to Lackawanna where thousands of unemployed steel workers wonder why we subsidized foreign steel while we surrender their dignity to unemployment and to welfare checks; maybe if you stepped into a shelter in Chicago and talked with some of the homeless there; maybe, Mr. President, if you asked a woman who'd been denied the help she needs to feed her children because you say we need the money to give a tax break to a millionaire or to build a missile we can't even afford to use—maybe then you'd understand. Maybe, Mr. President. But I'm afraid not. Because the truth is, this is how we were warned it would be.

President Reagan told us from the beginning that he believed in a kind of social Darwinism. Survival of the fittest. Government can't do everything, we were told. So it should settle for taking care of the strong and hope that economic ambition and charity will do the rest. Make the rich richer and what falls from their table will be enough for the middle class and those trying to make it into the middle class.

The Republicans called it trickle-down when Hoover tried it. Now they call it supply side. It is the same shining city for those relative few who are lucky enough to live in its good neighborhoods. But for the people who are excluded—locked out—all they can do is to stare from a distance at that city's glimmering towers.

It's an old story. As old as our history.

The difference between Democrats and Republicans has always been measured in courage and confidence. The Republicans believe the wagon train will not make it to the frontier unless some of our old, some of our young, and some of our weak are left behind by the side of the trail. The strong will inherit the land!

We Democrats believe that we can make it all the way with the whole family intact. We have. More than once. Ever since Franklin Roosevelt lifted himself from his wheelchair to lift this nation from its knees. Wagon train after wagon train. To new frontiers of education, housing, peace. The whole family aboard. Constantly reaching out to extend and enlarge that family. Lifting them up into the wagon on the way. Blacks and Hispanics, people of every ethnic group, and native Americans—all those struggling to build their families claim some share of America.

For nearly 50 years we carried them to new levels of comfort, security, dignity, even affluence. Some of us are in this room today only because this nation had that confidence. It would be wrong to forget that. So, we are at this convention to remind ourselves where we come from and to claim the future for ourselves and for our children.

Today, our great Democratic Party, which has saved this nation from depression, from fascism, from racism, from corruption, is called upon to do it again—this time to save the nation from confusion and division, most of all from fear of a nuclear holocaust.

In order to succeed, we must answer our opponent's polished and appealing rhetoric with a more telling reasonableness and rationality. We must win this case on the merits. We must get the American public to look past the glitter, beyond the showmanship, to reality, to the hard substance of things. And we will do that not so much with speeches that sound good as with speeches that are good and sound. Not so much with speeches that bring people to their feet as with speeches that bring people to their senses.

We must make the American people hear our "tale of two cities." We must convince them that we don't have one city, indivisible, shining for all its people. We will have no chance to do that if what comes out of this convention, what is heard throughout the campaign, is a babel of arguing voices.

To succeed we will have to surrender small parts of our individual interests, to build a platform we can all stand on, at once, comfortably, proudly singing out the truth for the nation to hear, in chorus, its logic so clear and commanding that no slick commercial, no amount of geniality, no martial music will be able to muffle it. We Democrats must unite so that the entire nation can. Surely the Republicans won't bring the convention together. Their policies divide the nation into the lucky and the left-out, the royalty and the rabble. The Republicans are willing to treat that division as victory. They would cut this nation in half, into those temporarily better off and those worse off than before, and call it recovery.

We should not be embarrassed or dismayed if the process of unifying is difficult, even at times wrenching. Unlike any other party, we embrace men and women of every color, every creed, every orientation, every economic class. In our family are gathered everyone from the abject poor of Essex County in New York to the enlightened affluent of the gold coasts of both ends of our nation. And in between is the heart of our constituency. The middle class, the people not rich enough to be worry-free but not poor enought to be on welfare, those who work for a living because they have to: white collar and blue collar, young professionals, men and women in small business desperate for capital and contracts they need to prove their worth.

We speak for the minorities who have not yet entered the mainstream: for ethnics who want to add their culture to the mosaic that is America; for women indignant that we refuse to etch into our governmental commandments the simple rule "thou shalt not sin against equality," a commandment so obvious it can be spelled in three letters: E.R.A.; for young people demanding an education and a future, for senior citizens terrorized by the idea that their only security, their Social Security, is being threatened; for millions of reasoning people fighting to preserve our environment from greed and stupidity. And fighting to preserve our very existence from a macho intransigence that refuses to make intelligent attempts to discuss the possibility of nuclear holocaust with our enemy. Refusing because they believe we can pile missiles so high that they will pierce the clouds and the sight of them will frighten our enemies into submission.

We're proud of this diversity. Grateful we don't have to manufacture its appearance the way the Republicans will next month in Dallas, by propping up mannequin delegates on the convention floor.

But we pay a price for it. The different people we represent have many points of view. Sometimes they compete and then we have debates, even arguments. That's what our primaries were.

But now the primaries are over, and it is time to lock arms and move into this campaign together. If we need any inspiration to make the effort to put aside our small differences, all we need to do is reflect on the Republican policy of divide and cajole and how it has injured our land since 1980.

The President has asked us to judge him on whether or not he's fulfilled the promises he made four years ago. I accept that. Just consider what he said and what he's done.

Inflation is down since 1980. But not because of the supply-side miracle promised by the President. Inflation was reduced the old-fashioned way, with a recession, the worst since 1932. More than 55,000 bankruptcies. Two years of massive unemployment. Two hundred thousand farmers and ranchers forced off the land. More homeless than at any time since the Great Depression. More hungry, more poor—mostly women—and a nearly $200 billion deficit threatening our future.

The President's deficit is a direct and dramatic repudiation of his promise to balance our budget by 1983. That deficit is the largest in the history of this universe; more than three times larger than the deficit in President Carter's last year. It is a deficit that, according to the President's own fiscal advisor, could grow as high as $300 billion a year, stretching "as far as the eye can see." It is a debt so large that as much as one-half of our revenue from the income tax goes to pay the interest on it each year. It is a mortgage on our children's futures that can only be paid in pain and that could eventually bring this nation to its knees.

Don't take my word for it—I'm a Democrat.

Ask the Republican investment bankers on Wall Street what they think the chances are this recovery will be permanent. If they're not too embarrassed to tell you the truth, they'll say they are appalled and frightened by the President's deficit. Ask them what they think of our economy, now that it has been driven by the distorted value of the dollar back to its colonial condition, exporting agricultural products and importing manufactured ones.

Ask those Republican investment bankers what they expect the interest rate to be a year from now. And ask them what they predict for the inflation rate then.

How important is this question of the deficit? Think about it: What chancce would the Republican candidate have had in 1980 if he had told the American people that he intended to pay for his so-called economic recovery with bankruptcies, unemployment and the largest government debt known to humankind? Would American voters have signed the loan certificate for him on election day? Of course not! It was an election won with smoke and mirrors, with illusion. It is a recovery made of the same stuff.

And what about foreign policy? They said they would make us and the whole world safer. They say they have. By creating the largest defense budget in history, one even they now admit is excessive, failed to discuss peace with our enemies. By the loss of 279 young Americans in Lebanon in pursuit of a plan and a policy no one can find or describe.

We give monies to Latin American governments that murder nuns, and then lie about it.

We have been less than zealous in our support of the only real friend we have in the Middle East, the one democracy there, our flesh and blood ally, the state of Israel.

Our policy drifts with no real direction, other than a hysterical commitment to an arms race that leads nowhere, if we're lucky. If we're not—could lead us to bankruptcy or war.

Of course we must have a strong defense! Of course Democrats believe that there are times when we must stand and fight. And we have. Thousands of us have paid for freedom with our lives. But always, when we've been at our best, our purposes were clear.

Now they're not. Now our allies are as confused as our enemies. Now we have no real commitment to our friends or our ideals to human rights, to the refusenicks, to Sakharov, to Bishop Tutu, and the others struggling for freedom in South Africa. We have spent more than we can afford. We have pounded our chest and made bold speeches. But we lost 279 young Americans in Lebanon and we are forced to live behind sand bags in Washington. How can anyone believe that we are stronger, safer or better? That's the Republican record. That its disastrous quality is not more fully understood by the Amerian people is attributable, I think, to the President's amiability and the failure by some to separate the salesman from the product.

It's now up to us to make the case to America. And to remind Americans that if they are not happy with all the President has done so far, they should consider how much worse it will be if he is left to his radical proclivities for another four years unrestrained by the need once again to come before the American people.

If July brings back Anne Gorsuch Burford, what can we expect in December? Where would another four years take us? How much larger will the deficit be? How much deeper the cuts in programs for the struggling middle class and the poor to limit that deficit? How high the interest rates? How much more acid rain killing our forests and fouling our lakes?

What kind of Supreme Court? What kind of court and country will be fashioned by the man who believes in having government mandate people's religion and morality? The man who believes that trees pollute the environment, that the laws against discrimination go too far. The man who threatens Social Security and Medicaid and help for the disabled.

How high will we pile the missiles? How much deeper will be the gulf between us and our enemies? Will we make meaner the spirit of our people?

This election will measure the record of the past four years. But more than that, it will answer the question of what kind of people we want to be.

We Democrats still have a dream. We still believe in this nation's future. And this is our answer—our credo: We believe in only the government we need, but we insist on all the government we need.

We believe in a government characterized by fairness and reasonableness, a reasonableness that goes beyond labels, that doesn't distort or promise to do what it knows it can't do. A government strong enough to use the words "love" and "compassion" and smart enough to convert our noblest aspirations.

We believe in encouraging the talented, but we believe that while survival of the fittest may be a good working description of the process of evolution, a government of humans should elevate itself to a higher order, one which fills the gaps left by chance or wisdom we don't understand.

We would rather have laws written by the patron of this great city, the man called the "world's most sincere Democrat," St. Francis of Assisi, than laws written by Darwin.

We believe, as Democrats, that a society as blessed as ours, the most affluent democracy in the world's history, that can spend trillions on instruments of destruction, ought to be able to help the middle class in its struggle, ought to be able to find work for all who can do it, room at the table, shelter for the homeless, care for the elderly and infirm, hope for the destitute.

We proclaim as loudly as we can the utter insanity of nuclear proliferation and the need for a nuclear freeze, if only to affirm the simple truth that peace is better than war because life is better than death.

We believe in firm but fair law and order, in the union movement, in privacy for people, openness by government, civil rights, and human rights.

We believe in a single fundamental idea that describes better than most textbooks and any speech what a proper government should be. The idea of family. Mutuality. The sharing of benefits and burdens for the good of all. Feeling one another's pain. Sharing one another's blessings. Reasonably, honestly, fairly, without respect to race, or sex or geography or political affiliation.

We believe we must be the family of America, recognizing that at the heart of the matter we are bound one to another, that the problems of a retired school teacher in Duluth are our problems. That the future of the child in Buffalo is our future. The struggle of a disabled man in Boston to survive, to live decently is our struggle. The hunger of a woman in Little Rock, our hunger. The failure anywhere to provide what reasonably we might, to avoid pain, is our failure.

For fifty years we Democrats created a better future for our children, using traditional democratic principles as a fixed beacon, giving us direction and purpose, but constantly innovating, adapting to new realities; Roosevelt's alphabet programs; Truman's NATO and the GI Bill of Rights; Kennedy's intelligent tax incentives and the Alliance for Progress; Johnson's civil rights; Carter's human rights and the nearly miraculous Camp David peace accord.

Democrats did it—and Democrats can do it again.

We can build a future that deals with our deficit.

Remember fifty years of progress never cost us what the last four years of stagnation have. We can deal with that deficit intelligently, by shared sacrifice, with all parts of the nation's family contributing, building partnerships with the private sector, providing a sound defense without depriving ourselves of what we need to feed our children and care for our people.

We can have a future that provides for all the young of the present by marrying common sense and compassion.

We know we can, because we did it for nearly fifty years before 1980.

We can do it again. If we do not forget. Forget that this entire nation has profited by these progressive principles. That they helped lift up generations to the middle class and higher: gave us a chance to work, to go to college, to raise a family, to own a house, to be secure in our old age and, before that, to reach heights that our own parents would not have dared dream of.

That struggle to live with dignity is the real story of the shining city. It's a story I didn't read in a book, or learn in a classroom. I saw it, and lived it. Like many of you.

I watched a small man with thick calluses on both hands work 15 and 16 hours a day. I saw him once literally bleed from the bottoms of his feet, a man who came here uneducated, alone, unable to speak the language, who taught me all I needed to know about faith and hard work by the simple eloquence of his example. I learned about our kind of democracy from my father. I learned about our obligation to each other from him and from my mother. They asked only for a chance to work and to make the world better for their children and to be protected in those moments when they would not be able to protect themselves. This nation and its government did that for them.

And on January 20th, 1985, it will happen again. Only on a much grander scale. We will have a new president of the United States, a Democrat born not to the blood of kings but to the blood of immigrants and pioneers.

We will have America's first woman vice president, the child of immigrants, a New Yorker, opening with one magnificent stroke a whole new frontier for the United States.

It will happen, if we make it happen.

I ask you, ladies and gentlemen, brothers and sisters—for the good of all us, for the love of this great nation, for the family of America, for the love of God. Please make this nation remember how futures are built.

SECOND INAUGURAL ADDRESS[1]
RONALD W. REAGAN[2]

When Ronald Reagan raised his right hand to take the oath of office on Monday, January 21, 1985, it was the 50th inauguration of an American president. Dating back to 1789, when George Washington assumed the nation's highest office and delivered the first inaugural address, such speeches have been presented by all of his successors. Although there is no constitutional requirement for such remarks, Washington felt it proper to use the occasion to present his views about the newly adopted Constitution. Since then the inauguration has become a national day of pomp and circumstance in which Americans celebrate a new beginning in hope that the next four years will be better than the last.

The circumstances of the 1985 ceremonies contrasted sharply with Mr. Reagan's first inauguration in 1981. (See *Representative American Speeches, 1980-1981*, pp. 9-18, for a description of his first inaugural address.) First, the actual 1985 swearing-in had taken place privately the day before, on January 20, the date specified by law; but because that was a Sunday the public inauguration was postponed to January 21. The second difference was occasioned by the severe weather in Washington at that time. Although they had been working on the inaugural activities since November, at the last minute the planning committee and Reagan decided to cancel the parade and move the inaugural ceremony indoors when the temperature dropped to 7 degrees Fahrenheit—causing dissappointment to many who had come from all over the country to participate in the parade or to observe the inauguration.

The ceremony was moved indoors to the Rotunda of the Capitol, where only 1,000 of the 140,000 who had purchased tickets for the outdoor event were able to attend. The immediate audience was composed of invited senators, representatives, government officials, diplomats, and friends. *The Christian Science Monitor* (January 22, 1985, p. 15) observed, "There is always something moving about such a tableau of national leaders—the members of the Supreme Court, the House and and Senate, and the executive branch." A vastly larger second audience observed the ceremony and speech on national television. Instead of the formal attire he chose in 1981, Reagan dressed in a dark blue suit, white

---

[1]Delivered in the Rotunda of the United States Capitol, Washington, D. C., at noon on January 21, 1985.

[2]For biographical note, see Appendix.

shirt, and striped red, white, and blue tie. Standing on a hastily installed wooden platform, he took his public oath of office from Chief Justice Warren E. Burger at 11:48 A.M., about fifteen minutes after Vice-President Bush had been sworn in to his second term. He read the 18-minute speech from a TelePrompTer. Bernard Weinraub reports that, "As the 73-year old president spoke—the oldest person ever to be sworn in as president—rays of sunlight poured through the frosted windows of the central dome into the Rotunda" (*New York Times,* January 22, 1985, p. 1).

Press response to the address was generally positive. Charlotte Saikowski of the *Christian Science Monitor* (January 22, 1985, p. 1) described it as "an inaugural speech suffused with optimism, hope, and patriotism . . . largely inspirational in content and strikingly bipartisan in tone." She noted that "Both Democrats and Republicans praised the conciliatory tone of the speech." The *Monitor,* in an editorial, described Reagan as "confident, at ease" and felt that he "struck a note of high purpose and good will appropriate for the occasion" (January 22, 1985, p. 15). Louise Sweeney, in the *New York Times* (January 22, 1985, p. 4.) wrote, "It was a more intimate and less stirring ceremony than his dramatic first inaugural." Veteran columnist James Reston observed:

> President Reagan made an eloquent address, full of glittering phrases and nostalgic dreams, but it didn't inaugurate a coherent discussion of his views or proposals, but merely a jumble of opinions to scattered audiences. (*New York Times,* January, 22, 1985, p. 17)

Other reporters described the speech as "subdued," "straight, even stern," and "sombre" and noted that it was "greeted by sporadic applause." Charlotte Saikowski provided an interesting insight into the way Reagan, who has been labeled by reporters as "the great communicator," prepares his speeches (*Christian Science Monitor,* February 7, 1985, p. 1). She notes that although he has a stable of six speech writers at the White House, when he delivers a major address it "rings with the cadences, rhythm, and clean phrases that are the hallmark of the Reagan style":

> Those who help Mr. Reagan draft and polish his speeches say he is extremely skillful at wielding the blue pencil—slicing off excess verbiage, removing repetition, tightening paragraphs, simplifying language. . . . [He] doesn't like repetition or high-hat words or embellished prose. He's a plain-spoken guy in person and likes plain-spoken speeches. . . . The catch phrases that go into presidential speeches are usually thought up by the writers. But Reagan often triggers an idea by his own comments.

"The President's editorial skills are not surprising," according to Saikowski. "He developed them throughout his career, from the time he was a radio broadcaster and wrote his own scripts to his years as Hollywood actor, as host for a General Electric television show, and on the lecture circuit."

President Reagan's speech: Senator Mathias, Chief Justice Burger, Vice President Bush, Speaker O'Neill, Senator Dole, reverend clergy, and members of my family and friends, and my fellow citizens: This day has been made brighter with the presence here of one who for a time has been absent. Senator John Stennis, God bless you and welcome back. There is, however, one who is not with us today. Representative Gillis Long of Louisiana left us last night. And I wonder if we all could join in a moment of silent prayer. Amen.

There are no words adequate to express my thanks for the great honor that you've bestowed on me. I will do my utmost to be deserving of your trust.

This is, as Senator Mathias told us, the 50th time that we, the people have celebrated this historic occasion. When the first president, George Washington, placed his hand upon the Bible, he stood less than a single day's journey by horseback from raw, untamed wilderness. There were four million Americans in a union of 13 states.

Today we are 60 times as many in a union of 50 states. We've lighted the world with our inventions, gone to the aid of mankind wherever in the world there was a cry for help, journeyed to the moon and safely returned. So much has changed. And yet we stand together as we did two centuries ago.

When I took this oath four years ago, I did so in a time of economic stress. Voices were raised saying that we had to look to our past for the greatness and glory. But we, the present-day Americans, are not given to looking backward. In this blessed land, there is always a better tomorrow.

Four years ago I spoke to you of a new beginning, and we have accomplished that. But in another sense, our new beginning is a continuation of that beginning created two centuries ago when, for the first time in history, government, the people said, was not our master. It is our servant; its only power that which we, the people allow it to have.

That system has never failed us. But for a time we failed the system. We asked things of government that government was not equipped to give. We yielded authority to the national government that properly belonged to the states or local governments or to the people themselves. We allowed taxes and inflation to rob us of our earnings and savings and watched the great industrial machine that had made us the most productive people on earth slow down and the number of unemployed increase.

By 1980 we knew it was time to renew our faith, to strive with all our strength toward the ultimate in individual freedom consistent with an orderly society.

We believed then and now there are no limits to growth and human progress when men and women are free to follow their dreams. And we were right to believe that. Tax rates have been reduced, inflation cut dramatically and more people are employed than ever before in our history.

We are creating a nation once again vibrant, robust and alive. But there are many mountains yet to climb. We will not rest until every American enjoys the fullness of freedom, dignity and opportunity as our birthright. It is our birthright as citizens of this great republic.

And if we meet this challenge, these will be years when Americans have restored their confidence and tradition of progress; when our values of faith, family, work, and neighborhood were restated for a modern age; when our economy was finally freed from government's grip; when we made sincere efforts a meaningful arms reductions by rebuilding our defenses, our economy, and developing new technologies helped preserve peace in a troubled world; when America courageously supported the struggle for individual liberty, self-government, and free enterprise thoughout the world and turned the tide of history away from totalitarian darkness and into the warm sunlight of human freedom.

My fellow citizens, our nation is poised for greatness. We must do what we know is right and do it with all our might. Let history say of us, these were golden years when the American Revolution was reborn, when freedom gained new life and America reached for her best.

Our two-party system has served us well over the years, but never better than in those times of great challenge, when we came together not as Democrats or Republicans but as Americans united in the common cause.

Two of our Founding Fathers, a Boston lawyer named Adams and a Virginia planter named Jefferson, members of that remarkable group who met in Independence Hall and dared to think they could start the world over again, left us an important lesson. They had become, in the years spent in government, bitter political rivals. In the presidential election of 1800, then years later, when both were retired and age had softened their anger, they began to speak to each other again through letters.

A bond was reestablished between those two who had helped create this government of ours.

In 1826, the 50th anniversary of the Declaration of Independence, they both died. They died on the same day, within a few hours of each other. And that day was the Fourth of July.

In one of those letters exchanged in the sunset of their lives, Jefferson wrote:

It carries me back to the times when, beset with difficulties and dangers, we were fellow laborers in the same cause, struggling for what is most valuable to man, his right of self-government. Laboring always at the same oar, with some wave ever ahead threatening to overwhelm us, and yet passing harmless we rode through the storm with heart and hand.

Well, with heart and hand, let us stand as one today: one people under God determined that our future shall be worthy of our past. As we do, we must not repeat the well-intentioned errors of our past. We must never again abuse the trust of working men and women by sending their earnings on a futile chase after the spiraling demands of a bloated federal establishment. You elected us in 1980 to end this prescription for disaster. And I don't believe you reelected us in 1984 to reverse the course.

The heart of our efforts is one idea vindicated by 25 straight months of economic growth: freedom and incentives unleash the drive and entrepreneurial genus that are the core of human progress. We have begun to increase the rewards for work, savings, and investment; reduce the increase in the cost and size of government and its interference in people's lives.

We must simplify our tax system, make it more fair, and bring the rates down for all who work and earn. We must think anew and move with a new boldness so every American who seeks work can find work; so the least among us shall have an equal chance to achieve the greatest things—to be heroes who heal our sick, feed the hungry, protect peace among nations, and leave this world a better place.

The time has come for a new American emancipation, a great national drive to tear down economic barriers and liberate the spirit of enterprise in the most distressed areas of our country. My friends, together we can do this, and do it we must, so help me God.

From new freedom will spring new opportunities for growth, a more productive, fulfilled and united people, and a stronger America, an America that will lead the technological revolution and also open its mind and heart and soul to the treasuries of literature, music and poetry, and the values of faith, courage, and love.

A dynamic economy, with more citizens working and paying taxes, will be our strongest tool to bring down budget deficits. But an almost unbroken 50 years of deficit spending has finally brought us to a time of reckoning.

We've come to a turning point, a moment for hard decisionss. I have asked the Cabinet and my staff a question and now I put the same question to all of you. If not us, who? And if not now, when? It must be done by all of us going forward with a program aimed at reaching a balanced budget. We can then begin reducing the national debt.

I will shortly submit a budget to the Congress aimed at freezing government program spending for the next year. Beyond this we must take further steps to permanently control government's power to tax and spend.

We must act now to protect future generations from government's desire to spend its citizens' money and tax them into servitude when the bills come due. Let us make it unconstitutional for the federal government to spend more than the federal government takes in.

We have already started returning to the people and to state and local governments responsibilities better handled by them. Now, there is a place for the federal government in matters of social compassion. But our fundamental goals must be to reduce dependency and upgrade the dignity of those who are infirm or disadvantaged. And here a growing economy and support from family and community offer our best chance for a society where compassion is a way of life, where the old and infirm are cared for, the young and, yes, the unborn, protected, and the unfortunate looked after and made self-sufficient.

Now there is another area where the federal government can play a part. As an older American, I remember a time when people of different race, creed, or ethnic origin in our land found hatred and prejudice installed in social custom and, yes, in law. There's no story more heartening in our history than the progress that we've made toward the brotherhood of man that God intended for us. Let us resolve: There will be no turning back or hesitation on the road to an America rich in dignity and abundant with opportunity for all our citizens.

Let us resolve that we, the people, will build an American opportunity society in which all of us—white and black, rich and poor, young and old—will go forward together, arm in arm. Again, let us remember that, though our heritage is one of blood lines from every corner of the earth, we are all Americans pledged to carry on this last best hope of man on earth.

And I have spoken of our domestic goals, and the limitations we should put on our national government. Now let me turn to a task that is the primary responsibility of national government: the safety and security of our people.

Today we utter no prayer more fervently than the ancient prayer for peace on earth. Yet history has shown that peace does not come, nor will our freedom be preserved, by good will alone. There are those in the world who scorn our vision of human dignity and freedom. One nation, the Soviet Union, has conducted the greatest military buildup in the history of man, building arsenals of awesome offensive weapons.

We've made progress in restoring our defense capability. But much remains to be done. There must be no wavering by us, nor any doubts by others, that America will meet her responsibilities to remain free, secure, and at peace.

There is only one way safely and legitimately to reduce the cost of national security and that is to reduce the need for it. And this we're trying to do in negotiations with the Soviet Union. We're not just discussing limits on a further increase of nuclear weapons. We seek, instead, to reduce their number. We seek the total elimination, one day, of nuclear weapons from the face of the earth.

Now for decades we and the Soviets have lived under the threat of mutual assured destruction; if either resorted to the use of nuclear weapons, the other could retaliate and destroy the one who had started it. Is there either logic or morality in believing that if one side threatens to kill tens of millions of our people, our only recourse is to threaten to killing tens of millions of theirs?

I have approved a research program to find, if we can, a security shield that will destroy nuclear missiles before they reach their target. It wouldn't kill people, it would destroy weapons. It wouldn't militarize space, it would help demilitarize the arsenals of earth. It would render nuclear weapons obsolete. We will meet with the Soviets hoping that we can agree on a way to rid the world of the threat of nuclear destruction.

We strive for peace and security, heartened by the changes all around us. Since the turn of the century, the number of democracies in the world has grown fourfold. Human freedom is on the march, and nowhere more so than in our own hemisphere. Freedom is one of the deepest and noblest aspirations of the human spirit. People worldwide hunger for the right of self-determination, for those inalienable rights that make for human dignity and progess.

America must remain freedom's staunchest friend, for freedom is our best ally, and it is the world's only hope to conquer poverty and preserve peace. Every blow we inflict against poverty will be a blow against the dark allies of oppression and war. Every victory for human freedom will be a victory for world peace.

So we go forward today a nation still mighty in its youth and powerful in its purpose. With our allies strengthened, with our economy leading the world to a new age of economic expansion, we look to a future rich in possibilities. And all of this is because we worked and acted together not as members of political parties, but as Americans.

My friends, we, we live in a world that's lit by lightning. So much is changing and will change, but so much endures and transcends time.

History is a ribbon, always unfurling; history is a journey. And as we continue on our journey we think of those who traveled before us. We stand again at the steps of this symbol of our democracy, or we would've been standing at the steps if it hadn't gotten so cold. Now, we're standing inside this symbol of democracy, and we see and hear again the echoes of our past.

A general falls to his knees in the hard snow of Valley Forge; a lonely president paces the darkened halls and ponders his struggle to preserve the union; the men of the Alamo call out encouragement to each other; a settler pushes west and sings a song, and the song echoes out forever and fills the unknowing air.

It is the American sound: it is hopeful, bighearted, idealistic— daring, decent and fair. That's our heritage, that's our song. We sing it still. For all our problems, our differences, we are together as of old. We raise our voices to the God who is the author of this most tender music. And may He continue to hold us close as we fill the world with our sand sound—the unity, affection and love. One people under God, dedicated to the dream of freedom that He has placed in the human heart, called upon now to pass that dream on to a waiting and a hopeful world.

God bless you and may God bless America.

RIGHTS AND RESPONSIBILITIES
UNDER THE LAW

HOW FARES THE FIRST AMENDMENT?[1]
Franklyn S. Haiman[2]

Public lectures by visiting scholars have long been an important part of the intellectual life of most colleges and universities. Recognizing the valuable contribution of such lectures, alumni, friends, and former students often have chosen to recognize an outstanding scholar or teacher by endowing a lecture series in his honor. One such series is the Giles Wilkeson Gray annual lecture at Louisiana State University (LSU). The lectures honor one of the pioneers and outstanding scholars and educators in the field of speech communication.

The first lecture was given in 1984. On Monday, March 11, 1985, Professor Franklyn S. Haiman of the Northwestern University School of Speech delivered the second lecture. his topic was, "How Fares the First Amendment?" In the field of speech communication, Professor Haiman is perhaps the foremost authority on free speech. His books and articles include *Speech and Law in a Free Society,* for which in 1982 he won both the Prize for Outstanding Scholarly Book given by the Speech Communication Association (SCA) and the James A. Winans–Herbert A. Wichelus Award for Distinguished Scholarship. He also received SCA awards for his scholarship in 1967 and 1972 and has been honored by several legal, civil liberties, and library organizations.

Haiman addressed an overflow audience of more than 250 students and faculty from throughout the university, townspeople, and members and friends of the Gray family at 4:00 P.M. in the Vieux Carre room of the LSU Union. Dr. Mary Frances HopKins, chairman of the Department of Speech Communication at LSU introduced the speaker. At the end of the lecture, Professor Haiman responded to questions from the audience, and at the conclusion of the session he was given an extended ovation.

Early in his address, Haiman announced that he believed the country should be proud of the developments that have occurred in the nearly two hundred years since the Founding Fathers declared, "Congress shall make no law abridging the freedom of speech, or of the press, or of the

---

[1]Delivered as the Giles Wilkeson Gray annual lecture in the Vieux Carre room of the LSU Union at Louisiana State University, Baton Rouge, Louisiana, at 4:00 P.M. on March 11, 1985.

[2]For biographical note, see Appendix.

right of people peaceably to assemble to petition the Government for a redress of grievances.":

> I believe it is fair to say, without fear of contradiction from any reasonably informed person, that we have developed in the United States the freest and most vigorous—some might even say the most licentious—system of public discourse ever known in any nation in the world.

Especially remarkable in Haiman's opinion was the great advance in freedom of speech since World War I.

However, he warned, we also have ample cause for concern about the prospects ahead of us. "I believe that developments are occurring in our society which should cause us concern about the future." Stating what would be the central thought for the remainder of his address, Haiman said, "I would like to discuss some of those phenomena with you and identify the hazards they pose to the continued well-being of our First Amendment rights."

Franklyn S. Haiman's speech: With 1984, the year for which George Orwell predicted the onset of Big Brotherism, now safely behind us; with only two years yet to go to arrive at the Bicentennial of the United States Constitution; and only four more beyond that until the 200th birthday of the Bill of Rights; this seems an appropriate interlude in which to take stock of how we are doing with respect to the First Amendment's guarantees of freedom of speech and press. Where have we come in the nearly two hundred years since our Founding Fathers penned those courageous words: "Congress shall make no law . . . abridging the freedom of speech, or of the press; or the right of the people peaceably to assemble and to petition the Government for a redress of grievances"? And what does the future appear to hold for us? I would like to suggest in these remarks, and hopefully to demonstrate, that we have ample basis for satisfaction over the developments that have occurred since that language was written in 1791, as well as ample cause for concern about the prospects that lie ahead of us.

To begin with, I believe it is fair to say, without fear of contradiction from any reasonably informed person, that we have developed in the United States the freest and most vigourous—some might even say the most licentious—system of public discourse ever known in any nation of the world. Just in our own lifetimes, or at least in the lifetimes of those of us with a few graying hairs, there has been tremendous growth in the extent to which the free expression of unpopular, avant-garde, or deviant messages is accepted, if not always appreciated.

We have come a long way from the days of the first World War, and the period immediately thereafter, when people like Eugene V. Debs were sent to the penitentiary for making speeches in opposition to our entry into that war, and when laboring men and women were enjoined by courts of law from engaging in peaceful picketing of their employers or were beaten by the police if they did so. Less than 35 years ago a movie could not be distributed in this country with the Motion Picture Producers Association seal of approval if it portrayed even a married couple in bed together or acknowledged the existence of alcoholism or drug addiction.

Today, in contrast, one may advocate extremist political doctrine, even the desirability of a revolution, so long as that advocacy stops short of direct incitement to immediate and likely lawless action. Your local governments may not prohibit the Jehovah's Witnesses or political canvassers from ringing your doorbell to solicit your support or your conversion; they may not exclude the Hare Krishna or pro-nuclear demonstrators from your airport terminal building lobby; they may not even bar a group of uniformed neo-Nazis from marching with swastikas on the sidewalk in front of your city hall. Not only may married people appear in bed together in a movie, but entirely nude couples, married or not, straight or gay, may be portrayed in the throes of sexual intercourse.

What accounts for our having come to such a permissive state of affairs, so much farther than at any other place or time in human history? I believe that there are primarily two reasons for it.

First, we in the United States are by and large more secure, both physically and economically, than any other society has ever been. Despite any alleged "window of vulnerability" that may or may not exist, we are clearly the foremost military power on earth; and despite our pockets of unemployment and desperate poverty, most of us enjoy unparalleled standards of living and economic well-being. These kinds of security breed a tolerance for dissent, just as insecurity breeds intolerance. It is no coincidence that the most repressive periods in the history of nations, including our own, have come at times of the greatest perceived external military danger or internal economic unrest. When one is strong and comfortable one worries less about looking for subversives under the bed.

The second factor which I believe accounts for the degree of tolerance we have achieved is that we in the United States have attained higher levels of education for a greater proportion of our population than anywhere else in the world, and all survey research of which I am aware has consistently shown a positive correlation between levels of education and tolerance for deviation from the norm. The reasons for that seem quite clear. In the first place, intolerance and the impulse to suppress alien ideas spring often from fear of the unknown and the more one knows and understands about other people, and the world in general, the less fearful one tends to be—unless, of course, there is realistic cause to be afraid. Intolerance and repression are also the offspring of lack of confidence in one's own values, and the more we know and understand ourselves and are able to articulate and defend our ideas the less worried we are that our beliefs will be undermined by the urgings of others.

Finally, the philosophy of Voltaire—that although he might disagree with what others said he would defend to the death their right to say it—is a philosophy of *enlightened* self-interest requiring the ability to think at a level of abstraction and complexity that may elude one who is lacking in education. It is not apparent to those who act only in terms of immediate gratification why, if they have the power, they should not strike out and smash that which they dislike. It is only by understanding the long-term consequences of such behavior—that it does not succeed in smashing anything, but only in driving it underground; and that there may also be a time in the future when one is the smashee rather than the smasher—in short, it is only by responding with one's mind instead of one's guts that one becomes a Voltairean. I cannot even recount the number of times, back in 1978, as I argued on behalf of the ACLU's defense of the projected Nazi march in Skokie, that people said to me that although they might agree with me in their heads, their hearts or their stomachs would not follow. That, incidentally, is one of the reasons we have courts, which are somewhat insulated from popular passions of the moment, to provide protection for constitutional rights.

Whatever the causes for the robust health which freedom of speech and press enjoy in America today, let us rejoice in it. But complacency about freedom has never been a wise course, and I believe that developments are occurring in our society which should cause us concern about the future. I would like to discuss some of those phenomena with you and identify the hazards that they pose to the continued well-being of our First Amendment rights.

Perhaps no change has characterized the past decade more dramatically than the explosion of new technologies of communication—cable television, communication satellites and direct broadcast transmissions from them, mini-computers, videocassette recorders, and a multitude of other gadgets which I do not even begin to comprehend. At first blush one would expect an enormous enrichment of the exercise of First Amendment rights as a result of these new tools—a broader spectrum of communication channels, the more rapid transmission of material, and the ability to individualize messages to a greater degree and direct them to specialized audiences. And indeed, in many ways, that is precisely what has been happening. There is an almost infinite variety of magazines available to satisfy the most unusual of interests and tastes. If one has cable television and wants to do nothing but watch sports, or news, or X-rated movies, that is now possible. If you write a letter to your Congressman about abortion, Nicaragua, or federal aid to education, your name, address, particular interest and point of view may all go into a computer which can spit out appropriate mail to you whenever the Congressman thinks that might be politically useful.

And here we begin to see the down side of these new technologies—letters which appear to be personalized but are really automated, and phone calls of the same ilk which are not far behind; specialization which facilitates the development of sports buffs, adult movie addict, or Jesus freaks but does precious little for the maintenance of well-rounded citizenship; local cable television franchises awarded by city councils, understandably, to those who offer the best service, but that is usually a small group of large national corporations, which means more and more channels of communication in fewer and fewer hands.

That pattern is the same in the print media, where for a good many years now four-, three- and two-newspaper towns have become one-newspaper towns, and the papers which remain are more likely than before to be owned and operated by the Gannett chain (which has joined Exxon and AT&T as one of the largest corporations in America), Time magazine, and even Rupert Murdoch (who has taken over the *New York Post, Chicago Sun-Times* and *Boston Herald,* in addition to the *Village Voice* and *London Times*) or the Reverend Moon who now runs one of the two major daily newspapers in our nation's capital. If you thought it was a joke two months ago when Senator Jesse Helms announced a campaign to urge his idealogical soul-mates to purchase CBS stock in order to become "Dan Rather's boss," you better take a second look and ask yourself how long the ever-increasing concentration of ownership of the mass media, so frighteningly documented in Ben Bagdikian's book, *Media Monopoly,* can go on without endangering the public's exposure to a variety of points of view.

One of the difficulties here is that the media are businesses which are subject to the same economic facts of life as all other businesses in our society, where forces—such as economies of scale—which lead to mergers, take-overs, and giant multinational corporations seem irreversible. Who, after all, can afford to put a communications satellite in space but a gigantic corporation or a major industrialized nation? How many publishers can field foreign correspondents to the four corners of the globe? To what extent can a locally owned and operated bookstore compete with the discounted prices of the Crown or B. Dalton national chains? How many Ted Turners are there who can swing the establishment of a successful cable network, and how many Gannett empires that can sustain the millions in dollars of losses of *USA Today* until it gains a profit-making foothold?

Now, centralization and monopolization of the *ownership* of media of communication are not necessarily and inevitably antithetical to the dissemination of a diversity of messages and the free marketplace of ideas contemplated by the First Amendment. That depends on whether the owners choose, or are required by law, to allow access to their media by others with whom they may not agree. Although we have had a history in the United States of newspaper owners like William Randolph Hearst and Colonel Robert McCormick, who did not so choose, and a legal tradition which has honored that choice, we have evolved an entirely different set of rules for radio and television broadcasters, for common carriers like telephone and telegraph companies, and for local cable television franchise winners.

Over-the-air broadcasters may lose their licenses if they do not cover controversial issues of public importance with a reasonable degree of fairness; they are required, with some exceptions, to grant free time for replies to personal attacks; they may not refuse to sell time for political campaign advertisements nor may they censor the content of such ads. Telephone and telegraph companies may not pick and choose the customers they will serve, nor the messages they will transmit. Most cable television franchises are granted only on condition that channels be sent aside for use by local schools or local government and for some first-come first-serve public access programming. And even though it is not required by law, most reputable major newspapers today carry letters to the editor, so-called op-ed pieces (i.e. guest editorials), and columnists of a variety of ideological predispositions.

Although it has been claimed by some that legal obligations on the electronic media such as the Fairness Doctrine and equal-time rules are violations of the First Amendment rights of broadcasters, the U.S. Supreme Court has said that the competing First Amendment interest of the public in being exposed to a diversity of ideas takes precedence—a point of view directly opposite to that which the Court holds regarding newspapers. The difference is rationalized on the gounds of a theoretically unlimited number of newspapers that can be published versus the presumed relative scarcity and public nature of the airwaves and the resultant necessity of assuring access to this more limited resource.

Whether that rationale is still valid in a day when we have a greater number and diversity of radio stations than newspapers is legitimately debatable. But what I believe to be indisputable is that where media monopolies do, *in fact,* exist—as is the case with

telephone lines and cable and is likely to be increasingly the case
with the newer technologies of communication—legally required
and guaranteed public access to these media is essential if the exercise of free-speech rights is to survive in any meaningful way.
Whether our legislators can withstand the pressure of lobbyists
claiming for these media owners a First Amendment right to do
what they please with their property is not a matter about which
I am entirely optimistic.

A second phenomenon of recent times which poses serious
dangers to freedom of speech and of the press is the growing number of libel suits being brought against the media by prominent
public figures, two of the most nteworthy being General Westmoreland's suit against CBS [1984-1985] for accusing him of having doctored enemy troop figures during the war in Vietnam, and
Ariel Sharon's suit against *Time* magazine [1984-1985] for having charged him with complicity in the massacre of Palestinians
by Lebanese Phalangists. Not only do such law suits, win or lose,
create a climate in which hard-hitting investigative journalism
may operate with an excess of caution for fear of punishment if
mistakes are made, but also such law suits, win or lose, open the
door for a plaintiff's lawyers to rummage through the files of reporters and editors, seeking out their sometimes confidential
sources of information, examining their unused drafts and film
clips, and exploring their memoranda and conversations to try to
uncover the guilty state of mind that must be shown in order to
meet the burden of proof that the law requires of the plaintiff—
either knowledge by the defendant that what was said was false
or reckless disregard for its truth or falsity.

I am well aware of the legitimate interest that people have in
protecting their reputations against false and damaging charges,
and I share the public sympathy that often exists for the victims
of such accusations (although I am troubled by the "get the press"
mentality of revenge which sometimes accompanies that sympathy). Here, as with so many other First Amendment issues, like
free press versus fair trial, there is a tension between competing
and valid interests, and ways must be found to accommodate both.
The U.S. Supreme Court attempted to steer such a course in its
landmark *New York Times v. Sullivan* decision on libel in 1964,

where it recognized that in order for there to be the "uninhibited, robust and wide open" debate on public issues that a democracy requires, there must be latitude for error, and that public officials who are verbally attacked ordinarily have ample access to the media to set the record straight. However, according to the Court, when falsehoods are deliberately or recklessly promulgated, the pendulum swings to the other side, reputation becomes more valuable than speech, and a libel suit is an appropriate remedy.

But that is not what is going on in the burgeoning of law suits like those of Westmoreland and Sharon, where it not only defies reason to believe that CBS or *Time* would *deliberately* or *recklessly* lie, but where there was a substantial likelihood, with persuasive supporting evidence, that what was said was essentially true. Make no mistake about it—these are politically motivated cases designed to inhibit and punish those who dare challenge the public policies and practices of powerful individuals who may have abused their position of authority, and to vindicate those policies and practices. The Westmoreland case was instigated and financed by an organization in Washington D.C. called the Capital Legal Foundation whose president, Dan Burt, was Westmoreland's lead attorney. That foundation has close ties to another organization, the Libel Prosecution Resources Center, which, as its name suggests, offers its help to people who feel wronged by the media and want to sue. Although most such lawsuits are ultimately unsuccessful, because of the difficult burden of proof imposed by the Supreme Court on libel plaintiffs, a substantial number of them are won before sympathetic juries and must be appealed to higher courts for the judgment to be overturned on legal grounds. All of this, even if the defendant wins at the jury trial level, is immensely costly in time, emotional energy and money to the media, who may think twice before they let their reporters take on another powerful public figure. That, I suggest, is a frightful First Amendment prospect.

A third area in which I see troublesome developments from a First Amendment point of view is the ever increasing role being played in our marketplace of ideas by government agencies and officials, to the point where there may be danger of communication from the state effectively drowning out or overwhelming competing ideas. I should hasten to add that there is a necessary and important place for government in the public dialogue. Government agencies must keep us abreast of their policies and programs so that whatever support or participation are called for by citizens can be forthcoming. Political leaders must be free to advocate new courses of action or to justify present ones. Many of the services provided to us by federal, state, and local authorities involve, or even consist entirely of, the transmission of information and ideas. What I am concerned about are not these normal and valuable interactions, but a possible flooding of the channels of communication by government to the near exclusion of all else, with the practical result of a brainwashed and compliant citizenry.

Let me provide some illustrations of what I mean. It is a well known fact that there are large sums of money in the budgets of virtually every department and agency of the federal government, including the White House and the offices of the members of Congress—and much the same can be said of state and local governments—for public relations, press secretaries, literature, films, broadcasting, and so on. Some of this is to perform the necessary and useful functions to which I have already alluded. But much of it is nothing more than propaganda machinery to make the agency and agency leaders look good (whether they have fouled up on their jobs or not), and to perpetuate or even expand the activities and influence of the bureaucracy in question (whether that is in the public interest or not). As our society becomes ever more communications conscious and the tools of communication become ever more sophisticated, we can expect these P.R. budgets to grow, when in truth they need drastic pruning.

A little over a decade ago a book was published, written by former Federal Communications Commission chairman Newton Minow, along with John Bartlow Martin and Lee Mitchell, entitled *Presidential Television* and documenting the vast expansion of presidential communication to the public through television which was started during the Nixon administration and, it can now be added, has continued ever since. It was not the purpose of that book to advocate the curbing of such speech, which would not be feasible in any case, but to warn of the need for measures to insure that alternative messages would also be aired and be heard as broadly as those of the president. Some feeble steps have been taken by the television networks in that direction, such as providing response time to opposition leaders for the most obviously partisan of the president's speeches, although not usually for his more "presidential" appearances like press conferences, or like speeches about foreign or domestic crises that arise from time to time. I believe that the combined effectiveness of presidential television, along with well orchestrated State and Defense Department public relations, and obliging supportive statements from prominent senators and congressmen explains, far better than the facts of the situation warranted, the approval by an overwhelming majority of the American people of the United States invasion of Grenada in 1983. Even our most conservative and uncritical allies, like Prime Minister Thatcher of Great Britain, exposed to different communication stimuli, were not so impressed.

A final indication of the troubling dominance in our marketplace of ideas of government speech is that, in our elections of public officials—the one time citizens participate directly in the public decision-making process—over 90% of incumbents, regardless of party, are victorious. To be sure, some of that is attributable to non-speech factors such as experience, services rendered to constituents, ideological compatibility with the views of the voters, or even a clear edge in competence. But we cannot ignore the tremendous communication advantages also enjoyed by incumbent officeholders, such as the free franking privilege for mail accorded to members of Congress, staff people whose salaries are paid by the taxpayers but who may devote much of their time to promoting the reelection of their boss, readier access to the media for interviews or press coverage of their activities that comes with being a public official, and the name recognition that can be enhanced by a welcome sign from the mayor at the airport, the secretary of state's signature on drivers' licenses, the sponsorship of a piece of legislation, the cutting of ribbons at a public ceremony, riding in a convertible at the head of the Fourth of July parade, and so on. When one adds to these traditional imbalances between incumbents and challengers the new element of the exorbitant financial costs of a modern mass media political campaign, for which incumbents in most cases have a far greater ability to raise Political

Action Committee and other special-interest money than do challengers, one has to wonder if such campaigns can be counted as constituting a free marketplace of ideas. Clearly they are not "free" in a monetary sense!

Ironically, at the same time that our government officials are talking more and more, they are in some ways telling us less and less—which brings me to the fourth phenomenon that endangers the exercise of First Amendment freedoms, namely creeping government secrecy. The father of our Constitution, James Madison, who presumably knew what a democracy is all about, once said that "a popular government, without popular information or the means of acquiring it, is but a prologue to a farce or a tragedy, or perhaps both." I cannot help but wonder what Mr. Madison, if he were alive in our time, would have to say about thousands of government documents classified as "confidential" or "top secret" by hundreds of bureaucrats, contracts requiring public employees to promise to submit for prior review anything they write or say for the rest of their lives about what they have learned on their government jobs, secret plots to assassinate foreign leaders or secret funds to assist in their overthrow, secret mining of Nicaraguan waters sponsored by the C.I.A., or a ban on press coverage of the first phase of the Grenada invasion.

Now there are many valid justifications for a government keeping some kinds of information from being publicly disseminated. We have a right to expect that the personal information we submit to the Internal Revenue Service or the Census Bureau will not appear on the front pages of the local newspapers unless we ourselves voluntarily release it to them. There is ordinarily no reason for the police to release the name of a rape victim to the press and good reason for not doing so. The plans that were made by the Carter administration for the attempted rescue of the Americans held hostage at our embassy in Iran had to be kept under careful wraps, as do the details of our military defenses. Delicate diplomatic negotiations cannot usually be conducted with success in a fish bowl, and a chief executive is entitled to maintain some degree of confidentiality with respect to the discussions he has with his closest advisors.

But for every case of justifiable government secrecy there seem to be increasing numbers of instances where information is withheld because bureaucrats are trying to cover up their mistakes, or because they believe that the public, unlike themselves, cannot be trusted to deal responsibly with difficult problems, or, worst of all, because they desire to engage in activities which they believe they might not be able to get away with if the public knew about them. The latter would appear to be the best explanation for events like the secret bombing of Cambodia by U.S. warplanes in 1968 or the most recent mining of Nicaraguan waters, since the targets of those operations knew full well what was going on, and it was only the American people who were kept in the dark until somebody leaked the information.

I think that probably the most disturbing thing I ever hear from college students—the best educated segment of our population—is when, in the course of a discussion about U.S. foreign policy or military affairs, they sometimes say that they really do not know enough to have an opinion and that they simply trust the wisdom and good faith of the administration in Washington to do what is best for the country. Without passing any judgment on that attitude, since it may reflect a reasonable accommodation to an unfortunate reality, and without questioning either the wisdom or good faith of this or any administration in Washington, I submit that such a state of affairs is incompatible with the fundamental principles of a democracy. To accept the premise that Big Brother knows best because only Big Brother is informed is to accept the premise of George Orwell's 1984.

The fifth development which I believe poses serious dangers to the First Amendment is the increasing militancy and power of the religious fundamentalists in our society who are pressing for access to the public schools for prayer, religious meetings, and the teaching of creationism, and are pressing for access to public buildings and parks for the display of Christian religious symbols such as crosses and creches. This movement raises constitutional problems of unusual complexity because of the superficially persuasive claim by its adherents that, far from endangering the First Amendment, all they are seeking is to exercise their own rights of freedom of speech and religious liberty under that amendment.

Why do I say that this claim is only superficially persuasive and that it will not withstand critical scrutiny? Let us first look to the language of the First Amendment itself to begin to answer that question. In the event that you have not read it lately let me read it to you, and remind you that, as important to our democracy as are freedom of speech and of the press, they are not what came first for the authors of the First Amendment. For those people, whose families had fled from Europe to America primarily to escape religious persecution, what they said *first* was that "Congress shall make no law respecting an establishment of religion," and then they went on, "or prohibiting the free exercise thereof; or abridging the freedom of speech, or of the press; or the right of the people peaceably to assemble, and to petition the Government for a redress of grievances."

It was not because they were anti-religious that our Founding Fathers placed highest priority on prohibiting the new government they were creating from establishing any officially endorsed religion. On the contrary, it was because they were deeply religious and knew that the only way to preserve their religious liberty and "the free exercise thereof" was to keep the government out of it—to not allow it, as kings and princes had done in Europe, to promote, support, or give the imprimatur of official approval to any religion or church, for that could only work to the detriment, if not persecution or destruction, of all other religions or churches. Thus the wall of separation between church and state that was mandated by the opening words of the First Amendment is an essential predicate to the remaining phrases of that amendment. There can be no safe and sure exercise of religious freedom—of the right to speak about one's religious beliefs, to pray and to hold religious meetings, to display and to honor religious symbols, to write and to publish religious tracts—unless those activities remain in the private sector, free from entanglement with the coercive authority and power of the state.

The application of this broad and abstract principle to concrete cases is not always easy, and the fine lines that sometimes have to be drawn may seem picayune to those who like simpler answers or who are somewhat insensitive to the religious feelings of others who do not happen to belong, with them, to the majority religion of a particular community. Thus, a group of students eating in the lunch room of a public school who spontaneously decide to pray together have a First Amendment free-speech right to do that, but the same activity in a classroom led by the teacher would violate the separation of church and state. Singing secular Christmas season music, like "Jingle Bells" or "Rudolph the Red Nosed Reindeer," in a compulsory public school assembly does not violate the First Amendment, but singing "Silent Night," with its references to the virgin birth and "Christ the Savior," really does. Forcing biology teachers, againt their scientific judgment, to give equal time to the theories of evolution and creationism is an impermissible establishment of religion, whereas telling students in a history of religion lesson that some people have faith in creationism is not. A creche prominently displayed on the front lawn of the local church is perfectly appropriate; it is not so on the front lawn of the city hall. Roman Catholics have as much of a First Amendment right to gather in a public park for a mass conducted by the Pope as the nuclear freeze movement has to conduct a nonreligious demonstration there, but the Pope is not allowed to lead a religious ceremony in a public school assembly, although a debate there on the nuclear freeze would be entirely acceptable. Unfortunately for the First Amendment, there seem to be growing numbers of people in our country who are impatient with these distinctions and are willing, even eager, to use the facilities and auspices of the state to advance their religious beliefs. They forget that this is a two-edged sword which could some day be used against them.

The sixth and concluding development that causes me concern for the continued good health of freedom of speech is another kind of impatience which seems to be spreading among our people, but this one for very good reason. It is an impatience with the pettiness, emptiness, irrationality and even fraudulence of more and more of the rhetoric of our political campaigns. If that growing impatience, and even disgust, were to lead to a recognition by candidates that they were turning voters off, and that they needed to mend their ways, I would be applauding this development rather than viewing it with alarm. There is, in my view, a crying need for improvement in the ethics of communication, not only in the political world but in commercial advertising and the entertainment world as well, and I am all for social pressures which may stimulate such change.

I worry, however, when the solution that is proposed for the low level of political rhetoric is to resort to legal remedies—to pass a "truth-in-campaigning" law, for example, which would establish a government agency to hear and adjudicate complaints about unfair messages; or to give radio and television stations the opportunity, which is now forbidden to them by the Federal Communications Act, to censor political advertisements for alleged falsity or bad taste. It has been seriously suggested that anything shorter than five-minute radio or television political messages be outlawed, on the theory that nothing substantive and rational can be communicated in the lesser amounts of time. And at least one legal scholar has argued that the First Amendment was intended to protect only civilized political discourse and that, contrary to a U.S. Supreme Court ruling in 1971, a young man who appeared in public with the words "Fuck the Draft" printed on the back of his jacket, should have been found guilty, as charged, for disturbing the peace.

My problem with *legal* requirements of truth, fairness, rationality, good taste or civilized discourse in the political arena is that they place in the hands of some state commission, judge or jury the power to decide what is true, what is rational, what is fair, what is civilized, what is in good taste. But it is my understanding of democracy that these are questions which only the public may decide—not a government agency or the courts.

Justice Louis Brandeis summed up what I believe to be the proper understanding of the First Amendment when he wrote, in *Whitney* v. *California* in 1927:

If there be time to expose through discussion the falsehood and fallacies, to avert the evil by the processes of education, the remedy to be applied is more speech, not enforced silence.

Or, as Thomas Jefferson put the same thought, in words now engraved on that beautiful memorial to him in our nation's capital, when referring to political rebels:

. . . let them stand undisturbed as monuments of the safety with which error of opinion may be tolerated where reason is left free to combat it.

If that philosophy prevails, the First Amendment will remain alive and well.

PRESIDENTIAL APPOINTMENTS TO THE SUPREME COURT[1]

WILLIAM H. REHNQUIST[2]

"There is no reason in the world" for a President not to try to pack the Supreme Court with justices "who are sympathetic to his political or philosophical principles," Associate Supreme Court Justice William H. Rehnquist told an audience of law students and faculty at the University of Minnesota College of Law in Minneapolis on October 19, 1984.

It is unusual for a Supreme Court justice to speak publicly about the relationship between the court and the White House. Justice Rehnquist's lecture was particularly striking since it came near the end of a presidential campaign in which the age of the justices (five were 75 years old or older) and the likelihood that the next president would fill several vacancies had been issues.

For a decade after his appointment to the Supreme Court by President Richard Nixon in 1971, Rehnquist often stood alone as a dissenter to judicial activism. During these years, he established himself as the court's conservative conscience. By 1985 a conservative majority had begun to emerge with Justice Rehnquist at its ideological center. Writing in *The New York Times Magazine,* John A. Jenkins said: "on a Court that has lacked powerful personalities and a firm sense of direction, Justice Rehnquist stands out" (March 3, 1985, p. 28).

Since his appointment, Rehnquist had delivered more speeches than any of his Supreme Court brethren with the possible exception of Chief Justice Warren Burger. Describing the 60-year-old justice at the time of his Minneapolis address, Jenkins wrote, "He is a bit heavier, his hair thinner and grayer, the brown eye glasses thicker than when he first arrived. His smile is quick and genuine. . . . He speaks slowly and carefully. . . . " (*New York Times Magazine,* March 3, 1985, p. 31).

Rehnquist delivered the address to an audience of 400 faculty, alumni, student lawyers, and the press in room 175 Willey Hall on the University of Minnesota west bank campus at 12:15 P.M. The speech concluded a week-long Jurists in Residence program during which Rehnquist and

---

[1]Delivered in room 175, Willey Hall, University of Minnesota Law School, Minneapolis, Minnesota, at 12:15 P.M., October 19, 1984.

[2]For biographical note, see Appendix.

Judge Myron H. Bright had met with law students in classes and workshops.

Justice Rehnquist's speech: One of the proud and just boasts of the constitutional system of government which we have in the United States is that even the President is not above the law. The justness of the boast is rooted in decisions such as the Steel Seizure Case, in which the Court rebuffed the claims of President Truman, and in the Nixon Tapes Case, in which the Court rebuffed the claims of President Nixon. But, though the President, the head of the executive branch, may be subject under our system to checks and balances administered by the judicial branch of government, the courts themselves are subject to a different form of check and balance administered by the President. Vacancies in the federal judiciary are filled by the President with the advice and consent of the United States Senate. Just as the courts may have their innings with the President, the President comes to have his innings with the courts. It seems fitting, particularly in the year of a presidential election, to inquire what history shows as to the propensity of presidents to "pack" the Court, and the extent to which they have succeeded in any such effort.

I use the word pack as the best verb available, realizing fullwell that it has a highly pejorative connotation. But it ought not to have such a connotation when used in this context; the second edition of Webster's unabridged dictionary, which happens to be the one I have in my study, defines the verb "pack" as "to choose or arrange (a jury, committee, etc.) in such a way as to secure some advantage, or to favor some particular side or interest." Thus a President who sets out to pack the Court seeks to appoint people to the Court who are sympathetic to his political or philosophical principles.

There is no reason in the world why a President should not do this. One of the many marks of genius which our Constitution bears is the fine balance struck in the establishment of the judicial branch, avoiding both subservience to the supposedly more vigorous legislative and executive branches on the one hand, and total institutional isolation from public opinion on the other. The performance of the judicial branch of the United States government for a period of nearly two hundred years has shown it to be remarkably independent of the other coordinate branches of that government. Yet the institution has been constructed in such a way that the public will, in the person of the President of the United States—the one official who is elected by the entire nation—have something to say about the membership of the Court, and thereby indirectly about its decisions.

Surely, we would not want it any other way. We want our federal courts, and particularly the Supreme Court of the United States, to be independent of popular opinion when deciding the particular cases or controversies which come before them. The provision for tenure during good behavior and the prohibition against diminution of compensation have proved more than adequate to secure that sort of independence. The result is that judges are responsible to no electorate or constituency. But the manifold provisions of the Constitution with which judges must deal are by no means crystal clear in their import, and reasonable minds may differ as to which interpretation is proper. When a vacancy occurs on the Court, it is entirely appropriate that that vacancy be filled by the President, responsible to a national constituency, as advised by the Senate, whose members are responsible to regional constituencies. Thus, public opinion has some say in who shall become judges of the Supreme Court.

The answer to the first question I posed—have Presidents in the past attempted to pack the Court?—is easy; the Presidents who have been sensible of the broad powers which they have possessed and been willing to exercise those powers have all but invariably tried to have some influence on the philosophy of the Court as a result of their appointments to that body. This should come as a surprise to no one.

The answer to the second question which I posed—how successful have Presidents been in their efforts to pack the Court?—is more problematical. I think history teaches us that those who have tried have been at least partially successful but that a number of factors militate against a President having anything more than partial success. What these factors are I will try to illustrate with examples from the history of the Court.

Very early in the history of the Court, Justice William Cushing, "a sturdy Federalist and follower of Marshall," died in September, 1810. His death reduced the seven-member Court to six, evenly divided between Federalist appointees and Republican appointees. Shortly after Cushing's death, Thomas Jefferson, two years out of office as President, wrote to his former Secretary of the Treasury, Albert Gallatin, in these unseemingly gleeful words:

I observe old Cushing is dead. At length, then, we have a chance of getting a Republican majority in the Supreme Judiciary. For ten years has that branch braved the spirit and will of the Nation. . . . The event is a fortunate one, and so timed as to be a godsend to me.

Jefferson, of course, had been succeeded by James Madison, who, though perhaps less ardently than Jefferson, also championed Republican ideals. Jefferson wrote Madison that "it will be difficult to find a character of firmness enough to preserve his independence on the same Bench with Marshall." When he heard that Madison was considering Joseph Story and Ezekiel Bacon, then Chairman of the Ways and Means Committee of the House of Representatives, he admonished Madison that "Story and Bacon are exactly the men who deserted us [on the Embargo Act]. The former unquestionably a Tory, and both are too young."

President Madison seems to have been "snake-bit" in his effort to fill the Cushing vacancy. He first nominated his Attorney General, Levi Lincoln, who insisted that he did not want the job, and after the Senate confirmed him still refused to serve. Madison then nominated a complete dark horse, one Alexander Wolcott, the Federal Revenue Collector of Connecticut, whom the Senate, controlled by his party, rejected by the mortifying vote of 24–9. Finally, in the midst of a cabinet crisis which occupied a good deal of this time, Madison nominated Joseph Story for the Cushing vacancy, and the Senate confirmed him as a matter of routine three days later.

Story, of course, fulfilled Jefferson's worst expectations about him. He became Chief Justice Marshall's principal ally on the great legal issues of the day in the Supreme Court, repeatedly casting his vote in favor of national power and against the restrictive interpretation of the Constitution urged by Jefferson and his state's rights school. And Joseph Story served on the Supreme Court for thirty-four years, one of the longest tenures of record.

Presidents who wish to pack the Supreme Court, like murder suspects in a detective novel, must have both motive and opportunity. Here Madison had both, and yet he failed. He was probably a considerably less partisan chief executive than was Jefferson, and so his motivation was perhaps not strong enough. After having botched several opportunities, he finally preferred to nominate someone who would not precipitate another crisis in his relations with the Senate, rather than insisting on a nominee who had the right philosophical credentials.

The lesson, I suppose, that can be drawn from this incident is that while for court-watchers the President's use of his appointment power to nominate people for vacancies on the Supreme Court is the most important use he makes of the executive authority, for the President himself the filling of the Supremem Court vacancies is just one of many acts going on under the "big top" of his administration.

Abraham Lincoln had inveighed against the Supreme Court's 1857 decision in the *Dred Scott* case during his famous debates with Stephen A. Douglas in 1858, when both sought to be elected United States Senator from Illinois. Lincoln lost that election, but his successful presidential campaign two years later was likewise marked by a restrained but nonetheless forceful attack on this decision and by implication on the Court's apparent institutional bias in favor of slaveholders. Within two months of his inauguration, by reason of the death of one justice and the resignation of two others, Lincoln was given three vacancies on the Supreme Court. To fill them Lincoln chose Noah Swayne of Ohio, David Davis of Illinois, and Samual F. Miller of Iowa. All were Republicans who had rendered some help in getting Lincoln elected President in 1860; indeed, Davis had been one of Lincoln's principal managers at the Chicago convention of the Republican Party.

In 1863, by reason of expansion in the membership of the Court, Lincoln was enabled to name still another justice, and he chose Stephen J. Field of California, a War Democrat who had been the chief justice of that state's Supreme Court. In 1864, Chief Justice Roger B. Taney finally died at the age of 88, and Lincoln had an opportunity to choose a new chief justice. At this time, in the fall of 1864, the constitutionality of the so-called greenback legislation, which the government had used to finance the war effort, was headed for a Court test, and Lincoln was very much aware of this fact. He decided to appoint his Secretary of the Treasury, Salmon P. Chase, who was in many respects the architect of the greenback legislation, saying to a confidant that "We wish for a chief justice who will sustain what has been done in regard to emancipation and the legal tenders. We cannot ask a man what he will do, and if we should, and he should answer us, we should despise him for it. Therefore, we must take a man whose opinions are known."

In all, then, Lincoln had five appointments. How successful was Lincoln at "packing" the Court with these appointments? The answer has to be, I believe, that he was very successful at first. In the all important "Prize Cases," decided in 1863, the three Lincoln appointees already on the Court—Swayne, Miller, and Davis—joined with Justices Wayne and Grier of the old Court to make up the majority, while Chief Justice Taney and Justices Nelson, Catron, and Clifford dissented. It seems obvious that this case would have been decided the other way had the same Justices been on the Court who had decided the *Dred Scott* case six years earlier. Charles Warren, in his *The Supreme Court in United States History,* describes these cases as being not only "the first cases arriving out of the Civil War to be decided by [the court], but they were far more momentous in the issue involved than any other case; and their final determination favorable to the government's contention was almost a necessary factor in the suppression of the war."

Immediately after the war, a host of new issues arose which could not really have been foreseen at the time that Lincoln made his first appointments to the Supreme Court. The extent to which military tribunals might displace civil courts during time of war or insurrection was decided by the Supreme Court in 1866 in the famous case of *Ex parte Milligan,* 4 Wall. 2. While the Court was unanimous as to one aspect of this case, it divided five to four on the equally important question of whether Congress might provide for trial by military commissions during time of insurrection even though the President alone could not. On this point, Justices

Field and Davis, Lincoln appointees, joined Justices Nelson, Grier, and Clifford of the old Court to hold that neither Congress nor the President might do so, while Chief Justice Chase and Justices Miller and Swayne (all appointd by Lincoln) joined Justice Wayne of the old court in holding that Congress might establish such courts even though the President alone could not.

During the post-war Reconstruction Era, three new amendments to the United States Constitution were promulgated, and the construction of those amendments was also necessarily on the agenda of the Supreme Court. The first important case involving the Fourteenth Amendment to come before the Court was that of the Slaughterhouse Cases, in which the applicability of the provisions of that amendment to claims not based on racial discrimination was taken up by the Court. Of the Lincoln appointees, Justice Miller wrote the majority opinion and was joined in it by Justice Davis, while Chief Justice Chase and Justices Field and Swayne were in dissent.

The ultimate irony in Lincoln's effort to pack the Court was the Court's first decision in the so-called Legal Tender Cases. In 1870 the Court held, in an opinion by Chief Justice Chase, who had been named Chief Justice by Lincoln primarily for the purpose of upholding the greenback legislation, that this legislation was unconstitutional. Justice Field joined the opinion of the Chief Justice, while the other three Lincoln appointees—Miller, Swayne, and Davis—dissented. Chief Justice Chase's vote in the legal tender cases is a textbook example of the proposition that one may look at a legal question differently as a judge than one did as a member of the executive branch. There is no reason to believe that Chase thought he was acting unconstitutionally when he helped draft and shepherd through Congress the greenback legislation, and it may well be that if Lincoln had actually posed the question to him before nominating him as Chief Justice, he would have agreed that the measures were constitutional. But administrators in charge of a program, even if they are lawyers, simply do not ponder these questions in the depth that judges do, and Chase's vote in the legal tender cases is proof of this fact.

In assessing Lincoln's success in his effort to pack the Court, it seems that with regard to the problems he foresaw at the time of his first appointments—the difficulties that the Supreme Court might put in the way of successfully fighting the Civil War— Lincoln was preeminently successful in his efforts. But with respect to issues which arose after the war—the use of military courts, the constitutionality of the greenback legislation, and the construction of the Fourteenth Amendment—his appointees disagreed with one another regularly. Perhaps the lesson to be drawn from these examples is that judges may think very much alike with respect to one issue, but quite differently from one another with respect to other issues. And while both Presidents and judicial nominees may know the current constitutional issues of importance, neither of them are usually vouchsafed the foresight to see what the great issues of ten or fifteen years hence are to be.

Probably the most obvious laboratory test for success in packing the Court is the experience of President Franklin D. Roosevelt with his judicial appointments. Franklin Roosevelt had both motive and opportunity in abundance. He was elected President in 1932, and his first term in office was notable for the enactment of many important social and economic regulatory measures. But it seemed during these four years that no sooner were these New Deal measures signed into law by the President than they were invalidated by the Supreme Court. That Court, referred to in those days as the "Nine Old Men," had on it Justices appointed by Presidents Taft, Wilson, Harding, Coolidge, and Hoover. Though the outcomes in many cases were close, during Roosevelt's first term the Court struck down such important pieces of New Deal legislation as the NRA and AAA.

In November, 1936, President Roosevelt won a landslide re-election victory, with the Republican opponent carrying only the states of Maine and Vermont. Frustrated during his first term by the lack of any vacancies on the Supreme Court, Roosevelt disdained to wait longer for vacancies and in effect took the bull by the horns. In his famous "Court packing plan" proposed in February, 1937, he sought authority from Congress to enlarge the membership of the Court to as many as fifteen Justices; the President would have the authority to appoint an additional Justice for each Member of the Court over seventy years of age who chose not to retire. This measure was shot down in flames in the Senate, a Senate which the Democrats controlled by a margin of 5-1. But in the very course of the battle over this legislation, Justice Van Devanter, who had been appointed to the Court by President Taft in 1910, announced his intention to retire, and during the next four years there occurred six additional vacancies on the Court. The power to remake the Court, which Roosevelt had unsuccessfully sought from Congress, was given him by the operation of the actuarial tables.

There is no doubt that President Roosevelt was keenly aware of the importance of judicial philosophy in a justice of the Supreme Court; if he were not, he never would have taken on the institutional might of the third branch with his court-packing plan. When it appeared during the battle in the Senate over the Court packing bill that a compromise might be achieved in which Roosevelt would be allowed to appoint two new justices, he pondered with several of his intimates whom he might choose, and there is little doubt that uppermost in his mind was a judicial outlook sympathetic to sustaining the New Deal legislation.

Within four years of the defeat of the Court-packing legislation, as I have indicated, seven of the nine members of the Court had been appointed by Roosevelt, and in the short run the effect of the change in Court personnel was immediate and predictable. Social and regulatory legislation, whether enacted by the states or by Congress, was sustained across the board against constitutional challenge that might have prevailed before the "old" Court. When Roosevelt in 1941 appointed Harlan F. Stone to succeed Charles Evans Hughes as Chief Justice, the periodical *United States News* commented that "The new head of the Court will also find no sharp divergence of opinion among his colleagues." The *Washington Post* echoed the same sentiment when it foresaw "for years to come" a "virtual unanimity on the tribunal."

These forecasts proved to be entirely accurate in the area of economic and social legislation. But other issues began to percolate up through the judicial coffee pot, as they have a habit of doing. The Second World War, which occupied the United States from 1941 until 1945, produced numerous lawsuits about civil liberties. During the War, the Court maintained a fair degree of cohesion in deciding most of these cases, but quite suddenly after the War, the predicted "virtual unanimity" was rent asunder in rancorous squabbling the like of which the Court had seldom seen before.

A part—but only part—of the differences were of judicial philosophy. Understandably, seven justices who agreed as to the appropriate constitutional analysis to apply to economic and social legislation might not agree with one another in cases involving civil liberties. These differences manifested themselves infrequently during the war years, but came into full bloom shortly afterwards. In a case called *Saia* v. *New York* (1948), the Court held by a vote of 5 to 4 that a local ordinance of the city of Lockport, New York, regulating the use of sound trucks in city parks was unconstitutional. Four of the five Justices in the majority were appointees of Franklin Roosevelt, but so were three of the four Justices in the minority. Seven months later the Court all but overruled the *Saia* case in *Kovacs* v. *Cooper,* with one of the *Saia* majority defecting to join the four dissenters for the *Kovacs* majority. These two cases provide but one of abundant examples of similar episodes in the Court's adjudication during the period from 1945 to 1949.

In 1949, two events of rather dramatic importance for court-watchers, if not for the public at large, occurred within a few months of each other. In July of that year, Justice Frank Murphy died at the age of 59, after having served on the Court for ten years. In September, Justice Wiley Rutledge died at the age of 55, after having served on the Court for six years. Both of these deaths may fairly be described as untimely, and the terms of service of both Justices Murphy and Rutledge were substantially below the average for Supreme Court justices.

Ironically, these two appointees were the most liberal of all of the Roosevelt appointees on issues such as civil rights and civil liberties. Harry Truman, then President, replaced them with Justices Tom Clark and Sherman Minton, respectively, who had no doubts about the constitutionality of New Deal economic and social legislation, but who had quite different views of the relationship of the Constitution to civil liberties and civil rights claims from Justices Murphy and Rutledge. Here was an element of blind chance which frustrated at least in part the unanimity that had been predicted for the so-called Roosevelt Court: two of President Roosevelt's eight appointees died well before they might have been expected to die, permitting another President to fill the vacancies. One is reminded of the statement of William Howard Taft, speaking with newspaper reporters as he stepped down from the Presidency. Numbering among his most important presidential acts the appointment of six justices to the Supreme Court, Taft said he had told these judges: "If any of you die, I'll disown you."

The final factor which frustrated President Roosevelt's complete success in his effort to pack the Supreme Court was a deep personal animosity which developed between several of his appointees. It originally arose between Justice Black and Justice Jackson, but then spread to ally Justice Douglas with Justice Black and Justice Frankfurter with Justice Jackson. The first public manifestation of this animosity was buried in the minute orders denying rehearing in the *Jewell Ridge* case when the Supreme Court adjourned for the summer in June, 1945. The petition for rehearing claimed that Justice Black should have disqualified himself in that 5–4 decision because it was argued by his one-time law partner; Justice Jackson's insistence upon separately stating his views as to the petition for rehearing caused a deep rift between the two Justices.

This unedifying controversy resurfaced the following spring in 1946. Chief Justice Stone died suddenly in April of that year, and President Truman delayed filling the vacancy for a number of weeks. Justice Jackson was at this time special prosecutor for the United States at the Nuremberg trials of the Nazi war criminals. He had just wound up his many months' work in Germany, but had not yet returned to the United States. In early June, President Truman announced the appointment of Fred M. Vinson as Chief Justice, and four days later Justice Jackson released an unprecedented statement to the press in Europe, although it was addressed nominally to the chairmen of the House and Senate Judiciary Committees. Jackson then, responding to what he thought were inspired columns in the Washington press reflecting Black's view of the controversy over the *Jewell Ridge* case, released to the public all the gory details of that case in a light favorable to him. The reaction of the American press and public was one of astonishment that Jackson would air dirty linen in this manner, and of "a plague on both your houses" insofar as the Black-Jackson "blood fued" was concerned.

Jackson and his ally, Frankfurter, had voted differently from Black and his ally, Douglas, in some of the cases to come before the Court before the *Jewell Ridge* controversy, but one cannot help wondering if the bitter public antagonism generated by that case might not have exacerbated these differences. The expected near unanimity which the Roosevelt appointees were supposed to bring to the Court was frustrated by these antagonisms as well as by the other factors which I have mentioned.

Thus history teaches us, I think, that even a strong president determined to leave his mark on the Court—a President such as Lincoln or Franklin Roosevelt—is apt to be only partially successful. Neither the president nor his appointees can foresee what issues will come before the Court during the tenure of the appointees, and it may be that none had thought very much about these issues. Even though they agree as to the proper resolution of current cases, they may well disagree as to future cases involving other questions when, as judges, they study briefs and hear arguments. Longevity of the appointees, or untimely deaths such as those of Justice Murphy and Justice Rutledge, may also frustrate a President's expectations; so also may the personal antagonisms developed between strong willed appointees of the same President.

All of these factors are subsumed to a greater or lesser extent by observing that the Supreme Court is an institution far more dominated by centrifugal forces, pushing towards individuality and independence, than it is by centripetal forces pulling for hierarchial ordering and institutional unity. The well known checks and balances provided by the framers of the Constitution have supplied the necessary centrifugal force to make the Supreme Court independent of Congress and the President. The degree to which a new Justice should change his way of looking at things when he "puts on the robe" is emphasized by the fact that Supreme Court appointments almost invariably come one at a time, and each new appointee goes alone to take his place with eight colleagues who are already there. Unlike his freshman counterpart in the House of Representatives, where if there has been a strong political tide running at the time of a particular election there may be as many as forty or fifty or eighty new members who form a bloc and cooperate with one another, the new judicial appointee brings no cohorts with him.

A second series of centrifugal forces is at work within the Court itself, pushing each member of the court to be thoroughly independent of his colleagues. The Chief Justice has some authority that the Associate Justices do not have, but this is relatively insignificant compared to the extraordinary independence that each Justice has from every other Justice. Tenure is assured no matter how one votes in any given case; one is independent not only of public opinion, of the President, and of Congress, but of one's eight colleagues as well. When one puts on the robe, one enters a world of public scrutiny and professional criticism which sets great store by individual performance, and much less store upon the virtue of being a team player.

James Madison, in his pre-presidential days when he was authoring political tracts, said in *The Federalist No. 51*:

But the great security against a gradual concentration of the several powers in the same department, consists in giving to those who administer each department the necessary constitutional means and personal motives to resist encroachments of the others. The provision for defense must in this, as in all other cases, be made commensurate to the danger of attack. Ambition must be made to counteract ambition. The interest of the man must be connected with the constitutional rights of the place.

Madison, of course, was talking about the principles necessary to secure independence of one branch of the government from another. But he might equally well have been talking about principles, at least in the case of the Supreme Court of the United States, designed to weaken and diffuse the outside loyalties of any new appointee, and to gradually cause that appointee to identify his interests in the broadest sense not merely with the institution to which he is appointed, but to his own particular place within the institution. Here again, this remarkable group of fifty-some men who met in Philadelphia in the summer of 1787 seem to have created the separate branches of the federal government with consummate skill. The Supreme Court is to be independent of the legislative and executive branch of the government; yet by reason of vacancies occurring on that Court, it is to be subjected to indirect infusions of the popular will in terms of the President's use of his appointment power. But the institution is so structured that a brand new presidential appointee, perhaps feeling himself

strongly loyal to the President who appointed him, and looking
for colleagues of a similar mind on the Court, is immediately beset
with the institutional pressures which I have described. He identifies more and more strongly with the new institution of which he
has become a member, and he learns how much store is set by his
behaving independently of his colleagues. I think it is these institutional effects, as much as anything, which have prevented even
strong presidents from being any more than partially successful
when they sought to pack the Supreme Court.

A PLEA FOR CORPORATE RESPONSIBILITY[1]
MILES W. LORD[2]

On February 29, 1984, the Minneapolis courtroom of United States
District Court Judge Miles W. Lord was the scene of an unusual and
highly controversial confrontation. The cause of controversy was a speech
delivered in a $4.6 million product-liability suit against the A. H. Robins
Company, manufacturers of the Dalkon Shield intrauterine contraceptive
device. The birth control device, on the market in the United States from
1970 to 1974, had been linked to severe pelvic infection and septic abor-
tions and had allegedly caused 18 deaths. (*Time,* July 24, 1984, p. 88)
Although the Dalkon Shield had not been sold since 1974, the company
never formally recalled it. By mid-1984, of more than 10,000 lawsuits
and claims filed by women against the company, over 4,000 remained un-
settled. (*Business Week,* July 16, 1984, p. 28) Believing that the A. H.
Robins Company had employed delay and obfuscation to wear down its
opponents in the current suit and others, Lord, Chief Judge of the U. S.
District Court for Minnesota, ordered the firm's president, E. Claiborne
Robins, Jr., its senior vice-president for research and development, Carl
D. Lunsford, and vice president and general counsel William A. Forrest,
Jr., to appear in his courtroom in Minneapolis. Once they were there,
in open court he insisted that the three read a lengthy speech on corporate
ethics he had once given to a church group. Then he delivered a stinging
rebuke of Robins' tactics in the Dalkon Shield cases. Enraged by Robins'
legal strategy in continuing to fight the suits in the face of what he called
overwhelming evidence, Lord said:

[1]Delivered in the United States District Court for Minnesota, Minneapolis, Minnesota, on February
29, 1984.
[2]For biographical note, see Appendix.

If one poor young man were by some act of his to inflict such damage upon one woman, he would be jailed for a good portion of the rest of his life. And yet your company, without warning to women, invaded their bodies by the millions and caused them injuries by the thousands. And when the time came for these women to make their claims against your company, you attacked their characters. . . . You have taken the bottom line as your guiding beacon and the low road as your route. This is corporate irresponsibility at its meanest.

Appointed to the federal bench in 1966, Lord had earned a reputation as an "outspoken," "blunt and strong-willed" populist "who has challenged large corporations both inside and outside the courtroom." (*Time,* July 23, 1984, p. 88) The judge's tongue-lashing was widely publicized in the press and attracted greater attention when *Harper's* published a two-page excerpt from the speech in its June 1984 issue. The Robins executives subsequently filed a complaint with the Eighth Circuit Court of Appeals, arguing that Judge Lord had "methodically destroyed their personal and professional reputations" and "grossly abused his office." Since federal judges can be removed only after impeachment by Congress, the complainants asked only that Lord be cited for misconduct. On November 2, 1984, the appeals court rules that Lord's public reprimand of the executive had been "highly injudicious," but took no action on Robins' request that the judge be cited for misconduct. Lord said he felt he had been vindicated. (*New York Times,* November 3, 1984, p. 11)

Judge Lord's speech: Mr. Robins Jr., Mr. Forrest and Dr. Lundsford: After months of reflection, study and cogitation—and no small amount of prayer—I have concluded it perfectly appropriate to make to you this statement, which will constitute my plea to you to seek new horizons in corporate consciousess and a new sense of personal responsibility for the activities of those who work under you in the name of the A. H. Robins Company.

It is not enough to say, "I did not know," "It was not me," "Look elsewhere." Time and time again, each of you has used this kind of argument in refusing to acknowledge your responsibility and in pretending to the world that the chief officers and the directors of your gigantic multinational corporation have no responsibility for the company's acts and omissions.

In a speech I gave several years ago (in the document which I have just asked you to read), I suggested to the hundreds of ministers of the gospel who constitute the Minnesota Council of Churches that the accumulation of corporate wrongs is in my mind a manifestation of individual sin.

You, Mr. Robins Jr., have been heard to boast many times that the growth and prosperity of this company is a direct result of its having been in the Robins family for three generations. The stamp of the Robins family is upon it. The corporatrion is built in the image of the Robins mentality.

You, Dr. Lunsford, as director of the company's most sensitive and important subdivision, have violated every ethical precept to which every doctor under your supervision must pledge as he gives the oath of Hippocrates and assumes the mantle of one who would help and cure and nurture unto the physical needs of the populace.

You, Mr. Forrest, are a lawyer, one who upon finding his client in trouble should counsel and guide him along a course which will comport with the legal, moral and ethical principles which must bind us all. You have not brought honor to your profession, Mr. Forrest.

Gentlemen, the results of these activities and attitudes on your part have been catastrophic. Today as you sit here attempting once more to extricate yourselves from the legal consequences of your acts, none of you has faced up to the fact that more than 9,000 women have made claims that they gave up part of their womanhood so that your company might prosper. It is alleged that others gave their lives so you might so prosper. And there stand behind them legions more who have been injured but who have not sought relief in the courts of this land.

I dread to think what would have been the consequences if your victims had been men rather than than women, women who seem through some strange quirk of our society's mores to be expected to suffer pain, shame and humiliation.

If one poor young man were by some act of his—without authority or consent—to inflict such damage upon one woman, he would be jailed for a good portion of the rest of his life. And yet your company, without warning to women, invaded their bodies by the millions and caused them injuries by the thousands. And when the time came for these women to make their claims against your company, you attacked their characters. You inquired into their sexual practices and into the identity of their sex partners. You exposed these women—and ruined families and reputations and careers—in order to intimidate those who would raise their voices against you. You introduced issues that had no relationship whatsoever to the fact that you planted in the bodies of these women instruments of death, of mutilation, of disease.

I wish to make it absolutely clear that I am specifically directing and limiting my remarks to that which I have learned and observed in these consolidated cases before me. If an incident arises involving another product made by the A. H. Robins Company, an independent judgment would have to be made as to the conduct of your company concerning that product. Likewise, a product made by any other company must be judged upon the individual facts of that case.

Gentlemen, you state that your company has suffered enough, that the infliction of further punishment in the form of punitive damages will cause harm to your ongoing business, will punish innocent shareholders and could conceivably depress your profits to the point where you could not survive as a competitor in this industry. When the poor and downtrodden in this country commit crimes, they too plead that these are crimes of survival and that they should be excused for illegal acts which helped them escape desperate economic straits. On a few occasions when these excuses are made, a contrite and remorseful defendant promises to mend his ways, courts will give heed to such a plea. But no court would heed this plea when the individual denies the wrongful nature of his deeds and gives no indication that he will mend his ways. Your company, in the face of overwhelming evidence, denies its guilt and continues its monstrous mischief.

Mr. Forrest, you have told me that you are working with members of the Congress of the United States to ask them to find a way of forgiving you from punitive damages which might otherwise be imposed. Yet the profits of your company continue to mount. Your last financial report boasts of new records for sales and earnings, with a profit of more than $58 million in 1983. And all the while, insofar as this court is able to determine, you three men and your company still engage in the self-same course of wrongdoing in which you originally commenced. Until such time as your company indicates that it is willing to cease and desist this deception and to seek out and advise victims, your remonstrances to Congress and to the courts of this country are indeed hollow and cynical. The company has not suffered, nor have you men personally. You are collectively being enriched by millions of dollars each year. There is as yet no evidence that your company has suffered any penalty whatsoever from these litigations. In fact, the evidence is to the contrary.

The case law indicates that the purpose of punitive damages it to make an award which will punish a defendant for his wrongdoing. Punishment traditionally involves the principles of revenge, rehabilitation and deterrence. There is no evidence I have been able to find in my review of these cases to indicate that any one of these factors has been accomplished.

Mr. Robins Jr., Mr. Forrest, Dr. Lunsford: You have not been rehabilitated. Under your direction your company has in fact continued to allow women, tens of thousands of them, to wear this device—a deadly depth charge in their womb, ready to explode at any time. Your attorney Mr. Alexander Slaughter denies that tens of thousands of these devices are still in the bodies of women. But I submit to you that Mr. Slaughter has no more basis for his denial than the plaintiffs have for stating it as truth, because we simply do not know how many women are still wearing these devices and your company is not willing to find out. The only conceivable reasons you have not recalled this product are that it would hurt your balance sheet and alert women who already have been harmed that you may be liable for their injuries. You have taken the bottom line as your guiding beacon and the low road as your route. This is corporate irresponsibility at its meanest. Rehabilitation involves an admission of guilt, a certain contrition, an acknowledgment of wrongdoing and a resolution to take a new course toward a better life. I find none of this in the instance of you and your corporation. Confession is good for the soul, gentlemen. Face up to your misdeeds. Acknowledge the personal responsibility that you have for the activities of those who work under you. Rectify this evil situation. Warn the potential future victims and recompense those who already have been harmed.

Mr. Robins Jr., Mr. Forrest, Dr. Lunsford: I see little in the history of this case that would deter others from partaking of like acts. The policy of delay and obfuscation practiced by your lawyers in courts throughout this country has made it possible for you and your insurance company, Aetna Casualty and Surety Company, to delay the payment of these claims for such a long period that the interest you earn in the interim covers the cost of these cases. You, in essence, pay nothing out of your pocket to settle these cases. What other corporate officials could possibly learn a lesson from this? The only lesson could be that it pays to delay compensating victims and to intimidate, harass and shame the injured parties.

Mr. Robins Jr., Mr. Forrest, Dr. Lunsford: You gentlemen have consistently denied any knowledge of the deeds of the company you control. Mr. Robins Jr., I have read your deposition. Many times you state that your management style was such as to delegate work and responsibility to other employees in matters involving the most important aspects of this nation's health. Judge Fran Theis, who presided over the discovery of these cases during the multidistrict litigation proceedings, noted this phenomenon in a recent opinion. He wrote, "The project manager for Dalkon Shield explains that a particular question should have gone to the medical department, the medical department representative explains that the question was really the bailiwick of the quality control department, and the quality control department representative explains that the project manager was the one with the authority to make a decision on that question." Under these circumstances, Judge Theis notes, "it is not at all unusual for the hard questions posed in Dalkon Shield cases to be unanswered by anyone from Robins."

Your company seeks to segment and fragment the litigation of these cases nationwide. The courts of this country are now burdened with more than 3,000 Dalkon Shield cases. The sheer number of claims and the dilatory tactics used by your company's attorneys clog court calendars and consume vast amounts of judicial and jury time. Your company settles those cases in which it find itself in an uncomfortable position, a handy device for avoiding any proceeding which would give continuity or cohesiveness to this nationwide problem. The decision as to which cases to try rests almost solely at whim and discretion of the A. H. Robins Company. In order that no plaintiff or group of plaintiffs might assert a sustained assault upon your system of evasion and avoidance, you time after time demand that able lawyers who have knowledge of the facts must as a price of settling their cases agree to never again take a Dalkon Shield case nor to help any less experienced lawyers with their cases against your company.

Minnesota lawyers have filed cases in this jurisdiction for women from throughout the United States. The cases of these women have waited on the calendar on this court for as many as three years. The evidence they will present at trial is predominantly generic evidence concerning the company's actions, which is as easy to produce in Minnesota as anywhere else. Yet your company's attorneys persist in asking that these cases be transferred to other jurisdictions and to other judges unfamiliar with the cases, there to wait at the bottom of the calendars for additional months and years before they have their day in court.

Another of your callous legal tactics is to force women of little means to withstand the onslaught of your well-financed, nationwide team of attorneys, and to default if they cannot keep pace. You target your worst tactics for the meek and the poor.

(I should point out that the Faegre & Benson law firm, local counsel for your company in the consolidated cases before me, has a high reputation for fair play, integrity and fidelity to the court. Faegre & Benson, and other local firms retained for trials across the country, are not responsible for the overall strategic decisions of your company.)

Despite your company's protestations, it is evident that these thousands of cases cannot be viewed in isolation, one at a time. The multidistrict litigation panel of the federal court system found these cases to have sufficient similarity on issues of fact and law to warrant their reference to a single judge who, for varying periods of time, conducted discovery, depositions and proceedings designed to devise an efficient method of handling these cases. In each of these thousands of cases, the focal point of the inquiry is the same: the conduct of your company through its acts and omissions. Indeed, Judge Gerald Heaney of the Court of Appeals for the Eight Circuit recently urged judges in Minnesota to work together to devise a coordinated system for dealing with all of their Dalkon Shield cases.

These litigations must be viewed as a whole. Were these wom-
en to be gathered together with their injuries in one location, this
would be dominated a disaster of the highest magnitude. The mere
fact that these women are separated by geography blurs the total
picture. Here we have thousands of victims—present and potential—whose injuries arise from the same series of operative facts.
You have made no effort whatsoever to locate them and bring
them together to seek a common solution to their plight.

If this were a case in equity, I would order that your company
make an effort to locate each and every woman who still wears
this device and recall your product. But this court does not have
the power to do so. I must therefore resort to moral persuasion and
a personal appeal to each of you. Mr. Robins Jr., Mr. Forrest and
Dr. Lunsford: You are the people with the power to recall. You
are the corporate conscience.

Please in the name of humanity lift your eyes above the bottom
line. You, the men in charge, must surely have hearts and souls
and consciences. If the thought of facing up to your transgression
is so unbearable to you, you might do as Roger Tuttle [former A.
H. robins in-house counsel who testified about the destruction of
company documents] did and confess to your maker, beg forgive-
ness, and mend your ways.

Please, gentlemen, give consideration to tracing down the victims and sparing them the agony that will surely be theirs.

THE OUTLOOK FOR AMERICAN EDUCATION

A "NOTION" AT RISK: THE GREATER CRISIS IN AMERICAN EDUCATION[1]
Jeffrey R. Holland[2]

"Education is in the news. For the past twelve months the nation has been awash in a flood of reports and studies on the state of American schools." Dr. Jeffrey R. Holland, President of Brigham Young University, used these words in a speech at one of the National Press Club's Newsmaker Breakfasts on March 12, 1984, to describe the publicity and controversy surrounding the country's educational system. Holland was referring to a spate of studies prepared by highly regarded groups which, in general, deplored a "rising tide of mediocracy" in the schools.

Paraphrasing one report, "A Nation at Risk," Dr. Holland titled his address, "A 'Notion' at Risk: the Greater Crisis in American Education." Holland said that, after nearly a year of reading reports criticizing our education system, his main concern was "the conspicuous and wholesale absence" from virtually every one of these reports of any mention of the importance of the moral and civilizing value of education and the substitution of "unabashedly utilitarian" economic and technological goals in their place. Responding to the various reports' demands for utilitarian education, Holland proclaimed: " . . . if our number one priority in this country is education devoted to economic growth, national defense, and increased productivity, important as they are, then God in Heaven cannot help us out of the severe straits we are in."

In his speech, Holland traced the history of education from early Greece and Rome, through the Middle Ages and the Renaissance and the founding of this country, up to the present. In so doing, he displayed an impressive familiarity with the ideas of philosophers, scholars, educators, and critics from the ancient past to today. Holland concluded his address with four recommendations designed to reaffirm traditional values in our schools.

Dr. Holland's speech: Thank you for your hospitality this morning. I am aware of the responsibility such an invitation carries, and I earnestly hope you will feel your time has been well spent.

[1]Delivered at a Newsmaker Breakfast at the National Press Club, Washington, D. C., on the morning of March 22, 1984.
[2]For biographical note, see Appendix.

Allen Drury once said that Washington, D.C. is a city of just-arriveds and only-visiting. I am guilty on both counts, but am delighted to be in the nation's capital.

Education is in the news. For the past twelve months the nation has been awash in a flood of reports and studies on the state of American schools. We have seen it examined by national commissions which say the "Nation [is] at Risk" and by task forces that insist on "Action for Excellence." We are coached along the way by the very formal Carnegie Foundation and the very informal Group of Fifty. And of course, these are only the evidence of national anguish. A gaggle of state and local reports pursue the agenda closer to our respective homes. Business barons and social scientists, public policy makers and skeptical taxpayers are wading into the swamp to grapple with educational reform in his or her own way. And more reports of their combat are yet to come, some of them already public through recently published iterim findings. Through it all education promises to be one of the three or four top domestic issues in the 1984 election campaign.

Although former U. S. Secretary of Education Harold Howe II terms this "heady wine for educators," he is also quick to note the "fickle ebb and flow of the tides of enthusiasm for education" which have been particularly evident for one-third of a century in this country. President Bart Giamatti of Yale University is even more biting:

The gaudy halftime show put on the last six months by the strutting incumbents and aspirants for office, followed as always by massed trombones and xylophones of the press, will probably do no real harm, although the racket will be tremendous for awhile. . . . [In fact] national opinion leaders and federal officials are paralyzed, baffled by the proper demands for partnership, lost in the joys of preemptive ideological strikes and in distrust of what their polls tell them is deeply important. As the country, fragmented, without serious moral authority from any quarter of public leadership, struggles to pay attention again to the means for elementary and secondary education, mistakes will be made [even as] some ideas will be trumpeted . . . as the panacea for all time, world without end.

Obviously the subject has touched a raw nerve or two, a little more painfully for some than others, but eliciting a marked response in every quarter just the same. Not all of the reports cover

the same ground or make the same recommendations but for our
purposes today, may I quote from the most publicized of them,
submitted to Secretary T. H. Bell just one year ago today by the
National Commission on Excellence in Education. Its title is in
its opening line.

Our nation is at risk. Our once unchallenged preeminence in commerce,
industry, science, and technological innovation is being overtaken by com-
petitors throughout the world. . . . The educational foundations of our
society are presently being eroded by a rising tide of mediocrity that
threatens our very future as a nation and a people. What was unimagin-
able a generation ago has begun to occur—others are matching and surpassing our educational attainments.
If an unfriendly foreign power had attempted to impose on America the
mediocre educational performance that exists today, we might well have
viewed it as an act of war. . . . We have, in effect, been committing the
act of unthinking, unilateral educational disarmament.
Our society and its educational institutions seem to have lost sight of the
basic purposes of schooling, and of the high expectations and disciplined
effort needed to attain them.

Then, to demonstrate that the "basic purposes of schooling"
have indeed been lost, the commission reports that the Japanese
make more automobiles than we do, the South Koreans make better steel mills than we do, the Germans make finer machine tools
than we do, and so forth. Thus, we are told, our nation is at risk.

My concern this morning, after nearly a year of reading such
reports and listening to them being discussed, is that while a nation may be at risk, it is manifestly clear that a very important
American notion is at even greater risk.

As evidenced by their conspicuous and wholesale absence from
virtually every one of these reports and proposals, we have obviously relegated all the moral and civic (read "civilizing") values
of education to the very back seat of the big yellow bus—if indeed
they are still being allowed to ride at all—while prominently seat-
ed up front are the real necessities, those which give primacy to
our economic needs, our escalating technological needs; in short
those that are "unabashedly utilitarian." As Professor Douglas
Sloan has said, "First a living, then art and morality; first [money
for] our financially beleaguered colleges and universities, then a
philosophy of education." If one doesn't believe it, just ask the Ed-

ucation Commission of the States. Last month a university president serving there said,

I really believe there has got to be a resurgence of public commitment to
education in this country, and I think it's fundamental if we really do
want to see economic growth, advancement in national defense, and an
increase in productivity. . . . This has got to become the nation's number
one priority.

Well, if our number one priority in this country is education
devoted to economic growth, national defense, and increased productivity, important as they are, then God in His heaven cannot
help us out of the severe straits we are in. No wonder Amitai Et-
zioni speaks of the 1980s as "the hollowing of America." Meg
Greenfield saw the wrong-headedness of it all when she wrote several months ago that "the values we bring to the effort to fight the
situation are precisely the ones that got us in trouble in the first
place and are only likely to perpetuate our grief."

Education as an "investment," education as a way to beat the Russians,
and best the Japanese, education as a way to get ahead of the fellow down
the street . . . you really do not generate the educational values that
count when you stress only these external, comparative advantages.

In the words of Robert Nash and Edward Ducharme, "[The
reports'] deficiencies are a direct outgrowth of what is essentially
a manpower-neeeds view of educational excellence, a view which
encourages a marketplace solution to complex spiritual and intellectual problems." What is missing, they say, is "the most irksome
(yet the most important) value question of all: what should education's short and long-term purposes be beyond [its] response
to . . . manpower needs."

It is as if Leo Strauss's classic *Natural Right and History*
speaks directly to his hour.

We can be . . . wise in all matters of secondary importance, but we have
to be resigned to utter ignorance in the most important respect. . . . We
are then in the position of beings who are sane and sober when engaged
in trivial business and who gamble like madmen when confronted with
serious issues—[it is] retail sanity and wholesale madness.

James Reston made just this point last fall in a *New York
Times* article about political leadership. "It's interesting to look

back," he says, "at the speeches and the Federalist Papers at the beginning of the American Republic. Their authors were tough politicians, but they were always referring to their responsibilities to 'future gnerations.' The talk here in modern times is mainly about the next election."

Then quoting Walter Lippman, Reston goes on.

Those in high places . . . are more than the administrators of government bureaus. They are more than the writers of laws. They are the custodians of a nation's ideals, of the beliefs it cherishes, of the faith which makes a nation out of a mere aggregation of individuals.

"Leaders do matter," Reston concludes. "Much depends on how they view themselves, what they say, whether they appeal to the best or the worst in the people." Well, if that kind of leadership matters in politics, I insist that it matters in education. Teachers and principals and superintendents and presidents of universities are in "high places." They are—or should most assuredly be—"custodians of a nation's ideals, of the beliefs it cherishes, of the faith which makes a nation out of a mere aggregation of individuals." That is, after all, why all those young Athenians went to Socrates in the first place. Educational leaders "do matter" and as a profession we need to appeal to "the best in the people." The nation is educationally at risk, all right, but not solely for the reasons expressed by the National Commission, indeed not even principally for the reasons they express. As a nation we have lost sight of "the basic purposes of schooling," but so, it seems to me, have far too many of our educators, including many who must have responded to the honest and important inquiries made by the National Commission. Where are the Thoreauvian men and women who will strike at the root of our educational, and national problem rather than hacking forever at the branches? Too many in our profession have forgotten what Socrates said in those original and purer groves of academe. "For the argument," he said to his students, "is not about just any question but about the way one should live." Losing the significant sense of that notion has put our nation at risk. It is the greater crisis in American education, for the "rising tide of mediocrity" is in morality and manners far more than in mathematics and manufacturing.

We know that at least Socrates' very best student tried to address the teacher's question. Against the Sophists, those itinerant charlatans who said they could teach fifth century B.C. Athenians how to be clever and win debates so long as they didn't worry about "the truth" (of which, relatively speaking, they felt certain there wasn't any), Plato held that not only was there truth but that the highest truth always had moral value. To know it and live accordingly to it was man's obligation and his virtue. Finally for him only education in virtue was worthy of the name. Plato's philosophy provided a justification not only for what students ought to be taught but also for how they ought to live.

That philosophy provided what Alston Chase calls "the paradigmatic rationale for scholarly activity" from the fifth century A.D. to the nineteenth century A.D. Even during the very darkest moments in our history it endured. St. Benedict, living at a time when Rome was threatened and finally overrun by vandals, simply retreated behind the stone walls of Monte Cassino, taking with him the spirit and valued traditions of Christianity. "While the barbarian invaders ran wild," note Calvin Woodard, "pillaging and destroying everything in sight, St. Benedict and his monks gently nourished the flickering flame of civilization."

St. Benedict's example reminds us that one of the purposes of education is not only to resist the wicked, the tawdry, and the profane, but to stand unalterably for the higher values of civilization—Plato's truths, if you will—and, when the turbulent world will not accept them, to preserve and keep them alive for the future, when and after the vandals have exhausted themselves.

And so it continued, out of the darkness and into the light. "Learning and training in virtue are peculiar to man," they would still write in the fifteenth century.

We call those students liberal that are worthy of a free man; those studies by which we obtained and practice virtue and wisdom; that education which calls forth, trains, and develops those higherst gifts of body and mind, which in noble men are rightly judged to rank next in dignity and virtue only.

From continental and English renaissance to the shores of the new world the universities were charged with holding the moral character of their students.

In the United States such personal beliefs as John Adams' "virtuous citizen" and Thomas Jefferson's "moral sense" and "aristocracy of talent and virtue," were the natural values upon which the republic was predicated. Jefferson always placed the individual man first in his philosophy and framed his entire social theory in the light of the moral nature of that human being.

The key to John Adams' optimism was his abiding belief in American virtue. He was irrepressible. Even during the darkest hours of the Revolution, he felt "the great difficulties which America faced, would 'lay the foundations of a full and flourishing people, deep and strong in great virtues and abilities.'" He believed firmly that history (under the direction of divine providence) was destined to become the next and greatest in the continuing succession of empires—a land where the two great bulwarks of liberty and knowledge would flourish.

But none of this meant that virtue was either automatic or inevitable. It required education and discipline. The Founding Fathers had read John Locke with a passion and believed with that "of all the men we meet with, nine parts of ten are what they are, good or evil, useful or not, by their education." The great danger to society then was not from any innate evil within the individual, but rather from ignorance born of sloth. Laziness, both moral and intellectual, was at the heart of the problem.

That is why Ben Franklin would believe that an individual, in devoting himself to his own intellectual and moral development in a disciplined way, not only insures his success in life but also determines his society's moral progress. "Virtue is an art," Franklin maintained, "as much as painting, architecture, or navigation. If a person wants to become a painter, a navigator, or an architect . . . one must learn 'the Principles of the Art.'" Even the pessimistic James Madison said,

I go on this great republican principle that the people will have virtue and intelligence to select men of virtue and wisdom. Is there no virtue among us? If there is not, we are in a wretched situation. No theoretical checks, no form of government can render us secure. To suppose any form of government will secure liberty or happiness without any virtue in the people, is a chimerical idea.

As Professor Douglas Sloan has so carefully documented (and to whom I am indebted for his writing on ethics and moral philosophy) the moral foundation for the republic both informed and encouraged the same foundation for the American educational experience. Until the very last decade of the nineteenth century, the most important course in the college curriculum was moral philosophy, taught usually by the college president and required of all senior students. It aimed to integrate, to give meaning and purpose to the student's entire college experience and course of study. In so doing it more importantly sought to equip the graduating seniors with the ethical sensitivity and insight needed if they were to put their newly acquired knowledge to use in ways that would benefit not only themselves and their own personal advancement, but the larger society as well.

So the foremost task of the moral philosopher was to demonstrate to his students that humans are fundamentally moral creatures. It was his task to exhort, admonish, and inspire students to recognize that the demands of morality were real and all-encompassing. Furthermore the entire college curriculum and campus environment had the same purpose. The entire college experience was meant above all to be an experience in character development and the moral life.

But the advent of the twentieth century brought decisive change: including the rise of the modern university. Yet Daniel Coit Gilman, President of Johns Hopkins, the model of the research university, could still speak for most of his fellow university reformers when he said, "The object of the university is to develop character—to make men." But there was change in the wind.

Diversity and specialization, trained experts, the rise of scholarly societies, the elective principle introduced under Charles W. Eliot at Harvard, the growth of university departments, undergraduate specialization, vocationalism, professional education, and research—all of these shattered the vision of a unified curriculum and culture of learning. The ethical, social, and character concerns, once central to higher education, were giving way to an emphasis on research and specialized training as the primary purpose of the university.

With the new status and scholarly achievements of the faculties came an academic style that was becoming, in the words of Frederick Rudolph, "indifferent to undergraduates," "removed from moral judgment," and to an increasing degree "unrelated to the traditional social purposes of higher education."

There was increasing emphasis on "value-free inquiry," and for good reason. By dispensing with such ethical questions, the scholars also eliminated a major source of potential controversy. The teaching of ethics was relegated to the department of philosophy, where there was little danger that anyone would enroll in it. The classic texts by America's nineteenth century moral philosophers had all been almost totally abandoned. "With the world calling for moral power and efficiency, and with the adolescent of college years in the nascent period of moral adjustment," wrote one early student of the teaching of ethics, "how insufficient, foreign, barbarian, do the arid ethic logomachies of most textbooks appear?"

Some sensing the loss, tried anxiously to reclaim their cultural and indeed religious heritage. The general education movement in the first half of the 20th century were experiments that declared their "central concern was moral education, the turning out of persons with the breadth of knowledge, intellectual discipline, and ethical sensitivity needed to grapple with the personal and social problems of the modern world."

One of the earliest efforts was made at Columbia in 1917. Harry Carman said:

The college, we agreed, would be concerned with education for effective citizenship in a democratic society: citizens with broad perspective and a critical and constructive approach to life, who are concerned about values in terms of integrity of character, motives, attitudes, and excellence of behavior; citizens who have the ability to think, to communicate, to make intelligent and wise judgments, to evaluate moral situations, and to work effectively to good ends with others.

Twenty-five years later, following the lead of Robert Hutchins at Chicago, President James Conant of Harvard appointed a committee to study "the objective for general education in a free society." In 1945 they issued their report. "The impulse to rear students to a received idea of the good," it read, "is in fact necessary to education. It is impossible to escape the realization that our society, like any society, rests on common beliefs and that a major task of education is to perpetuate them."

But it was very hard work and we seemed to be failing. As Walter Lippman wrote at the time:

We reject the religious and classical heritage, first, because to master it requires more effort than we are willing to compel ourselves to make and, second, because it creates issues that are too deep and too contentious to be faced with equanimity. We have abolished the old curriculum because we are afraid of it, afraid to face any longer in a modern democratic society the severe discipline and the deep disconcerting issue of the nature of the universe and of man's place in it and of his destiny.

Then came the "effortless barbarism" of the third quarter of this century when grand educational institutions, and more than a few grand educators, were savaged by the very students who had come to those centers to be civilized. The late sixties and early seventies were the darkest hours in the history of American higher education, a dark night of the institutional soul from which we have not yet, and may not ever, fully recover. In their disdain for standards and the demand for relevance, our cultural continuity was eroded and any institutional sense of morality regarding a student's course work, conversation, conduct, or sexual conquest was obliterated. Our Benedictine walls around campus were not thick enough, and neither were our convictions.

Now, in the eighties we are trying to pick up the pieces. In our time it is obligatory upon us to see that schools in this nation forcefully renew their committment to the inseparability of living and learning, and the sooner the better. If we are not diligent, it will be as Montaigne wrote, "They teach us to live, when life is past. A hundred students have caught syphilis before they came to Aristotle's lesson on temperance."

The moral decline of higher education in the twentieth century was both representative of and cause for decline elsewhere in society, especially the primary and secondary schools. President Reagan has chosen to focus on at least one rather obvious, and universally deplored, manifestation of the present problem there. Every year for 15 years respondents to the annual Gallup Poll have listed "lack of discipline" as their number one concern in elementary and secondary schools. In August of 1983, President Reagan and Secretary Bell, concerned about persistent reports of a school discipline/violence problem in the school, directed the Human Resources Cabinet Council to establish a working group on the issue. The report of that working group and its recommendations were presented to the President on January 3, 1984. Four days later Mr. Reagan took to the airwaves in his first radio address of this new year to decry the trouble pointed out in the report. Citing a 1978 report by the National Institute of Education, he revealed that each month three million secondary school children were victims of in-school crime. Two and one-half million were, each month, victims of robberies and thefts, and more than 250,000 students suffered physical attacks. At the same time 6,000 teachers were being robbed each month, and at least 1,000 teachers each month were assaulted with violence so severe they required medical care. That was 1978. A study released in 1983 suggests that the earlier report probably understated the problem.

Elsewhere we read of a teacher in California forced by an intruder in her classroom to undress and then be sexually assaulted as her second grade class looked on in horror. We read of a New Orleans teacher who watched while two boys threw a smaller child off a second-floor balcony, afraid to interfere because she thought the boys might then attack her. We read of high school girls in Los Angeles who set fire to their teacher's hair because of low grades she had given them.

We read of a school in Alexandria which was slashed, ripped, smashed, soaked, snipped, rammed and detonated before it was burned to the ground, presumably by school vandals. We read that in New York City high schools on a normal day only 71% of enrolled students are in school. Crime against property, malicious mischief, and vandalism cost taxpayers $600 million yearly, the equivalent of a vandalism tax of $13 levied on every public school student in the nation.

It is alarming to open a professional journal as we did some months ago and read: "The Testimony of a Battered Teacher." (The neurologist was 90% certain she would recover, which must have been reassuring.) It cannot be entirely incidental in any discussion of excellence in education in America, or the lack of it, to

note that as the violent trend moves into schools that have traditionally been calm, more teachers are opting to leave the field altogether. Early retirements and resignations had by 1979 reduced
the number of teachers with 20 years or more experience by half
over a period of less than two decades. Teachers surveyed in Chicago listed nervous tension, ulcers, high blood pressure, migraine
headaches, and coronary stress as health hazards faced in their
profession. Alfred Bloch, a Los Angeles psychiatrist who has
treated nearly 500 public school teachers, 243 of whom were physically beaten, concluded that the syndrome of these teachers'
symptoms was "classical battle fatigue." Why not, when a recent
survey of California schools found that teachers "spend between
30% and 80% of their time on discipline." Of course the only other
answer is crushing compromise. In the words of Ernest Boyer:

Beaten down by some of the students and unsupported by the parents,
many teachers have entered into an unwritten, unspoken corrupting contract that promises a light work load in exchange for cooperation in the
classroom. Both the teacher and the students get what they want. Order
in the classroom is preserved, and students neither have to work too hard
nor are too distracted from their preoccupations. All of this at the expense
of a challenging and demanding education.

Consider these other manifestations of the problem: more than
half of all serious crimes in the United States are now committed
by youths 10 to 17 years of age; juvenile delinquency is increasing
so fast that one of every nine children will appear in court by age
18, and studies by the National Council on Crime and Delinquency show that criminal acts are as common among youth of middle-
class families as they are among those from low-income homes.

Teachers everywhere agree that students of all ages have far
less respect for authority than they once had. Children and teenagers defy and swear at their teachers. Says one substitute teacher
who has worked for ten years in an affluent suburb: "Every ob-
scene word you can possibly think of has come out of the mouths
of elementary school students. And these aren't 'bad' schools."

Says a veteran elementary school principal: "We're seeing
more just plain meanness. On the playground kids don't seem to
play like they used to; they rove around in gangs. They're quick
to identify the weak ones, kids on the fringe, kids who don't wear

the right sneakers or jeans. They go after them, taunt them; there's a vicious edge to it. We've tried to stop it, but we haven't been very successful."

There's hardly a community in America that doesn't face the problems of teenage drug abuse and drinking. The number of teenage alcoholics is estimated to be 2.5 million. During the 1970s, the number of 12- to 17-year-olds experimenting with marijuana and cocaine doubled. Often it starts even younger. Says a mother of two boys in a white collar town: "The elementary schools in this community are full of drugs. Our kids were into it before we knew what was happening."

The age at which teenagers begin to have sexual relations gets younger all the time. One in five has had intercourse by 15. Teenagers account for 25% of the one million reported cases of gonorrhea each year. Half of all illegitimate babies in this country are now born to teenage mothers.

Says a 15-year-old girl: "All my friends are cheating on tests and getting good grades as a result." In one high school survey 95% of juniors and seniors admitted cheating. At the college level, according to a survey of research by psychologist Roger Burton, 50% to 80% of students, given the chance, will cheat on a test. Many colleges and universities have had to abandon honor codes because of the frequency of violations. In some cases, students have been found bribing custodians to get copies of an exam and then selling them to their fellow students.

North Carolina State University Professor Hattye Liston says that "cheating is an American pastime, involving 30 to 50% of the nation's higher education students. (We use 'higher education' advisedly.)" Speaking at a recent conference of the American Psychological Association he noted that one West Los Angeles company working "the term paper flimflam" has been operating since 1969, and boasts a catalog of over 14,000 titles, taking pride in adding several hundred new titles every year.

The company employs 50 professional writers, each with an advanced degree and specializing in a particular field. All academic topics are covered. Business is brisk. The product is a finished term paper, complete with footnotes, bibliography, and covers. The price? A very reasonable $5.00 a page.

Or what of the 131 U.S. business students recently surveyed. Nearly all expected to face pressure toward unethical behavior, and fully one-half of them anticipated, not resistance to that invitation, but accommodation and compromise. I suppose then that it is no surprise to learn that two years ago white-collar crime in the retail industry alone in this nation was an $8 billion-a-year business. That's $26 million a day, every day, taken I suppose by those like the young business students who were quite prepared to compromise, even before they got out to that first job.

Two years before that $23 million was taken out the front door of banks in armed robbery while three times this amount, about $80 million, was taken out the back door in fraud and embezzlement. Where did those clerks and accountants and loan officers and vice presidents go to school? And what were they taught? As one writer said, "If English literature courses can teach the distinction between Shakespeare and comic books, the school should also be able to take a stand on what is ethically sound." But that is clearly a notion at risk in the 1980's.

April 15th is just around the corner. "Taxes," said Justice Oliver Wendell Holmes, Jr., "are what we pay for civilized society." Ever since 1913, when the income tax system became law, there has been the expected grumbling as well as the classic debates about just who should pay and how much, but civilized people paid. At least we assumed so. During a three month "tax amnesty" program in Massachusetts that ended last January, more than $54.6 million was received. This amount shattered even the most optimistic forecasts for payment. In a poll conducted for *Time* by Yankelovich, Shelly, and White, Inc., 43% of those questioned found cheating on taxes "acceptable." In an Oregon state survey, one out of four citizens revealed that they had cheated on their taxes and felt that most everyone would cheat if they had the chance and felt they could get away with it.

Well, enough of the jeremiad. Surely some criticism from our present plight has to be directed toward me and my fellow presidents who should have been in the forefront all these years, "custodians of the nation's ideals," declaring the difference between right and wrong.

Consider this story told to me personally by Alston Chase. A friend of his was teaching at a small liberal arts college. One of his students, living off campus, vandalized his apartment to the tune of several thousand dollars and then refused to reimburse the landlord. As the college did nothing to encourage her to pay the damages, the professor took matters into his own hands. He gave her an "F" in the course she was taking from him and told her that he would not change it until she paid the landlord. He justified this, he told the college, on the solid Socratic grounds that if a student did not know right from wrong she should not pass a college course. Well the college authorities, naturally, were incensed. The grievance committee overruled him, expunged the "F" from the student's record and did not renew his contract.

On that note of what is right and what is wrong I draw to a close. For all that I've said, there is hope, and a courageous teacher like this proves it. There is a national battalion of them out there, from Seattle to Savannah and from Bangor to Burbank. The most sensational of the problems we have mentioned are limited, but they are increasing and we must act boldly. Fortunately there is an increasing number of private voices giving an ever clearer call to arms. I believe several chapters of Alston Chases's *Group Memory* to be the best examination of moral issues facing, and in some sense stemming from, higher education in the 80s. For slightly different purposes one would add President Derek Bok's *Beyond the Ivory Tower*. A third would be Warren Bryan Martin's *College of Character,* and earlier Alexander W. Astin's *Four Critical Years.* A provocative look at the college student (rather than the college per se) is Arthur Levine's *When Dreams and Heroes Died.*

For primary and secondary education I would commend Neil Postman and Jonathon Kozol for their persuasive effort to claim a moral base to our educational efforts, one which underscores the continuity of the human enterprise. Like most people I don't know exactly what to do with Mortimer Adler's *Paideia Proposal* but three other very recent books on the public schools are encouraging: Ernest Boyer's *High School,* John Goodlad's *A Place Called School,* and Theodore Sizer's very new *Horace's Compromise.* None deals as directly with the continuity of moral tradition in

education as I would like but they are good books written by good
men who are pointing in the right direction. And the rest of us
must do more. Our schools and those who teach there need the
support, as Secretary Bell said to the National Commission, "of
all who care about the future." I suggest the following:

(1) For one thing we can talk about and expect more and indeed demand more virtue in our lives and in our schools. The remarkable Barbara Tuchman once wrote:

Standards of . . . morality need continued reaffirmation to stay alive, as
liberty needs eternal vigilance. . . . To recognize and to proclaim the difference between the good and the shoddy, the true and the fake, as well
as between right and wrong . . . is the obligation . . . of persons who
presume to lead or are thrust into leadership or hold positions of authority.

We can have exactly what we want in this matter of morality.
SAT scores in mathematics have finally improved after 19 years
of decline, due largely, I think, to the fact that enough people
talked about it and expected it and indeed demanded it. We can
do the same regarding the civilizing of our children's minds, if we
want it badly enough.

(2) Schools, and especially universities, have to again be keep-
ers of what Chase calls the group memory, remembering the unity, continuity, and values which have marked the teaching of the
liberal arts for nearly 2500 years.

At Brigham Young University we have recently completed a
review of our twelve academic schools and colleges in which we
are trying to evaluate and encourage the unifying principles that
should characterize any true university and, more specifically in
our case, a true Christian university. We are determined not to
be sadly secularized, nor to fracture our institutional unity
through departmental isolation or increasingly specialized technologies. And because we teach future teachers, as well as future
doctors and lawyers and mothers and fathers, we intend to send
them out into the world with a sound sense of where they fit in
the scheme of things.

We are also initiating a massive reorientation of our Student
Life organization. We are moving to have these young student
leaders create for themselves the kind of campus milieu which will

communicate an expectation of virtue and moral growth to every student who comes on campus. An initial group of several hundred students are being monitored as they identify their individual values (within the context of Judeo-Christian values) and then set personal goals, short and long term, that flow from those values.

We have committed five full-time and two part-time professionals to design and implement this student experiment. It has been underway for one year and will have a major evaluation after one more. If it works we will tell you about it; if it doesn't we probably won't.

(3) With just a little more groundwork to lay, we will be proposing a conference on the moral foundations of higher education to be hosted, if no one else wishes to do so, at Brigham Young University. Such a conference could convene one year from now, and we have every reason to believe there are many who would be interested.

(4) Lastly the parents of this nation need to care about the moral quality of their schools—K through college—because there is preciously little chance that a willing but increasingly weary band of underpaid school teachers or beleaguered administrators will have either the will or the way to do it without you. We need to put back into those civics texts the teachings that were once so central to our national experience. We've thrown accusations and insults and statistics—and have always wanted to throw—money at this problem. What we really need to throw at it is ourselves.

The task before us is staggering. The social and cultural and economic and political problems that complicate it seem nearly insoluable. It all looks very difficult and demanding and dark.

When Mother Teresa was once asked whether she got discouraged in the face of seemingly endless poverty, disease, and misery in the cities of India, she said, "My job is not to succeed, but to be faithful to my mission." With so very much in American life at risk, we ought to stiffen our educational spine and be faithful to the moral notions inherent in our mission. I pray God's blessing that we will.

HOPE, VISION, AND DEDICATION: THE FUTURE
OF AMERICAN EDUCATION[1]
Ernest L. Boyer[2]

The searching reexamination of America's educational system sparked by several critical reports in 1983 (See "Suggested Priorities and Goals for American Education," speech by T. H. Bell, *Representative American Speeches, 1983–84,* pp. 8–14) continued into 1985. While the earlier reports and conferences had focused on alleged inadequacies of elementary and secondary schools, now the school reform movement expanded to criticism of the education that prospective teachers were getting at the nation's colleges and universities.

The status of the teaching profession was a matter of major concern at the annual convention of the American Federation of Teachers (AFL-CIO) on August 21–23, 1984. The AFL, founded in 1857, is a professional organization and union of 1,600,000 elementary and secondary school teachers, college and university professors, administrators, principals, and others concerned with education. The more than 3,000 delegates to the federation's meeting discussed higher education's lack of support for the teaching profession, the low pay of teachers, and teachers' lack of status and authority. Of particular concern to the members was a report issued earlier in the week by the Rand Corporation which predicted a shortage of teachers so severe that the least qualified academically would be responsible for teaching the next two generations of American school children.

Keynote speaker at the opening session of the AFT's annual convention on the morning of August 21, 1984, was Ernest L. Boyer, president of the Carnegie Foundation for the Advancement of Teaching, an organization devoted to conducting educational studies, publishing essays, and issuing policy statements. The foundation's 1983 report was one of the major studies contributing to debate on the state of American education. Dr. Boyer addressed approximately 2,500 convention delegates in the International Ballroom of the Washington Hilton Hotel in Washington, D. C.

Dr. Boyer told his listeners:

> I suggest, then, that after all the discussion and debate there remain four simple propositions: To me the search for quality will be achieved as we discover the importance of critical thinking through

[1]Delivered as the keynote address at the opening session of the American Federation of Teachers' national convention in the International Ballroom of the Washington Hilton Hotel in Washington, D. C., on August 21, 1984.
[2]For biographical note, see Appendix.

the centrality of language; as we sort out the curriculum and give the focus to a core that is not only national, but global; as we give recognition to teachers who are performing outstandingly in the classroom; and as we give more authority at the local level where the job genuinely must be done.

The delegates interrupted Dr. Boyer with applause twenty-six times during the course of his address.

Dr. Boyer's speech: As everyone in this room certainly must know by now, it has been just sixteen months since the National Commission on Excellence in Education said this nation was at risk and declared that we had unilaterally disarmed. Then, twelve months later, the President of the United States assured us that suddenly, just in time for the national election, the nation's public schools were being fixed.

The truth is, of course, our schools were never quite as bad as the hyperbole would suggest. Indeed, after completing our study of high schools from coast to coast, I became convinced that the nation's schools deserve not just Fs, but As as well.

And I also concluded that most school critics could not survive one week in the classrooms they so eloquently condemn.

It also seems abundantly clear to me that in some communities at least, the public school is the most stable, not the least stable institution to be found. Several weeks ago, Benjamin Dumott, writing in *The New York Times*, talked about what he called the killer decade of the 1960s. It was in an era when every institution in America was being battered and abused as all of us can recall too well. And while there were assassinations and riots in the streets and a loss of confidence in our most cherished institutions, still the nation's public schools were opening their doors and serving 50 million children every single day—a minor miracle, I might add.

During the decade of the sixties, I happened to have been in higher education. I was locked in and locked out of office. I was shouted down by students; I was trying to control riots on the campus; I was wondering if I should call the State Police.

And I must confess now that, in the quiet hours before dawn, it did not occur to me to check the SATs. Indeed, looking back on those traumatic times, I wish I had an SAT score on higher education.

Having been in Washington for a time, I also wish I had an SAT score on the Congress. And that I had an SAT score on the nation's courts, which Warren Burger tells us are not in the finest shape.

I wish I had an SAT score on the medical profession, which itself is sick. And perhaps more to the point, I wish I had an SAT score on the nation's families and homes.

The simple truth is that a report card on the nation's schools is, in larger measure, a report card on the nation, and increasingly we expect teachers to do what the homes and the communities and the churches have not been able to accomplish.

The point is this. I am convinced that with all of our talk about school renewal it is time to recognize that the public school is a connected institution and that we cannot have an island of academic excellence in a sea of indifference and neglect.

At the same time, I am convinced that in education there is much work to do, public schools are more than passive actors in this process. And so this morning I should like this convention to focus on four priorities for school renewal that I believe are absolutely crucial. We conclude in the Carnegie report, high school, that the first priority of education is critical thinking through the mastery of language.

In the National Commission's report there was an urgent call for more math and science in order for the United States to maintain its competitive advantages. I support that view, but it seems to me we are confusing a specialized problem with a general problem in the nation's colleges and schools.

I do not believe that every student will grow up to be a scientist, an engineer. I do believe, however, that every student must become linguistically proficient. Language is not just another subject; it is the skill by which all other subjects are pursued.

I recognize, of course, that happily we have God's help in the development of language. It is a God-given trait imprinted in the genes. And language begins long before the child moves on to formal education.

My wife, Kay, who is a certified nurse midwife and delivers many children including five grandchildren of our own, insists that language begins *in utero,* as the unborn infant begins to monitor the mother's voice and then after birth turns instinctively to see the face behind the voice.

Well, I happen to believe that my wife is right, and there are data to support that fact. We do know, that the three bones of the middle ear, the hammer, anvil, and stirrup are the only bones fully formed at birth, and we do know that the child *in utero* responds to the startle of the environment that surrounds us.

Children listen to language before they are born, but certainly with the first breath of birth there comes the miracle of language. First with the gurgles, then with phonemes that are crudely formed, then with utterances we call words and then sentences to convey subtle shades of meaning.

Now that I am a grandfather and watch this process more objectively than I did when there were diapers and burpings late at night, I think we should be much more reverential of this process that begins in infancy and in quantum leaps establishes the identity of every human being.

One of my favorite essayists is Lewis Thomas. He was reflecting in recent writing about the fact that in the human species the child remains so dependent so very long, while in other life forms the newborn moves out rapidly and becomes independent.

Thomas said it occurred to him that "childhood is for language." I believe this is true. As children stay in touch with older folks they listen to signals and begin to define reality through the symbol systems that we create.

Indeed, I am convinced any child who can speak and listen can also read and write and schools should build on the marvelous linguistic system already well established. And let the record show that while our own study focuses on high school and while most of the debate during the past 18 months talked about secondary education, I do believe that the early years are absolutely crucial, that it is there that the successes of education will be won or lost.

Here I should like to pay special tribute to my first grade teacher. I was on my way to school about 100 years ago with my mother in Southwest Ohio and I asked my mother if I would learn to read that day. My mother, in a burst of caution, said "No, not today, but you will before the year is out."

Well, my mother did not know Miss Rice, my first-grade teacher, who stood at the door, half-human and half divine. In fact, for months I assumed in the afternoon Miss Rice just ascended into heaven and descended every morning to teach the class. And to add to the mystique she was a maiden lady. It was against the law in Ohio 100 years ago to teach and also be married. It had something to do with not mixing business and pleasure. In any event, Ms. Rice looked at 20 frightened awestruck children and said "Good morning, class; today, we learn to read," and not one child said, no, not today, let's string beads." If Miss Rice said we learn to read, we learn to read, and we spent all day on just the words "I go to school." We played them, we sang them, we even prayed them. The one prayer, I understand, that is acceptable to all faiths is "Dear God, don't let her call on me today." I ran home that night ten feet tall and I announced proudly to my mother "Today I learned to read."

Well, to be honest, I learned to memorize. But that day Miss Rice taught me something much more essential. She taught me that excellence in the language is the key to learning.

The Carnegie report also gives top priority to writing. Writing, we say is the most important and most neglected language process because language is frozen thought. It is the means by which we discover what is or is not in our head.

We hear a lot these days about the process of critical thinking. I can only say that to me it is a process taught through writing, when students expose what it is they have in their minds and hearts and then are guided to think more subtly and more carefully about the issues.

I believe that every student, then, before he or she graudates from high school, should be asked to write a thoughtful, coherent statement on a consequential topic and if after twelve years of formal education students cannot write English prose with clarity and convention, then I sugggest we lock the doors and start again.

I am often asked now to measure the impact of education. Well, certainly not through the SATs which were not created to measure schools. My conclusion is that school quality is measured by the capacities of students to communicate with clarity and conviction. And if I had one wish in this debate about school renewal it would be that every child during his or her first day of school would hear some teacher say "Good morning, class, today we learn to read."

In the Carnegie report we also call for a core of common learning. We say that two-thirds of the high school program should be required, not to preserve the academic disciplines but to promote a common discourse in our culture. Certainly, as I suggested, we need mathematics and science strengthened to help our students understand numeracy and the miracles of science, but we also need citizens who know something about our human heritage, our civic institutions, about literature and the arts. And in our report we suggest that all students also should study a non-Western culture so their vision will not be just national but global.

About twelve years ago, I was shuffling through my third-class mail in Albany, New York, and I found a copy of the latest issue of the Stanford *Student Daily*. The headlines reported that the faculty at Stanford had introduced a required course in Western civilization after having abandoned all requirements three years before. The students were mightily offended by this action and in a front page editorial said the required course was an "illiberal act" and they concluded by asking how dare they impose uniform standards on nonuniform people.

I was absolutely stunned. I wondered, is it possible that after fourteen years of formal education the students in our best colleges and universities have not understood that while we are "nonuniform" we are still connected? Have they failed to learn that growing up not only involves the discovery of who you are as an individual but also how we are connected to each other?

I am suggesting that, at boottom, education has two major missions: to create the independence of the students and to remind them of the interdependence that will shape their world as well.

The truth is we are all alone and we are all together and a core curriculum is essential in order to help our students gain a perspective. And I happen to believe every student, if properly taught, can understand and appreciate that larger vision, too.

Dr. Lewis Thomas of the Sloan-Kettering Cancer Center wrote on one occasion that if this century does not slip forever through our fingers it will be because education will have directed us away from "splintered dumbness" and will have helped us see our common goals.

I am suggesting that in addition to the centrality of language we must also give priority to those subjects that are absolutely crucial in developing civic and social and cultural literacy, as well. So, we don't need more Carnegie units, we need a large vision to help all students discover their connection to others on the planet earth.

This brings me, then, to priority number three. Yes, critical thinking through emphasis on language. Yes, a larger vision through a carefully designed curriculum in the schools. But in the final analysis, we say that excellence in education means excellence in teaching. And after talking with thousands of teachers from coast to coast, we can conclude that the basic problem is not salary, although teachers are notoriously underpaid; it is not merit pay, President Reagan notwithstanding; the basic problems are the depressing working conditions of the teacher and the lack of recognition and rewards.

Teachers burn out because of too little backing by the parents, too much paperwork, too little time for preparation, and too many mindless interruptions.

And I am not being facetious or trivial when I say that the public address system has become a symbol of all that has gone wrong in the public education system. We were reminded by a previous speaker that George Orwell has not overtaken us yet. I remind him that Orwell's 1984 is the nation's classroom with the idiot box that barks out without warning, every single day.

I was in a classroom several months ago and the PA system interrupted three separate times in a 50-minute hour, including an announcement about a pep rally and about one of the students' lunch money being delivered to the office. And I must tell you— my own pacifist inclinations notwithstanding—if the teacher would have said, "I am going to march to the central office to find the person behind the voice," I would have joined the march and would have delighted to watch him twist slowly in the wind.

I have a concrete proposal to make. I propose that we unplug the PA systems to stop these mindless interruptions.

Incidentally, several weeks ago I was speaking to a group of teachers in which I said that the PA system goes on without warning. Afterward one of the teachers corrected me. she said, "That's not right, because in my school the principal blows into the microphone before the announcement is made."

Every cloud has a silver lining.

I am often asked how we can get rid of bad teachers in the public schools and I say wrong question. The first question is how do we reward the good ones.

No institution, just like no individual, is made healthy by focusing only on the bad. Now, I acknowledge there are poor teachers in the classroom, but I believe the time has come first to give recognition to those gifted teachers who perform heroic acts every single day.

When I was Commissioner of Education one of the last and most rewarding things I did was invite a group of students to the office for the day and ask them to talk about their teachers and their schooling. I was enormously reassured. When we ended the conversation I said, "How many of you have had a teacher that has genuinely changed your life?" and every hand went up, and then I said, "How many of you ever thanked the teacher?" and not one hand was raised. And then one of the young women rather sheepishly said, "Well, you see, it is not the thing to do." And I said, "You just defined the nature of the problem."

"How many of you could go to a classroom where 30 come in and stare at you day after day as if you were a brontosaurus warmed over and then leave without a signal of response? And then how many of you could continue to try to present yourselves and your ideas to others without getting some signal of response? And without being too clever, I said: "Before you graduate, I would like for you to take a teacher to lunch instead of have one for lunch." And they all agreed they would.

I also have a footnote to convey. I believe that colleges and universities have enormous responsibilities to help give new status to the teacher and that is one of the reasons we have now moved on at the Carnegie Foundation to a study of higher education.

I can't tell you how discouraging it is to go to a college campus and hear students say that they planned to be teachers but could not tell their senior professors because they would be discouraged from the task. Yet, it is those very academics who run around the country and discuss the "facts" that schools have gone down the drain.

How can we expect to attract good students and teachers if universities and colleges themselves are not supportive of the process and do not help give dignity to the work?

Several years ago, I was having dinner here in Georgetown with Father Healy, President of Georgetown, and I was describing what I thought were the inadequacies of higher education, in not only training but in attracting good people to the posts. Father Healy said, "Well, if you will pause for just a moment, I have a story that may warm your heart." And indeed it did.

Tim Healy said several years ago he noticed fifteen of the incoming freshmen at Georgetown University were graduates of Bronx High School of Science, a public high school in New York, and he was so intrigued that they had attracted such a strong array of graudates from that institution he asked them to join him in his office. And after a pleasant conversation, Father Healy said, "Could you agree on a teacher who has been absolutely outstanding in your lives?" And after quick consultation, they all agreed on one name at Bronx who had been an influence in shaping them academically and socially as well. So Father Healy called the principal of Bronx High School of Science and confirmed yes, there is such a man; yes, he does teach here and he has been a science teacher for seventeen years.

That evening, Father Healy called the man at home and said, "This is Father Healy, President of Georgetown," and, he said, "on the authority of the Board of Trustees, I would like to invite you to our commencement next spring and award you an honorary degree for what you have done for Georgetown and the nation."

He said there was absolute silence but next spring the man arrived with his family and after they had awarded several degrees to those who were edging their way towards the pearly gates, he said, "I'm pleased to announce that the last awardee is a teacher in the public schools, one who has helped shaped the lives of students here at Georgetown." Without warning, there was a spontaneous response. For one fleeting moment the students reflected on the fact that they should perhaps support the schools. And, for one fleeting moment the faculty reflected on the fact that perhaps education did not begin with them.

I was at Monmouth College in New Jersey about six weeks ago where students had been asked to nominate a great teacher they had had. From that nomination process a group of students and faculty chose one teacher to symbolize the rest. At commencement I was deeply moved as the head of the Math Department in Asbury Park—a magnificent teacher—addressed 5,000 people, telling them about the agonies and ectasies of teaching in public schools.

I believe that speech did more to advance education for that audience than all of the education reports.

I am suggesting, then, and I mean to be clear about this, we will have better schools when we in this nation find ways to give more authority and more status to the teacher.

Finally, I am convinced that in our push for excellence in education we must not impose more rules and regulations on the local school and in the process ignore the people who meet with children every day.

Four months ago, Secretary Bell presented a summary of school reform in all fifty states called *The Nation Responds.* The vast majority of these initiatives focused on more testing, more teaching preparation. And let me say I believe many of these initiatives were appropriate and overdue. But I am also deeply troubled that of the 20 school improvement categories cited in the secretary's report, only two are concerned primarily with the renewal of the teacher. And it is ironic to me that while American business is beginning to recognize the importance of the worker, in education, we still are trying to fix the system from the top.

In an airplane magazine several days ago I read an interview with Philip Caldwell, President of Ford Motor Company. Caldwell said in the interview, "Why kick the man downstream who can't put the parts together because the parts really weren't designed properly." And then he said, "Now, two years before production of the new vehicle, the plans are taken to the plants where they are going to be made, and the people who are actually going to make them have a chance to go through the whole process and make suggestions."

The sad fact is that with all of our new mandates, virtually none of the proposed reforms have been taken to teachers for suggestions to see if they will truly work in the schools and the classrooms where they will meet with the children.

In the Carnegie report we call for a Teacher Excellence Fund for every school, a discretionary grants program to help teachers quickly implement a good idea. We also call for a Teacher Travel Fund in every school to make it possible for teachers to stay in touch with new ideas. And, through The Carnegie Grants Program for High School Improvement, we are giving grants to local schools to give teachers and principals a little discretionary money rather than just more mandates from above. And above all, I believe at this crucial time we need leadership at the Federal level as well, leadership that will support the teachers rather than condemn them.

It seems to me that a report entitled "A Nation at Risk" calls for more than tuition tax credits or prayer in schools or a shootout over merit pay.

If the nation truly is at risk, then the nation should respond. And if the President is serious about helping the nation's schools I suggest a national fellowship program for classroom teachers, similar to the NDEA enrichment program President Eisenhower launched nearly thirty years ago.

I am suggesting it is time to recognize that excellence in education will be accomplished, not by experts on leave from Mount Olympus, but by teachers in the classroom who urgently need not more paperwork and more regulation, but more support. Teachers are the solution, not the problem; and if they are given more responsibilities they must be given more authority as well.

Above all, I hope in the midst of this great debate, we will reaffirm our commitment not just to excellence but to equity, as well. I do have a nagging fear that if we impose requirements without providing more support that at the end we will have more students failing rather than succeeding.

I don't know how many of you saw William Buckley's PBS program "Firing Line" several months ago, Mortimer Adler was the guest, and they were discussing an idea or proposal. Mortimer was arguing aggressively that all students should be involved in the process and Mr. Buckley remained quite skeptical throughout. Near the end of the interview Bill Buckley turned to Mr. Adler and said "What makes you so sure that all children can learn?" At which point Mortimer Adler, stuck his finger in Buckley's face and said, "Well, I am not confident that all children can learn, but, on the other hand, you are not absolutely confident that they can't. I would rather live by my hope than by your doubt."

I cannot be absolutely confident that we can achieve both equality and excellence for all. I only know that the moment we start shaping public policy based on doubt rather than on hope, that is the moment the future of this nation is imperiled.

One of my favorite 20th century authors is James Agee, who wrote on one occasion that with every child who is born under no matter what circumstance, the potentiality of the human race is born again.

This is the vision of the educators at this conference and I am here to extend my deep thanks and admiration for your dedicated service which will go on long after the reports have gathered dust.

THE HUMANITIES AND THE DEFENSE
OF A FREE SOCIETY[1]
Sidney Hook[2]

In 1972 the National Endowment for the Humanities established the Jefferson Lecture as the highest official award the federal government bestows for distinguished intellectual achievement in the humanities. The lecture provides an opportunity for an outstanding thinker to explore, in a public forum, matters of broad concern in the humanities and to affirm

---

[1]Delivered as the annual National Endowment for the Humanities Jefferson Lecture first in the Department Auditorium of the National Endowment for the Humanities in Washington, D. C., at 8:00 P.M. on May 14, 1984, and subsequently on May 17, 1984, at New York University's Fischman Auditorium.

[2]For biographical note, see Appendix.

the relationship between the great works of the humanities and the intellectual, moral, and political traditions of our civilization. The award includes a $10,000 prize. The lecturer is chosen each year by the National Council on the Humanities.

Dr. Sidney Hook, professor emeritus of philosophy at New York University and a senior research fellow at the Stanford University Hoover Institution on War, Revolution, and Peace, was chosen to deliver the 1984 lecture. In announcing the choice, William J. Bennett, chairman of the endowment, called Hook "our global philosopher of freedom through more than a half-century's continuous struggle against the totalitarian ideologies of the left and right." Carol Innerst, of the *Washington Times*, described Hook as "one of the world's leading philosophers of freedom." (May 14, 1984, p. 12B).

Hook, himself, says, "I have always been, so to speak, in opposition to some dominant trend or fad." Few would dispute this. A former student, Paul Kurtz, wrote of Hook: "Like Socrates, he is a gadfly, focusing on the contradictions and hypocrisies, the fads and fallacies of the reigning orthodoxies in the marketplace of ideas" (Zoe Ingalls, *Chronicle of Higher Education*, May 16, 1984, p.7). Then the 81-year old philosopher, born in New York City, the son of Russian-Jewish immigrants, grew up in and attended the public schools of Brooklyn. He studied for a Ph.D. in philosophy under John Dewey and taught for more than 40 years at New York University. At one time a fervent Marxist, Hook has changed his opinions. Currently, he has been described as a philosopher of pragmatism, ardent democrat, passionate anti-Communist, and neo-conservative. Hook rejects the "neo-conservative" label, calling himself a "flaming liberal." An avowed atheist, since the 1930s he has been one of the country's most brilliant, influential, and controversial intellectuals.

Professor Hook delivered the Jefferson lecture twice, first to an audience of more than 1,200 representatives of cultural and academic institutions, government officials, Congress, the judiciary, and the general public in the Department Auditorium of the National Endowment for the Humanities on Constitution Avenue in Washington, D.C., at 8:00 P.M. on Monday, May 14, 1984. The second delivery was on Thursday May 17, 1984, at New York University's Fischman Auditorium. In Washington, William J. Bennett, Chairman of the National Endowment for the Humanities, welcomed the audience. In New York, New York University President John Brademas delivered the welcome.

Although Hook was recovering from a heart attack and stroke that occurred a year earlier, reporters described him as "back on his feet again, his flesh somewhat weaker but his spirit still as feisty and willing as ever" (John Gallagher, *Chicago Tribune*, May 20, 1984, section 6, p. 11); and "a small, grandfatherly mustachioed man who wears spectacles and a warm smile that makes his voice rise when he speaks." (Penny Pagano, *Los Angeles Times*, May 22, 1984, part VI, p. 1).

Several major newspapers carried articles on the lecture. National

Public Radio and the broadcast service of the *Christian Science Monitor* taped the lecture and distributed it to their affiliates. The Voice of America broadcast the speech and an interview with Hook throughout the world.

Dr. Hook's speech: As we approach the bicentenary of the American Constitution, it seems to me fitting and fruitful to explore two related themes in the intellectual legacy of Thomas Jefferson, the first philosopher-statesman of the fledging American republic to call himself a democrat. These themes are, first, his conception of a free self-governing society; and second, his faith in the processes of education to guide, strengthen, and defend this free self-governing society from the dangers—internal and external—that might threaten its survival. Since Jefferson's own time, discussion of the relation between democracy and education has not been absent from political discourse, but as a rule, it has been subordinated to narrow curricular issues. Periodically, however, the question becomes focal whenever we seek, as we are doing today, to rethink, revise, and reform the educational establishment of the nation.

Jefferson was not a systematic thinker and his rhetoric sometimes carried him beyond the bounds of good sense. A revolution every twenty years or so which he advocated to nourish the tree of liberty, would have destroyed the American republic long before the Civil War came near to doing so. Nor were all elements of his thought consistent. Jefferson once wrote that man was "the only animal which devours its own kind." Yet in the very passage in which man is so characterized, he declared that "were it left to me to decide whether we should have a government without newspapers or newspapers without a government, I should not hesitate for a moment to prefer the latter." The case for a free press does not rest on such an absurd position, which overlooks the fact that in a state of anarchy, one without government, there would be no press at all. It would be destroyed by mob rule when it exercised its critical functions, as indeed happened during some stormy years of American history in various regions of the country. Of course, government is not a sufficient condition of a free press, but it is a necesary condition not only of press freedom but of any freedom. For how can any freedom be exercised unless those who would violate it are not free to do so?

Rhetorical excesses and logical inconsistencies apart, the most profound feature of Jefferson's political philosophy, and what all major political groups in American life today regard as possessing a perennially valid significance, is its emphasis on self-government. Self-government in Jefferson's conception has three central features. It is based on freely given or uncoerced consent. Secondly, freely given consent entails the guaranteed right to dissent, to wit, the freedoms of speech, press, association, and assembly, and all other freedoms legitimately derived from them. It is this feature that distinguishes the Jeffersonian, or modern, conception of self-government from the ancient and transient democratic orders of the past which recognized no limits on government power, and treated opponents within the democratic system as enemies. Finally, given the recognition of the right to dissent, a *sine qua non* of a self-governing community is the principle of majority rule. In the absence of a consensus, rarely to be expected in the inescapable conflicts of human interests and opinions, this rule is the only way to reach orderly decision and effect a peaceful succession of government. Jefferson stressed this, as did many years later the uncompromising individualist, William James. "The first principle of republicanism," writes Jefferson, "is that the *lex majoris partis* is the fundamental law of every society of individuals of equal rights. To consider the will of society enunciated by a single vote, as sacred as if unanimous, is the first of all lessons in importance. This law, once disregarded, no other remains but the use of force."

Jefferson was acutely aware, as are we all, that majorities may go astray, be injudicious, and even be morally tyrannical within the letter of the law. For this he had only one remedy: not the rule of presumably enlightened minorities, but the education of experience. His not unreasonable assumption is that, given access to knowledge, most adult human beings are better judges of their own interests than are others. However, to be able to learn effectively from their present experience, to make it available for their future experience, citizens should have access to education of a narrower kind—to schooling that develops the intellectual skills and imparts the relevant knowledge necessary to sustain a free society. The people themselves, Jefferson continually observes, are "the only safe depositories" of non-oppressive rightful government.

One may ask, of course, whether such government is not only safe, but whether it is sound, not only whether it is right, but whether it is good. Jefferson's reply indicates where he puts his faith: "To render them (the people) safe, their minds must be improved to a certain degree. This is indeed not all that is necessary though it be essentially necessary. An amendment of our Constitution must here come in aid of the public education. The influence on government must be shared by all the people."

How far we have come from the Jeffersonian faith that the people or their representatives are the only safe depositories of a free society is evidenced by current discussion of a constitutional convention. I am not a partisan of any particular measure advocated for the agenda of such a convention and I disapprove of most. But I am appalled at the reasons offered by some who oppose its convocation and who cry out in alarm that it will run amok and even abolish the Bill of Rights. No more flagrant contradiction of the Jeffersonian faith is imaginable than such a sentiment. It confidently predicts that measures threatening the foundations of a free society will not only be adopted by a majority of the delegates but also by three-quarters of our fifty states, and by both freely elected legislative assemblies in those states. If such a thing were to come to pass, it would certainly establish that a majority of citizens are either too obtuse or too vicious to be entrusted with self-government. And if this were indeed true, as some philosophers from Plato to Santayana have asserted, why should anyone be in favor of a politically free society? The current state of civic education and behavior is indeed deplorable. But the situation is not so far gone as to make the case for a free society a lost cause.

Far from fearing a constitutional convention, I believe its convocation, timed for our bicentenary, could become the occasion for a great historic debate. Reviewing and interpreting the experience of two centuries, it might strike a more adequate balance among the branches of our government and clarify some central ambiguities in present constitutional provisions that sometimes generate dangerous deadlocks.

Jefferson, as we know, was in advance of his time. He provided the rationale for the systems of public education that developed in the United States after his day, especially for instruction going beyond the fundamentals of literacy—reading, writing, and the arts of calculation. He even ventured on the outlines of a curriculum of studies, mainly based on science and history, to strengthen faith in a free society and safeguard it from the corruptions of human ambition and power.

Now suppose that, in the spirit of Jefferson, we wanted to devise an educational system that would indeed strengthen allegiance to our self-governing democratic society: how would we do this today? One possible way—consistent with Jefferson's own prescriptions—would be to modify our educational system so that its central emphasis became the detailed study of the sciences. But is there really any convincing reason to believe that this would result in an increase of support for a free self-governing society? After all, the subject matters and techniques of the sciences can be mastered in any kind of society. Even though it is true that the greatest burgeoning and bursts of creative discovery in science have occurred during the last two centuries in modern democratic countries, it does not tax our imagination to conceive a world in which, once political freedom has been lost, the sciences become not only the organon of continuous inquiry into nature but also the instrument of enforcing a cruel and ruthless despotism over society. The domination man exercises over nature has often been used to fasten bonds of domination over other men.

To be sure, as John Dewey often pointed out, there is much in the process of scientific inquiry—its openness, sense of evidence, tentativeness, and cooperative intelligence—that when carried over into the discussion and practice of human affairs vitalizes the free society. But Dewey also never ceased to remind us that, desirable as it is to carry over scientific methods in the pursuit and testing of human ends, science and politics differ in several crucial respects. For one thing, not everyone is qualified to be a scientist or has a right to a scientific judgment, while all citizens of a free society are deemed qualified to participate in determining judgments of political policy. Deny this and and one is committed to the view of government by experts, which is incompatible with the premises of a self-governing society. For those premises imply that on crucial questions of policy one does not have to be an expert to judge the work of experts or choose among their oft-conflicting proposals.

Further, scientists are united in one overriding interest—the interest in the pursuit of truth; human affairs, on the other hand, are a field of conflicting interests. The agreements scientists reach are ultimately determined by the compulsions of fact; in human affairs, even when there is agreement on facts, the resolution of differences may require tolerance and compromise of interest. In a free society, it may be necessary to forgo demands for the full measure of justified claims in order to preserve the process by which future claims may be peacefully negotiated. Science develops by the elimination of error. But the life of a free society consists not so much in elimination of interests as in their reconciliation. In science, a wrong judgement loses all value as soon as it is shown to be wrong; in a democracy, even the interest which is outvoted has value. It must be respected in defeat if only because it has submitted itself to the arbitrament of argument and persuasion.

In short, a curriculum concentrating entirely on science could not be expected to achieve the aim Jefferson sought. Not that Jefferson himself was a simple-minded believer in the effect of science and science education on the moral estate of humanity. He called freedom "the firstborn daughter of science"; yet he was aware that science could "produce the bitter fruits of tyranny and rapine." He never wavered in his belief that through the diffusion of scientific knowledge the human condition could be advanced. And if by the advance of human condition we mean the material improvement of the human estate, the extension of longevity, and the increase of our power over nature, none can gainsay him. Yet even if we grant the dubious proposition that all knowledge is good, surely not all of it is relevant for our political purpose. Henry Adams to the contrary notwithstanding, no law of physics has any bearing on the justification for a free society. Einstein's theory overthrew Newton's, not the Declaration of Independence.

It is a commonplace but an important one that is not science and technology that are fateful to man, but the uses to which they are put. When we speak of uses, we imply purposes and ends, goals and policies. We therewith find ourselves in the realm of values. The humanities, broadly speaking, are concerned with the exploration of this realm. Though Jefferson prescribed a mainly scientific course of study for the intellectual elite, a curriculum built on the humanities is roughly what he had in mind for the ordinary citizen, whose studies should, he thought, be chiefly historical. Might not such a curriculum today provide what the sciences cannot—a strengthened faith in a free self-governing society?

I wish to declare at once that regardless of how we answer this question, the humanities—primarily the disciplines of language and literature, history, art, and philosophy—should have a central place in the education of any society. For their subject matter is perennial and transcends, even when it touches on, the temporalities of politics.

The reasons for this are manifest and heralded in many ways from ancient days to the present. The study of the humanities nurtures an understanding and appreciation of the great and often unfamiliar visions and modes of life. Within any mode of life, they present "the problems of the human heart in conflict with itself" (William Faulkner). They therefore embrace but go beyond the dimensions of the political and ideological. They strike no consensus. They have no flag or creed, even when they celebrate ways of life and death fought under warring battle cries. They take us out of ourselves and enable us to see with the eyes and minds of others in us. Define the humanities and limit their concerns for curricular purposes as one will, their cultivation leads to the permanent enrichment of the internal landscape of the mind in any clime or social station. For they provide an ever-renewed source of delight, consolation, insight, sometimes hope.

Surely this is merit enough to justify the place of the humanities in any curriculum of liberal studies. Surely this justifies us in maintaining that their absence is the sign of a truncated, one-sided, and impoverished education—whatever other virtues such education may have.

Nonetheless, we cannot honestly maintain that the study of the humanities of itself generates allegiance to the free society. Two considerations prevent us from doing so. The first is the historical fact that the student population of Western Europe, who until recently were brought up in their lycees and gymnasia largely on classical studies, were certainly not noteworthy for their ardor and enthusiasm for free democratic societies. Indeed, not infrequently in countries like Spain, Italy, France, and Germany, it was students who provided the intellectual shock troops for anti-democratic movements.

There is a second troubling reason why we cannot maintain that an organic relationship exists between the humanist tradition in life and letters and commitment to the free or liberal society. This is the fact that many of the monumental writers of the past regarded the promise of democratic progress as a threat to the life of the mind and to the creative spirit, as the political gloss on the mechanisms that were leveling and standardizing culture and taste. No one can reasonably dispute the record. From the age of Plato to the present, the dominating figures in the humanistic disciplines have been critical of, sometimes even hostile to, the extension of political power to the masses, even when safeguards against the excesses of popular sovereignty have been adopted. In the 19th century, writers like Dickens, George Eliot, and Shelley were sympathetic to the advance of the democratic idea, but their influence was more than counterbalanced by Wordsworth, Balzac, Goethe, Dostoevsky, and many others. In our own time, such major literary figures as T. S. Eliot, Yeats, Pound, Faulkner, and D. H. Lawrence typify the distrust and suspicion of democratic society prevalent among the creative vanguard.

Why there should be this adversary relationship, as Lionel Trilling called it, between the sympathies and values of so many great humanists and the democratic tendencies of their culture, and why there should be a corresponding bias toward the aristocratic tradition, is hard to explain. A partial answer may lie in the greater receptivity among aristocratic classes to the novel and experimental than is generally found in the larger public ("Nothing is so foreign to the plain man," observes Santayana, "as the corrupt desire for simplicity.") To this may be added the fact that where the people are sovereign they have sometimes been less tolerant of heresies that challenge accepted beliefs than have some benevolent despotisms, which under the mantle of a patronizing *narrenfreiheit,* the freedom accorded to the court jester, sometimes sheltered purveyors of doctrines dangerous to the state.

Whatever the explanation, we cannot plausibly deny that the outstanding humanist figures have rarely been protagonists of the ordered freedoms we associate with democratic life and republican virtue in a self-governing society. The growth of such a society in the West owes more to the dissident, nonconformist religious sects, to the agitation and battles of the early trade unions and other manifestations of class struggle than to the classical humanist tradition. It was not a scholar inspired by Plato or Aristotle, Aquinas or Dante, or any figures of the Renaissance, but a spokesman of the Protestant Levellers who proclaimed that "the poorest he that is in England has a life to live as the greatest he," and therefore argued for the right "to choose those who are to make the laws for them to live under."

In pointing to the considerations that prevent us from making the easy inference that a liberal-arts education centered around the study of the humanities is integral to the existence and survival of a liberal society, I do not mean to suggest that there is a simple causal relation between curricular study and political behavior. A contemprary literary critic, George Steiner, has written in a tone of bitter discovery: "We know now that a man can read Goethe and Rilke in the evening, that he can play Bach and Schubert, and go to his day's work at Auschwitz in the morning." But he could have added that those who studied Euclid and Newton also built the crematoria at Auschwitz. And he undoubtedly is aware that those in previous times who led the massacres of innocents in their holy wars against heretics or infidels invoked the blessings of the God of love on their dedicated work. This is an old story. The face of evil can wear the mask of learning. The devil can play the role not only of gentleman but of a scholar—but this does not make learning or manners evil or less desirable. The guilt of a criminal does not stain the means by which he commits or conceals his crime. As well maintain that the abuse of language is an argument for permanent silence.

Moreover, after one has said everything there is to be said to the contrary, there still remains at least some positive connection between the expressions of the human spirit in art and literature. Regardless of their specific political orientation, these works are usually animated by a passion or vision of opposition to the customary. They move by challenging complacency. They are essentially nonconformist. To reach their mark they must disturb, upset, and sometimes frighten.

To the extent, then, that a free society thrives on diversity, the play and struggle of varied perspectives, the dialectic of confrontation, it is served by the humanities, just as in turn the free society often serves the humanities better than the authoritarian societies some humanists tend to favor. For a free society offers an unlimited theater for works of the spirit to develop, in contrast with authoritarian societies that always in some crucial area of the mind invoke the Augustinian dictum that "error has no rights," as a bar to further inquiry and experiment.

To be sure, free societies sometimes sin against the light of cultural freedom. But when they do, they are violating their own ethos. Conversely, some unfree societies may tolerate, even encourage, experiment and variation in some restricted area, but never in all the realms of the human spirit. I am struck by a story told about General de Gaulle. In refusing to endorse the arrest of Sartre for an infraction of the law, he is reputed to have said: "In a free society one does not arrest Voltaire." Sartre was no Voltaire, and he was to boot an apologist for Stalinism; but we know what his fate would have been as a dissident under a Stalinist regime.

I do not want to go beyond the modest claim that there is no essential or necessary hostility between the humanities and a free society, and that there need be no conflict between a love of the humanities and a commitment to liberal democracy. But I believe I have also shown that a curriculum concentrating on the humanities can no more be expected to achieve the Jeffersonian objective of strengthening faith in the free society than a curriculum based on the sciences.

I have brought up Jefferson's ideas about the relation between education and freedom not out of an academic concern with those ideas, but rather in the hope that examining them might yield some guidance in dealing with our urgent contemporary crisis. It is a crisis that threatens the very survival of a free self-governing society in the United States. For it consists precisely of an eroding allegiance to the ideals of a free self-governing society itself. It would require volumes to document the failure to abide by the democratic ethos in American life today. Restricting ourselves only to phenomena observable without enlisting batteries of research teams to report on them, we find: (1) the vehement assertion of rights and entitlements without the acceptance of corresponding duties and obligations; (2) the invocation of group rights to justify overriding the rights of individuals; (3) the growth of violence, and the tolerance of violence, in schools and local assemblies; (4) the open defiance of laws authorized by democratic process, and the indulgence of courts themselves into the legislative process; (5) the loss of faith in the electorate as the ultimate custodian of its own freedom.

Each reflective observer can make his own list of the multiple threats from within our own society to the health, security, and civility of the processes of self-government. However conceived, they raise the question of whether we possess the basic social cohesion and solidarity today to survive the challenge to our society from without, particularly that posed by the global expansion of Communism. Although there are different views of the immediacy and magnitude of the Communist threat to the free world, it is plain political folly to deny its existence. The map of the world from 1945 to the present bears witness to the fact that the policy of containment, initiated by President Truman after Baruch-Lilienthal and the Marshall Plan had been rejected by the Kremlin, does not contain.

The threat of Communist expansion is compounded by the fear that the defensive use of nuclear weapons will result in a nuclear holocaust. The artful, unremitting, and often unscrupulous propaganda by fanatical groups, exemplified by television programs like "The Day After" and by terrifying classroom scenarios on every level of our school system from kindergarten to university, has generated a mood of fear not far removed from hysteria. The fallout from this sustained propaganda has often short-circuited reflection. It has led to the mistaken belief in some circles that we are confronted by the stark alternatives of unilateral disarmament or inevitable war, and to disregard of the well-grounded position that an effective deterrent is the best way of preserving peace without sacrificing freedom. Clarity, however, requires recognition that to renounce in advance the retaliatory use of a deterrent is to proclaim in effect that we have no deterrent, thus inviting the very aggression the policy of deterrence was designed to discourage.

In our precarious world every policy has risks. What shall we risk for freedom? What shall we sacrifice for mere survival? If our nation were confronted by a nuclear ultimatum, would there be enough loyalty to a free society to generate the necessary resolution to cope with the threats without bluster or paralyzing panic? To many the answer seems doubtful, and this in itself is an alarming sign of the state of the national mind. Past generalizations about the American character are no guide, whether drawn from de Tocqueville, Whitman, or Lord Bryce.

What then must be done? Not long ago our President proposed and our Congress approved the organization of a National Endowment for Democracy to encourage the spread of democratic forces abroad. As welcome as such a program is, I submit that it is even more necessary to organize a National Endowment for a Democracy at home. The first goal of such an endowment would be to develop programs to study the basic elements of a free society, and suggest them as required parts of instruction on every educational level.

Today it is widely agreed that fundamental educational reforms are needed to improve the levels of skill and literacy of American students so that they may cope with present and future problems arising from multiple changes in our complex world. Agreeing with this proposition, I am suggesting that it is just as important to sharpen the students' understanding of a free society, its responsibilities and opportunities, the burdens and dangers it faces. Instead of relying primarily on the sciences and humanities to inspire loyalty to the processes of self-government, we should seek to develop that loyalty directly through honest inquiry into the functioning of a democratic community, by learning its history, celebrating its heroes, and noting its achievements. Integral to the inquiry would be the temporary totalitarian societies, especially the fate of human rights in those areas where Communism has triumphed.

The first retort to such a proposal is sure to be that it is just a variant of the propaganda and indoctrination we find so objectionable in Communist society. As to propaganda, Karl Jaspers somewhere says that the truth sometimes needs propaganda—a dark saying. I interpret it to mean that we require courage to defend the truth when challenged and the skill both to make it more persuasive and to combat its distortions. But as to indoctrination, the retort misses the basic difference between the open and closed society. This lies not in the presence or absence of indoctrination, but in the presence or absence of the critical, questioning spirit. Indoctrination is the process by which assent to belief is induced by non-rational means, and all education in all societies at home and in school in the tender years is based on it. The habits of character, hygiene, elementary sociality and morality are acquired by indoctrination and become the basis of all further learning. In a free society, however, such methods are, and always should be, accompanied by, and gradually become subordinate to, the methods of reflective, critical thought at every appropriate level. When students achieve greater maturity they are able to assess themselves step by step the validity of the beliefs and the justifications of the habits in which they have been nurtured. A free society not only permits but encourages questioning, commensurate with the intellectual powers of students, as integral to learning.

In a closed society indoctrination induces assent by irrational as well as non-rational means, beyond the early years, and throughout the entire course of study in all except certain technical areas. It never permits a critical study of its first principles and the alternatives to them. The unfree society regards its subjects as in a permanent state of political childhood; it controls what they read and hear by the monopoly of all means of communication. The free society can live with honest doubt and with faith in itself short of certainty. Skeptical of perfect solutions, it eschews the quest for absolutes. In contrast with the closed society, it can live with the truth about itself.

I am not making the utopian claim that anything we do in the schools today will itself redeem or rebuild our society. Continued institutional changes must be made to strengthen the stake of all groups in freedom. But of this I am convinced. In our pluralistic, multi-ethnic, uncoordinated society, no institutional changes of themselves will develop that bond of community we need to sustain our nation in times of crisis without a prolonged schooling in the history of our free society, its martyrology, and its national tradition. In the decades of mass immigration in the 19th and 20th centuries that bond was largely forged by the American public school. What I propose is that our schools, reinforced by our colleges and universities, do the same job today in a more intelligent, critical, and sophisticated way.

There was a time when most Americans understood that the free self-governing society bequeathed to them by Jefferson and the other founding fathers was the "last best hope on earth." If anything, the experience of the 20th century, and especially of the past fifty years, should have made that truth even more evident than it was to Jefferson himself. During that period, our own society has been able to make gigantic strides in the direction of greater freedom, prosperity, and social justice, while its totalitarian enemies—first Nazi Germany and then the Soviet Union—have produced war and holocaust, economic misery, cultural starvation, and concentration camps. Yet in spite of that record, the paradox is that faith and belief in the principles of liberal democracy have declined in the United States. Unless that faith and that belief can be restored and revivified, liberal democracy will perish. Jefferson thought that proper education was necessary to the birth and establishment of a free society. He would not have been surprised to discover that it is also necessary to its perpetuation, and indeed to its very survival.

DETERMINING FOREIGN POLICY

REDEFINING OUR PROBLEMS WITH THE SOVIET UNION[1]

DANIEL PATRICK MOYNIHAN[2]

The United States "should be less obsessed with the Soviets," because "the Soviet idea is spent—history is moving away from it with astounding speed," Senator Daniel Patrick Moynihan told an audience of 12,000 people at New York University's commencement exercises in Washington Square Park on May 24, 1984. Our grand strategy, the New York Democrat said, should be to wait out the Soviet Union—"its time is passing." Moynihan was the principal speaker and one of seven recipients of honorary doctoral degrees.

"With violet pennants flying at entrances around its perimeter, the park became an academic outdoor theater—and a sea of violet robes—as the surrounding university presented more than 7,500 bachelor's and advanced degrees to candidates ranging in age from 19 to 84" (Laurie Johnson, *New York Times,* May 25, 1984, p. 14).

"Receiving his honorary Doctor of Humane Letters degree, Moynihan was cited for his rise from "the streets of New York, where you shined shoes as a boy." The citation added, "Your enduring place in our national life will rest not only on the offices you held but on the ideas you have generated."

Senator Moynihan, the senior United States Senator from New York, held cabinet or sub-cabinet positions under Presidents Kennedy, Johnson, Nixon and Ford. He served as ambassador to India from 1973 to 1975 and U.S. permanent representative to the United Nations in 1975-1976. Moynihan is professor of government at Harvard University and director of the Joint Center for Urban Studies of MIT and Harvard.

Senator Moynihan's speech: The theologian, Georges Bernanos, once observed that "the worst, the most corrupting lies are problems poorly stated." This is in a way a kindly view of the human condition, but it makes a special claim on those whose education is much concerned, as yours has been, with the art of problem solving.

---

[1]Delivered at the commencement exercises of New York University in Washington Square Park in New York City on May 24, 1984.

[2]For biographical note, see Appendix.

It would appear that once again, as a nation, we are in the process of defining the nature of our problems with the Soviet Union. This is a recurrent process, things change. An early period of intense hostility was followed by a measure of normalcy, next by a wartime alliance, thereafter by a period of alternating cooperation and competition accompanied by the accumulation on both sides of unimagined levels of nuclear weaponry which now presents itself as the central concern of mankind.

This period of redefinition has been brought about by a number of events, some transient, as in the styles of political rhetoric, but some far more real. Of these, the single largest fact is the obsessive accumulation by the Soviets not just of more nuclear weapons, but ever newer weapon systems. This behavior seems unrelated to anything we do. A recent Secretary of Defense put it: "When we build, they build; when we don't build, they build."

Of late, the Soviets have begun to deploy these weapons in ways that have no conceivable military purpose but are, rather, singularly political. In Europe, they have deployed far more SS-20 missiles, or rather warheads, than there are targets they might wish to destroy. Here on the east coast of the United States, our week began with an announcement by Marshal Ustinov that the Soviet Union has deployed an increased number of nuclear armed submarines off our shores, with missiles aboard capable of reaching their targets in "ten minutes." President Reagan has replied there is nothing new in this; that if there were he would not have slept in the White House Tuesday night.

Now, indeed, there is nothing new in the deployment of Soviet submarines close to our shores. Their Yankee class boats began to appear there some fifteen years ago, and in fact they have been moving further off shore ever since. Their newest submarine, the Typhoon class, half again as large as our Trident, will spend much of its time under Arctic ice.

Even so, the question arises how it has come about that our relations have deteriorated to the point that responsible Soviet officials talk of war as if it were coming, and, as in Europe, direct their remarks not to governmentrs but to the publics. This is new and ominous.

In less dangerous times, it would be sufficient that if something ominous developed in our relations with the Soviet Union it was because they wanted it to. Certainly that is the experience of the last forty years. But at this moment, it seems necessary to ask the degree to which the United States shares some responsibility. Such a case can be made.

In the aftermath of World War II finding ourselves the ascendant, indeed almost the only economic and military power in the world, the United States, under a succession of presidents of both parties, conceived a world politics based on a remarkably enlightened perception of our own national interests. (Which is to say interests not inimical to others and thus having the potential of forming an enduring system.)

These world politics were based on three central concepts. In the order they emerged: first, the idea of law governing the conduct of nations; second, the doctrine of nuclear deterrence; and, third, growing out of the first two, the quest for arms control agreements so that the world might back away from the nuclear brink. The Soviets came to understand these to be our politics; and to a degree participated in them.

Then of a sudden, it began to appear that the United States was abandoning these former positions. Certainly, our friends began to ask whether we were. We must assume our adversaries have done so as well.

In the realm of law, the United States seems almost to have forgotten our once deep and abiding commitment ot the rules of international conduct. In Washington, where toughness and ignorance are frequently confused, the view is heard that for us to abide by such rules when the Soviets do not, is to submit to a permanent and possibly fatal disadvantage. Former Ambassador Richard N. Gardner, now teaching at Columbia, has describerd this as a contention "that we must be free to 'fight fire with fire,'" and admits its undoubted political appeal, even, in cases, its utility. But, he asks, if nations such as the United States "accept the Soviet standard of international behavior as their own, do they then forfeit any claim before the rest of the world to stand on a higher plane of morality?" And, of course, we do. And if such a claim is thought not to matter, then indeed we have changed.

The doctrine of strategic deterrence emerged in the 1950s when it became clear that the Soviets, also, would have nuclear weapons and missiles. It was a simple doctrine: the United States would defend itself: a right, incidentally, fundamental to international law.

We would never use our strategic weapons first, but we would deploy them in such a manner that if attacked, we could always attack back. And yet a year ago, as if no such history existed, the administration proposed, and Congress agreed, to deploy the giant MX missile in the old Minuetman silos in Wyoming and Nebraska, the very sites which, having become vulnerable to a Soviet attack, led us to the decision to build the new missile and deploy it elsewhere.

The MX in Minutemen silos can be instantly destroyed by a Soviet first strike. Which means that in a crisis, our only choice, as the phrase goes, is to "use 'em or lose 'em." Which the Soviets know is our only choice, and which allows them ten minutes to preempt. The moment those missiles are deployed, the world goes on a ten-minute trigger, called "launch on warning." Wise men protest. McGeorge Bundy of this university has written that the MX decision:

> . . . violated the fundamental rule first laid down in the Eisenhower Administration: the object of any new strategic system is to deter, and to deter safely it must be able to survive.

Professor Bundy goes on to echo Ambassador Garner's remark. True, he writes, the Soviets deploy their land-based missiles in a first-strike mode: it has ever been such. It follows that "the most important thing we can do, is not imitate the Russians." But with an amnesiac innocence, we seem bent on just that.

Arms-control ageeements got off to a fast start in the 1960s, beginning with the Limited Test Ban Treaty negotiated under President Kennedy; the critical Non-Proliferation Treaty of the Johnson Administration, culminating in the SALT I agreement reached under President Nixon. Then, of a sudden, the momentum broke. The Soviets have watched us sign, in succession, the Threshold Test Ban Treaty of 1974, the Peaceful Nuclear Explosions Treat of 1976, and the SALT II Treaty of 1979—but not

finally ratify any of them. For the moment we are not even negoti-
ating. That the United States is prepared to negotiate, no one
doubts. But we can no longer bring the Soviets to do so. And we
don't know why. In the meantime, we commence talking of sta-
tioning nuclear weapons in space.

And so the question arises: are we stating the problem poorly?

Let me offer the thought that the desired outcome of the world
politics the Untied States pursued in the period of its great ascendancy a generation ago is that ascendancy would gradually merge
into an ascendant world community of like-minded, above all
democratic, nations. This has happened. Our politics worked.
Now this change, of course, causes problems, too. We have now
to pay a great deal more heed to other nations than we once did.
Fine. That is the mark of our success. But somehow of late, we
seem to be mistaking it for a sign of weakness, and attributing that
weakness to the rise of Soviet strength.

What pitiful stuff that is. The truth is that the Soviet idea is
spent. It commands some influence in the world; and fear. But it
summons no loyalty. History is moving away from it with astounding speed. I would not press the image, but it is as if the
whole Marxist-Leninist ethos is hurtling off into a black hole in
the universe. They will be remembered for what? The death of
Andrei Sakharov? Yelena Bonner?

Are there Marxist-Leninists here and about in the world?
Yes: especially when the West allows Communism to identify
with nationalism. But in truth, when they do succeed, how well
do they do? And for how long?

We should be less obsessed with the Soviets. If we must learn
to live with military parity, let us keep all the more in mind that
we have consolidated an overwhelming economic advantage. The
24 members of the Organization for Economic Cooperation and
Development, knows as the O.E.C.D.—a quintessential initiative
in world politics of the post-war United States—now produce
60% of the world's GNP [gross national product]. The Soviet bloc
produces 19%. What is the rest of the world to think?

The historical outcome is certain if we can keep the nuclear
peace and attend to our own arrangements in a manner that they
continue to improve. The world monetary system, which the Unit-

ed States put in place forty years ago is badly in need of adjustment, lest it becomes an instrument for draining wealth for the nations that are least wealthy.

The culture of terror, a peculiar mutant of the totalitarian age, threatens democratic societies across the globe: in my own ancestral home in Ireland; in Italy; Israel; now India. That the governments and peoples of these nations show surpassing resources of firmness and courage does not make of terror any less a trial. (The Soviets, of course, contribute greatly to terrorist movements. Here we have no choice but to confront them. But surely, with a sense of proportion.) And, lastly, a kind of latent tribalism is sweeping much of the Earth challenging the traditions of modernity in which we have invested so much hope. This, too, is to be understood and confronted. But now, are these not challenges enough for one generation?

I suggest they are, and I offer a closing thought: our grand strategy should be to wait out the Soviet Union; its time is passing. Let us resolve to be here, our old selves, with an ever surging front of ideas. When the time comes, it will be clear that in the end freedom did prevail.

TERRORISM AND THE MODERN WORLD[1]
GEORGE P. SHULTZ[2]

An increasingly disturbing fact in international relations has been the growth of terrorism. In a speech to the Jonathan Institute on June, 1984, Secretary of State George P. Shultz traced its recent growth:

> Over these past five years terrorism has increased. More people were killed or injured by international terrorists last year than in any year since governments began keeping records. In 1983 there were more than 500 such attacks, of which more than 200 were against the United States. For Americans the worst tragedies were the destruction of our Embassy and then the Marine barracks in Beruit. But

[1]Delivered as the annual Sherr Lecture at the Park Avenue Synagogue in New York, New York, in the sanctuary at 8 P.M., October 25, 1985.
[2]For biographical note, see Appendix.

around the world, many of our close friends and allies were also victims. The bombing of Harrods in London, the bombing at Orly Airport in Paris, the destruction of a Gulf Air flight in the U.A.E., and the Rangoon bombing of South Korean officials are just a few examples, not to mention the brutal attack on a West Jerusalem shopping mall this past April.

What we have learned about terrorism, first of all, is that it is not random, undirected, purposeless violence. It is not, like an earthquake or hurricane, an act of nature before which we are helpless. Terrorists and those who support them have definite goals; terrorist violence is the means of attaining those goals (*Congressional Record,* June 29, 1984, E3100).

Although the Reagan Administration had been highly critical of President Jimmy Carter's handling of the Iranian hostage crisis, once in office it took a more cautious stance, stressing means of defending against and preventing terrorism, and arguing that the United States could not hit out at terrorists unless we were certain we were hitting the perpetrators.

In a speech on October 25, 1984, Secretary of State Shultz challenged administration policy, arguing that the United States should stop equivocating and adopt a policy to use military force against terrorist groups, even if it led to the death of American servicemen and innocent people. Shultz praised the way Israel had handled terrorists and called for a public campaign to win support for a policy of "swift and sure measures" against terrorists, both to prevent attacks and to retaliate for them. His speech was remarkable for several reasons, including the fact that it was given in the midst of an election and seemed to contradict statements by incumbent President Ronald Reagan in a presidential campaign debate. Vice President George Bush, in Ohio, publicly disagreed with Mr. Shultz's contention that American military force should be used against terrorists even if it led to the death of innocent civilians.

Secretary Shultz delivered the speech as the Sherr Lecture, an annual address of major moral or religious interest which begins the program of adult Jewish studies each year at the Park Avenue Synagogue in New York City, at 8:00 P.M., on October 25, 1985, in the sanctuary of the synagogue. His audience of 1,000 consisted of members of the Park Avenue Synagogue, their guests, and reporters.

The speech attracted widespread media coverage. It was a front-page story in the *New York Times, Chicago Tribune, Washington Post,* and other major newspapers and was covered by *Newsweek* and other news magazines. Reporters described the address as "his sharpest attack yet on terrorism" and a "harshly worded speech." *Newsweek* said, "It sounded as if Secretary of State George Shultz was adopting the new "Hill Street Blues" roll-call admonition: "Let's do it to them before they do it to us.""

Secretary Shultz's speech: Someday terrorism will no longer be a timely subject for a speech, but that day has not arrived. Less than two weeks ago, one of the oldest and greatest nations of the Western world almost lost its prime minister, Margaret Thatcher, to the modern barbarism that we call terrorism. A month ago the American Embassy annex in East Beirut was nearly destroyed by a terrorist truck bomb, the third major attack on Americans in Lebanon within the past two years. To list all the other acts of brutality that terrorists have visited upon civilized society in recent years would be impossible here because that list is too long. It is too long to name and too long to tolerate.

But I am here to talk about terrorism as a phenomenon in our modern world, about what terrorism is and what it is not. We have learned a great deal about terrorism in recent years. We have learned most about the terrorists themselves, their supporters, their diverse methods, their underlying motives, and their eventual goals. What once may have seemed the random, senseless, violent acts of a few crazed individuals has come into clearer focus. A pattern of terrorist violence has emerged. It is an alarming pattern, but it is something that we can devise concrete measures to combat. The knowledge we have accumulated about terrorism over the years can provide the basis for a coherent strategy to deal with the phenomenon, if we have the will to turn our understanding into action.

We have learned that terrorism is, above all, a form of political violence. It is neither random nor without purpose. Today, we are confronted with a wide assortment of terrorist groups which, alone or in concert, orchestrate acts of violence to achieve distinctly political ends. Their stated objectives may range from separatist causes to revenge for ethnic grievances to social and political revolution. Their methods may be just as diverse: from planting homemade explosives in public places to suicide car bombings to kidnappings and political assassinations. But the overarching goal of all terrorists is the same: they are trying to impose their will by force, a special kind of force designed to create an atmosphere of fear. The horrors they inflict are not simply a new manifestation of traditional social conflict; they are depraved opponents of civilization itself, aided by the technology of modern weaponry. The terrorists want people to feel helpless and defenseless; they want people to lose faith in their governments' capacity to protect them and thereby to undermine the legitimacy of the government itself, or its policies, or both.

The terrorists profit from the anarchy caused by their violence. They succeed when governments change their policies out of intimidation. But the terrorist can even be satisfied if a government responds to terror by clamping down on individual rights and freedoms. Governments that overreact, even in self-defense, may only undermine their own legitimacy, as they unwittingly serve the terrorists' goals. The terrorist succeeds if a government responds to violence with repressive, polarizing behavior that alienates the government from the people.

We must understand, however, that terrorism, wherever it takes place, is directed in an important sense against us, the democracies, against our most basic values and often our fundamental strategic interests. Because terrorism relies on brutal violence as its only tool, it will always be the enemy of democracy. For democracy rejects the indiscriminate or improper use of force and relies instead on the peaceful settlement of disputes through legitimate political processes.

The moral bases of democracy—the principles of individual rights, freedom of religion—are powerful barriers against those who seek to impose their will, their ideologies, or their religious beliefs by force. Whether in Israel or Lebanon or Turkey or Italy or West Germany or Northern Ireland, a terrorist has no patience for the orderly processes of democratic society, and therefore, he seeks to destroy it. Indeed, terrorism seeks to destroy what all of us here are seeking to build.

The United States and the other democracies are morally committed to certain ideals and to a humane vision of the future. Nor is our vision limited to within our borders. In our foreign policies, as well, we try to foster the kind of world that promotes peaceful settlement of disputes, one that welcomes beneficial change. We do not practice terrorism, and we seek to build a world which holds no place for terrorist violence, a world in which human rights are respected by all governments, a world based on the rule of law.

And there is yet another reason why we are attacked. If freedom and democracy are the targets of terrorism, it is clear that totalitarianism is its ally. The number of terrorist incidents in totalitarian states is minimal, and those against their personnel abroad are markedly fewer than against the West. And this is not only because police states offer less room for terrorists to carry out acts of violence. States that support and sponsor terrorist actions have managed in recent years to co-opt and manipulate the terrorist phenomenon in pursuit of their own strategic goals.

It is not a coincidence that most acts of terrorism occur in areas of importance to the West. More than 80% of the world's terrorist attacks in 1983 occurred in Western Europe, Latin America, and the Middles East. Terrorism in this context is not just criminal activity but an unbridled form of warfare.

Today, international links among terrorist groups are more clearly understood. And Soviet and Soviet-bloc support is also more clearly understood. We face a diverse family of dangers. Iran and the Soviet Union are hardly allies, but they both share a fundamental hostility to the West. When Libya and the PLO (Palestine Liberation Organization) provide arms and training to the communists in Central America, they are aiding Soviet-supported Cuban efforts to undermine our security in that vital region. When the Red Army Faction in Germany assault free countries in the name of communist ideology, they hope to shake the West's self-confidence, unity, and will to resist intimidation. The terrorists who assault Israel—and, indeed, the Marxist Provisional IRA (Irish Republican Army) in Northern Ireland—are ideological enemies of the United States. We cannot and we will not succumb to the likes of Khomeini and Qadhafi.

We also now see a close connection between terrorism and international narcotics trafficking. Cuba and Nicaragua, in particular, have used narcotics smugglers to funnel guns and money to terrorists and insurgents in Colombia. Other communist countries, like Bulgaria, have also been part of the growing link between drugs and terrorism.

We should understand the Soviet role in international terrorism without exaggeration or distortion. One does not have to believe that the Soviets are puppeteers and the terrorists marionettes;

violent or frantic individuals and groups can exist in almost any society.

But in many countries, terrorism would long since have withered away had it not been for significant support from outside. When Israel went into Lebanon in 1982, Israeli forces uncovered irrefutable evidence that the Soviet Union had been arming and training the PLO and other groups. Today, there is no reason to think that Soviet support for terrorist groups around the world has diminished. Here as elsewhere, there is a wide gap between Soviet words and Soviet deeds, a gap that is very clear, for instance, when you put Soviet support for terrorist groups up against the empty rhetoric of the resolution against so-called "state terrorism" which the U.S.S.R. has submitted to this year's UN General Assembly. The Soviets condemn terrorism, but in practice they connive with terrorist groups when they think it serves their own purposes, and their goal is always the same: to weaken liberal democracy and undermine world stability.

The stakes in our war against terrorism, therefore, are high. We have already seen the horrible cost in innocent lives that terrorist violence has incurred. But perhaps even more horrible is the damage that terrorism threatens to wreak on our modern civilization. For centuries mankind has strived to build a world in which the highest human aspirations can be fulfilled.

We have pulled ourselves out of a state of barbarism and removed the affronts to human freedom and dignity that are inherent to that condition. We have sought to free ourselves from that primitive existence described by Hobbes where life is lived in "continual fear and danger of violent death . . . nasty, brutish, and short." We have sought to create, instead, a world where universal respect for human rights and democratic values makes a better life possible. We in the democracies can attest to all that man is capable of achieving if he renounces violence and brute force, if he is free to think, write, vote, and worship as he pleases. Yet all of these hard-won gains are threatened by terrorism.

Terrorism is a step backward: it is a step toward anarchy and decay. In the broadest sense, terrorism represents a return to barbarism in the modern age. If the modern world cannot face up to the challenge, then terrorism, and the lawlessness and inhumanity that come with it, will gradually undermine all that the modern world has achieved and make further progress impossible.

The magnitude of the threat posed by terrorism is so great that we cannot afford to confront it with half-hearted and poorly organized measures. Terrorism is a contagious disease that will inevitably spread if it goes untreated. We need a strategy to cope with terrorism in all of its varied manifestations. We need to summon the necessary resources and determination to fight it and, with international cooperation, eventually stamp it out. And we have to recognize that the burden falls on us, the democracies—no one else will cure the disease for us.

Yet clearly we face obstacles, some of which arise precisely because we are democracies. The nature of the terrorist assault is, in many ways, alien to us. Democracies like to act on the basis of known facts and shared knowledge. Terrorism is clandestine and mysterious by nature. Terrorists rely on secrecy, and, therefore, it is hard to know for certain who has committed an atrocity.

Democracies also rely on reason and persuasive logic to make decisions. It is hard for us to understand the fanaticism and apparent irrationality of many terrorists, especially those who kill and commit suicide in the belief that they will be rewarded in the afterlife. The psychopathic ruthlessness and brutality of terrorism is an aberration in our culture and alien to our heritage.

And it is an unfortunate irony that the very qualities that make democracies so hateful to the terrorists—our respect for the rights and freedoms of the individual—also make us particularly vulnerable. Precisely because we maintain the most open societies, terrorists have unparallelled opportunity to strike at us. Terrorists seek to make democracies embattled and afraid, to break down democratic accountability, due process, and order; they hope we will turn toward repression or succumb to chaos.

These are the challenges we must live with. We will certainly not alter the democratic values that we so cherish in order to fight terrorism. We will have to find ways to fight back without undermining everything we stand for.

There is another obstacle that we have created for ourselves that we should overcome, that we must overcome, if we are to fight terrorism effectively. The obstacle I am referring to is confusion.

We cannot begin to address this monumental challenge to decent, civilized society until we clear our heads of the confusion about terrorism, in many ways the moral confusion, that still seems to plague us. Confusion can lead to paralysis, and it is a luxury that we simply cannot afford.

The confusion about terrorism has taken many forms. In recent years, we have heard some ridiculous distortions, even about what the word terrorism means. The idea, for instance, that denying food stamps to some is a form of terrorism cannot be entertained by serious people. And those who would argue, as recently some in Great Britain have, that physical violence by strikers can be equated with "the violence of unemployment" are, in the words of *The Economist*, "a menace to democracy everywhere." In a real democracy, violence is unequivocally bad. Such distortions are dangerous, because words are important. When we distort our language, we may distort our thinking, and we hamper our efforts to find solutions to the grave problems we face.

There has been, however, a more serious kind of confusion surrounding the issue of terrorism: the confusion between the terrorist act itself and the political goals that the terrorists claim to seek.

The grievances that terrorists supposedly seek to redress through acts of violence may or may not be legitimate. The terrorist acts themselves, however, can never be legitimate. And legitimate causes can never justify or excuse terrorism. Terrorist means discredit their ends.

We have all heard the insidious claim that "one man's terrorist is another man's freedom fighter." When I spoke on the subject of terrorism this past June, I quoted the powerful rebuttal to this kind of moral relativism made by the late Senator Henry Jackson. His statement bears repeating today: "The idea that one person's 'terrorist' is another's 'freedom fighter,'" he said, "cannot be sanctioned. Freedom fighters or revolutionaries don't blow up buses containing non-combatants; terrorist murderers do. Freedom fighters don't set out to capture and slaughter school children; terrorist murderers do. Freedom fighters don't assassinate innocent businessmen, or hijack and hold hostage innocent men, women, and children; terrorist murderers do. It is a disgrace that democracies would allow the treasured word 'freedom' to be associated with acts of terrorists." So spoke Scoop Jackson.

We cannot afford to let an Orwellian corruption of language obscure our understanding of terrorism. We know the difference between terrorists and freedom fighters, and as we look around the world, we have no trouble telling one from the other.

How tragic it would be if democratic societies so lost confidence in their own moral legitimacy that they lost sight of the obvious: that violence directed against democracy or the hopes for democracy lacks fundamental justification. Democracy offers the opportunity for peaceful change, legitimate political competition, and redress of grievances. We must oppose terrorists no matter what banner they may fly. For terrorism in any cause is the enemy of freedom.

And we must not fall into the deadly trap of giving justification to the unacceptable acts of terrorists by acknowledging the worthy-sounding motives they may claim. Organizations such as the Provisional IRA, for instance, play on popular grievances, and political and religious emotions, to disguise their deadly purpose. They find ways to work through local political and religious leaders to enlist support for their brutal actions. As a result, we even find Americans contributing, we hope unwittingly, to an organization which has killed—in cold blood and without the slightest remorse—hundreds of innocent men, women, and children in Great Britain and Ireland; an organization which assassinated senior officials and tried to assassinate the British Prime Minister and her entire cabinet; a professed Marxist organization which also gets support from Libya's Qadhafi and has close links with other international terrorists. The Government of the United States stands firmly with the Government of the United Kingdom and the Government of Ireland in opposing any action that lends aid or support to the Provisional IRA.

Moral confusion about terrorism can take many forms. When two Americans and twelve Lebanese were killed at our Embassy Annex in East Beirut last month, for instance, we were told by some that this mass murder was an expression, albeit an extreme expression, of Arab hostility to American policy in the Middle East. We were told that this bombing happened because of a vote we cast in the United Nations, or because of our policies in Lebanon, or because of the overall state of our relations with the Arab nations, or because of our support for Israel.

We were advised by some that if we want to stop terrorism, if we want to put an end to these vicious murders, then what we need to do is change our policies. In effect, we have been told that terrorism is in some measure our own fault, and we deserved to be bombed. I can tell you here and now that the United States will not be driven off or stayed from our course or change our policy by terrorist brutality.

We cannot permit ourselves any uncertainty as to the real meaning of terrorist violence in the Middle East or anywhere else. Those who truly seek peace in the Middle East know that war and violence are no answer. Those who oppose radicalism and support negotiation are themselves the target of terrorism, whether they are Arabs or Israelis. One of the great tragedies of the Middle East, in fact, is that the many moderates on the Arab side, who are ready to live in peace with Israel, are threatened by the radicals and their terrorist henchmen and are thus stymied in their own efforts for peace.

The terrorists' principal goal in the Middle East is to destroy any progress toward a negotiated peace. And the more our policies succeed, the closer we come toward achieving our goals in the Middle East, the harder terrorists will try to stop us. The simple fact is, the terrorists are more upset about progress in the Middle East than they are about any alleged failures to achieve progress. Let us not forget that President Sadat was murdered because he made peace, and that threats continue to be issued daily in that region because of the fear, yes, fear, that others might favor a negotiated path toward peace.

Whom would we serve by changing our policies in the Middle East in the face of the terrorist threat? Not Israel, not the moderate Arabs, not the Palestinian people, and certainly not the cause for peace. Indeed, the worst thing we could do is change our principled policies under the threat of violence. What we must do is support our friends and remain firm in our goals.

We have to rid ourselves of this moral confusion which lays the blame for terrorist actions on us or on our policies. We are attacked not because of what we are doing wrong but because of what we are doing right. We are right to support the security of Israel, and there is no terrorist act or threat that will change that firm determination. We are attacked not because of some mistake we are making but because of who we are and what we believe in. We must not abandon our principles, or our role in the world, or our responsibilities as the champion of freedom and peace.

While terrorism threatens many countries, the United States has a special responsibility. It is time for this country to make a broad national commitment to treat the challenge of terrorism with the sense of urgency and priority it deserves.

The essence of our response is simple to state: violence and aggression must be met by firm resistance. This principle holds true whether we are responding to full-scale military attacks or to the kinds of low-level conflicts that are more common in the modern world.

We are on the way to being well prepared to deter an all-out war or a Soviet attack on our principal allies; that is why these are the least likely contingencies. It is not self-evident that we are as well prepared and organized to deter and counter the "gray area" of intermediate challenges that we are more likely to face—the low-intensity conflict of which terrorism is a part.

We have worked hard to deter large-scale aggression by strengthening our strategic and conventional defenses, by restoring the pride and confidence of the men and women in our military and by displaying the kind of national resolve to confront aggression that can deter potential adversaries. We have been more successful than in the past in dealing with many forms of low-level aggression. We have checked communist aggression and subversion in Central America and the Carribbean and opened the way for peaceful, democratic processes in that region. And we successfully liberated Grenada from Marxist control and returned that tiny island to freedom and self-determination.

But terrorism, which is also a form of low-level aggression, has so far posed an even more difficult challenge, for the technology of security has been out-stripped by the technology of murder. And, of course, the United States is not the only nation that faces difficulties in responding to terrorism. To update President Rea-

gan's report in the debate last Sunday, since September 1, 41 acts
of terrorism have been perpetrated by no less than 14 terrorist
groups against the people and property of 21 countries. Even Israel has not rid itself of the terrorist threat, despite its brave and pro-
digious efforts.

But no nation had more experience with terrorism than Israel,
and no nation has made a greater contribution to our understanding of the problem and the best ways to confront it. By supporting
organizations like the Jonathan Institute, named after the brave
Israeli soldier who led and died at Entebbe, the Israeli people have
helped raise international awareness of the global scope of the terrorist threat.

And Israel's contribution goes beyond the theoretical. Israel
has won major battles in the war against terrorism in actions
across its borders, in other continents, and in the land of Israel itself. To its great credit, the Israeli Government has moved within
Israel to apprehend and bring to trial its own citizens accused of
terrorism.

Much of Israel's success in fighting terrorism has been due to
broad public support for Israel's antiterrorist policies. Israel's
people have shown the will, and they have provided their government the resources, to fight terrorism. They entertain no illusions
about the meaning or the danger of terrorism. Perhaps because
they confront the threat every day, they recognize that they are at
war with terrorism. The rest of us would do well to follow Israel's
example.

But part of our problem here in the United States has been
our seeming inability to understand terrorism clearly. Each successive terrorist incident has brought too much self-condemnation
and dismay, accompanied by calls for a change in our policies or
our principles or calls for withdrawal and retreat. We should be
alarmed. We should be outraged. We should investigate and strive
to improve. But widespread public anguish and self-condemnation
only convince the terrorists that they are on the right track. It only
encourages them to commit more acts of barbarism in the hope
that American resolve will weaken.

This is a particular danger in the period before our election.
If our reaction to terrorist acts is to turn on ourselves instead of

against the perpetrators, we give them redoubled incentive to do it again and to try to influence our political processes.

We have to be stronger, steadier, determined, and united in the face of the terrorist threat. We must not reward the terrorists by changing our policies or questioning our own principles or wallowing in self-flagellation or self-doubt. Instead, we should understand that terrorism is aggression and, like all aggression, must be forcefully resisted.

We must reach a consensus in this country that our responses should go beyond passive defense to consider means of active prevention, preemption, and experience has taught us over the years that one of the best deterrents to terrorism is the certainty that swift and sure measures will be taken against those who engage in it. We should take steps toward carrying out such measures. There should be no moral confusion on this issue. Our aim is not to seek revenge but to put an end to violent attacks against innocent people, to make the world a safer place to live for all of us. Clearly, the democracies have a moral right, indeed a duty, to defend themselves.

A successful strategy for combating terrorism will require us to face up to some hard questions and to come up with some clearcut answers. The questions involve our intelligence capability, the doctrine under which we would employ force, and, most important of all, our public's attitude toward this challenge. Our nation cannot summon the will to act without firm public understanding and support.

First, our intelligence capabilities, particularly our human intelligence, are being strengthened. Determination and capacity to act are of little value unless we can come close to answering the questions: who, where, and when. We have to do a better job of finding out who the terrorists are; where they are; and the nature, composition, and patterns of behavior of terrorist organization. Our intelligence services are organizing themselves to do the job, and they must be given the mandate and the flexibility to develop techniques of detection and contribute to deterrence and response.

Second, there is no question about our ability to use force where and when it is needed to counter terrorism. Our nation has forces prepared for action, from small teams able to operate virtually undetected, to the full weight of our conventional military might. But serious issues are involved—questions that need to be debated, understood, and agreed if we are to be able to utilize our forces wisely and effectively.

If terrorists strike here at home, it is a matter for police action and domestic law enforcement. In most cases overseas, acts of terrorism against our people and installations can be dealt with best by the host government and its forces. It is worth remembering that just as it is the responsibility of the U.S. Government to provide security for foreign embassies in Washington, so the internationally agreed doctrine is that the security of our embassies abroad in the first instance is the duty of the host government, and we work with those governments cooperatively and with considerable success. The ultimate responsibility of course is ours, and we will carry it out with total determination and all the resources available to us. Congress, in a bipartisan effort, is giving us the legislative tools and the resources to strengthen the protection of our facilities and our people overseas, and they must continue to do so. But while we strengthen our defenses, defense alone is not enough.

The heart of the challenge lies in those cases where international rules and traditional practices do not apply. Terrorists will strike from areas where no governmental authority exists, or they will base themselves behind what they expect will be the sanctuary of an international border. And they will design their attacks to take place in precisely those "gray areas" where the full facts cannot be known, where the challenge will not bring with it an obvious or clear-cut choice of response.

In such cases we must use our intelligence resources carefully and completely. We will have to examine the full range of measures available to us to take. The outcome may be that we will face a choice between doing nothing or employing military force. We now recognize that terrorism is being used by our adversaries as a modern tool of warfare. It is no abberation. We can expect more terrorism directed at our strategic interests around the world in the years ahead. To combat it, we must be willing to use military force.

What will be required, however, is public understanding before the fact of the risks involved in combating terrorism with overt power.

The public must understand before the fact that there is potential for loss of life of some our our fighting men and the loss of life of some innocent people.

The public must understand before the fact that some will seek to cast any preemptive or retaliatory action by us in the worst light and will attempt to make our military and our policymakers—rather than the terrorists—appear to be the culprits.

The public must understand before the fact that occasions will come when their government must act before each and every fact is known—and the decisions cannot be tied to the opinion polls.

Public support for U.S. military actions to stop terrorists before they commit some hideous act or in retaliation for an attack on our people is crucial if we are to deal with this challenge.

Our military has the capability and the techniques to use power to fight the war against terrorism. This capability will be used judiciously. To be successful over the long term, it will require solid support from the American people.

I can assure you that in the administration our actions will be governed by the rule of law; and the rule of law is congenial to action against terrorists. We will need the flexibility to respond to terrorist attacks in a variety of ways, at times and places of our own choosing. Clearly, we will not respond in the same manner to every terrorist act. Indeed, we will want to avoid engaging in a policy of automatic retaliation which might create a cycle of escalating violence beyond our control.

If we are going to respond or preempt effectively, our policies will have to have an element of unpredictability and surprise. And the prerequisite for such a policy must be a broad public consensus on the moral and strategic necessity of action. We will need the capability to act on a moment's notice. There will not be time for a renewed national debate after every terrorist attack. We may never have the kind of evidence that can stand up in an American court of law. But we cannot allow ourselves to become the Hamlet of nations, worrying endlessly over whether and how to respond. A great nation with global responsibilities cannot afford to be hamstrung by confusion and indecisiveness. Fighting terrorism will not be a clean or pleasant contest, but we have no choice but to play it.

We will also need a broader international effort. If terrorism is truly a threat to Western moral values, our morality must not paralyze us; it must give us the courage to face up to the threat. And if the enemies of these values are united, so, too, must the democratic countries be united in defending them. The leaders of the industrial democracies, meeting at the London summit in June, agreed in a joint declaration that they must redouble their cooperation against terrorism. There has been followup to that initial meeting, and the United States is committed to advance the process in every way possible. Since we, the democracies, are the most vulnerable, and our strategic interests are the most at stake, we must act together in the face of common dangers. For our part, we will work whenever possible in close cooperation with our friends in the democracies.

Sanctions, when exercised in concert with other nations, can help to isolate, weaken, or punish states that sponsor terrorism against us. Too often, countries are inhibited by fear of losing commercial opportunities or fear of provoking a bully. Economic sanctions and other forms of countervailing pressure impose costs and risks on the nations that apply them, but some sacrifices will be necessary if we are not to suffer even greater costs down the road. Some countries are clearly more vulnerable to extortion than others, surely this is an argument for banding together in mutual support, not an argument for appeasement.

If we truly believe in the values of our civilization, we have a duty to defend them. The democracies must have the self-confidence to tackle this menacing problem or else they will not be in much of a position to tackle other kinds of problems. If we are not willing to set limits to what kinds of behavior are tolerable, then our adversaries will conclude that there are no limits. As Thomas Jefferson once said, when we were confronted with the problem of piracy, "an insult unpunished is the parent of others." In a basic way, the democracies must shown whether they believe in themselves.

We must confront the terrorist threat with the same resolve and determination that this nation has shown time and again throughout our history. There is no room for guilt or self-doubt about our right to defend a way of life that offers all nations hope for peace, progress, and human dignity. The sage Hillel expressed it well: "If I am not for myself, who will be? If I am for myself alone, who am I?"

As we fight this battle against terrorism, we must always keep in mind the values and way of life we are trying to protect. Clearly, we will not allow ourselves to descend to the level of barbarism that terrorism represents. We will not abandon our democratic traditions, our respect for individuals rights, and freedom, for these are precisely what we are struggling to preserve and promote. Our values and our principles will give us the strength and the confidence to meet the great challenge posed by terrorism. If we show the courage and the will to protect our freedom and our way of life, we will prove ourselves again worthy of these blessings.

A TIME TO REMEMBER

DAYS OF REMEMBRANCE[1]
ELIE WIESEL[2]

In 1984, as it has each year since 1979, the United States Holocaust Memorial Council led the nation in remembering the six million Jews who perished in the Holocaust and the millions of others murdered by the Nazis. The solemn Days of Remembrance, organized by the Council's Day of Remembrance Committee, served to link the vanished past and the unknown future: "We remember the past, not only to mourn, but for the sake of the future, for the sake of life."

The weekend of remembrance opened on Sunday, April 29, with an Evening of Commemoration through the Performing Arts at the John F. Kennedy Center for the Performing Arts in Washington, D. C. Artists, musicians, and journalists—including Helen Hayes, Orson Welles, Lorne Greene, The American Symphony Orchestra, the Howard University Choir, Sherill Milnes, James Earl Jones, Tom Brokaw, Ted Koppel—gave voice to the legacy of words and music from the Holocaust. At the conclusion of the concert, Elie Wiesel briefly addressed the audience. Author, professor, and himself a survivor of concentration camps, Weisel is chairman of the United States Holocaust Council.

Early the next morning, Holocaust survivors gathered at the site for the United States Holocaust Memorial Museum for a symbolic ground-breaking ceremony to begin the process of creating an institution to preserve the history of the past and hopes for the future.

At noon, survivors were joined in the Rotunda of the United States Capitol by senators and congressmen of both parties, by leaders of both houses of Congress, and by Vice President George Bush for a National Civic Commemoration of the Holocaust. Speaking at the ceremony were Senate Majority Leader Howard Baker, Representative Sidney R. Yates of Illinois, Vice President Bush, and Elie Wiesel. Congressman Tom Lantos described the occasion as follows:

> . . . at noon in the rotunda of the Capitol Building, hundreds gathered in a solemn and heart-wrenching service to remember the nightmare of the Holocaust. There were survivors, whom this generous and great nation accepted with open arms, their second genera-

[1] Delivered in the Rotunda of the United States Capitol in Washington, D. C., at noon on April 30, 1984.

[2] For biographical note, see Appendix.

tion American-born children, and other Americans committed to the prevention of a repetition of this ultimate example of man's inhumanity to man.

Elie Wiesel delivered a moving statement on that occasion. More than any other he has helped us to understand—to the extent that understanding is possible—the significance of that nightmare. His voice has been the clearest in calling for us to create conditions to prevent the repetition of that outrage. His thoughtful and moving words have significance for all of us. (*Congressional Recond,* May 3, 1984, p. E1948)

Ever since he emerged from a Nazi death camp in April 1945, Wiesel has dedicated his life to telling the incredibly brutal story of the German World War II concentration camps. It was Wiesel who first used the word "holocaust" to described the treatment of the victims. Known as the "conscience of the Holocaust," Wiesel has worked to insure that mankind never forgets the horrors of that darkest episode in human history.

Elie Wiesel's speed: Mr. Vice President, Congressman Yates, distinguished members of the House and Senate, fellow survivors, friends:

For some of us, this is the most solemn and awesome day of the year. We delve into the darkest recesses of our memory only to confront and evoke a vanished universe surrounded by flames and penetrated by silence. The living and the dead locked together as they are during Kol Nidre services, young and old, pious and secular, princes and madmen, sages and wanderers, beggars and dreamers. On this day, Mr. Vice President and friends, we close our eyes and we see them—an erie procession which slowly, meditatingly, walks toward angels of death carried on wings of night into night. We see them as you see us. We are the link between you and them.

And, therefore, we thank you, members of the House and Senate, and Mr. Vice President, for allowing us to be that link. We thank you, people of the United States, for creating a framework in which we could share visions and memories that intrude, defy language and comprehension. On behalf of the Holocaust Memorial Council, its members, its Board of Advisers, its Second Generation Advisers, its staff, its friends and allies, we thank all of you for joining us today.

It is symbolic that our commemoration takes place in this august hall of legislation and commitment to law, and commitment to humanity. What we are teaching the world from this room, thanks to you, Members of the House and the Senate, is that laws must be human. Laws are to serve humanity and not destroy it. Laws are given to human beings to perfect life and not to profane it. Laws, too, became corrupt once upon a time. And here with your deed and our words, we shall shield laws in the future.

And so once more, as we have done since 1979, on this Day of Remembrance we gather from all the corners of exile to tell tales—tales of fire and tales of despair and tales of defiance—tales that we must tell lest we are crushed by our memories. In remembering them, remembering the victims in the ghettos and camps and the prisons, we become aware of man's singular vulnerability but also of his stunning ability to transcend it.

We remember the killers and we lose our faith in humanity. But then we remember the victims and, though scarred, our faith is restored—it must be. The fact that the Jewish victims never became executioners, that they never victimized others, that they remained Jewish to the end—human to the end—that inside ghettos and death camps, my God, inside gas chambers, they could speak of God, to God. They could say: *S'hma Yisroael Adonai Elohenu, Adonai Echad*—God is God and God is One and God is the Lord of Creation. To say those words there on the threshold of death and oblivion must restore our faith in them and therefore in humankind. We think of the victims and we learn that despair is not the solution. Despair is the question. And that is why we gather year after year—to fight despair; and not only mine—ours.

As a son of the Jewish people, as a citizen who is proud to be a member of the American people, I live with a memory of Jewish children and their parents. It has been our task, it will remain our task, to maintain that memory alive. But then we remember not because we seek vengeance; we don't believe in it. We only seek justice. We do not aim to hurt, only to sensitize. We believe that by retelling our tales we might help our contemporaries by making them aware of what could happen to human beings when they live in an inhuman society surrounded and penetrated by indifference on one hand, evil on the other, with so few opposing evil and indifference. That is why I allow myself at times to see in the Holocaust an analogy only to itself, meaning that nothing should be compared to it but that everything must be related to it. It is because of what we endured that we must try to help victims everywhere today: the Bahais in Iran who are being murdered by the dictatorship in Iran; the Miskitos on the border of Nicaragua; we must help the Boat People who are still seeking refuge; the Camodian refugees; and the prisoners, so many of them, in Communist jails. It is because we remember what has been done to our people that we must plead at every oppurtunity, in this House and in all other houses, for Anatoly Scharansky, Iosif Begun, Vladmir Slepack, and all the dissidents and prisoners who are in jail waiting for someone to shake off humankind's indifference. If they were to lose faith in us, we should be damned. It is because we remember the solitude of Jews in those times that we feel so linked to and proud of the state of Israel today. We survivors, our friends and allies, are grateful to Israel, grateful to a people simply for existing, for inspiring us to keep faith in a certain form of humanity and tradition.

While we remember the victims we also remember those who tried to help us—the Raoul Wallenbergs and the Oskar Shindlers, as Congressman Yates said. They were so few and they were so alone. It breaks our heart to think of their solitude, of their sacrifice. Memory is not exclusive. Memory is inclusive. It is because we remember the singular aspect of the tragedy that we remember its universality. We must also think of tomorrow as though it would be part of our memory. I think the world unleashed madness forty years ago and that madness is still dominating spirits and minds of too many countries. There are too many signals of danger—racism, anti-semitism, bigotry, fanaticism. We are scared of what humankind could do to itself. Therefore, we tell the story.

In conclusion, Mr. Vice President, may I quote to you a legend of the great masterwork of human civilizaton and culture, the Talmud. The Talmud tells us that when God gave the law to the people of Israel he lifted up Mount Sinai over the heads of the Jewish people and said: "If you accept the law, you shall live. If not, you shall die." And so, we accepted the law.

I have the feeling today, Mr. Vice President and friends, that God has lifted above our heads a mountain of fire, and it is as though God were to say to us: If you obey the law—if you remember that we are all children of one father, if you remember that whatever happened to one people must affect all other people, if you remember that stupid cruelty is absurd and grotesque, and it is not in hurting people that one can redeem oneself—if you remember, you shall live and if not—but we must remember.

THE REMARKABLE MAN FROM MISSOURI: HARRY S. TRUMAN[1]

ALAN WHEAT and MARGARET TRUMAN DANIEL[2]

In a two-hour ceremony, former President Harry S. Truman was recalled as an "uncommon common man" by those who knew him best at an emotional joint meeting of the United States House of Representatives and Senate on the 100th anniversary of his birthday on May 8, 1984.

Congress only once before had held such an observance for the birthday centennial of a former president. That was in 1982 to honor Franklin D. Roosevelt, whose mantle Truman assumed in 1945 when Roosevelt died. The joint meeting was part of a series of nationwide centennial observances, including pageants, symposiums, ceremonies, and special exhibits of Truman memorabilia.

Among those who paid tribute to the plain-spoken Missourian were Stuart Symington, the first secretary of the Air Force under Truman and, like him, a Missouri senator; Clark Clifford, Truman's special counsel and later Secretary of Defense under Lyndon Johnson; and Truman biographer Robert Donovan.

Presiding over the session with House Speaker Thomas P. O'Neill, Jr., was Senate President pro tem Strom Thurmond, who had split with Truman in 1948 in a bitter dispute over Truman's civil rights policies and had run against him for the presidency as a "Dixiecrat." Others present included four former Truman cabinet members, several White House staff members, and his daughter, Margaret Truman Daniel, and her husband and four sons.

The ceremony in the House chamber featured the U. S. Army Band and Chorus playing, among other selections, the Harry S. Truman March, and pianist Daniel Pollack with two Chopin pieces that were fa-

---

[1]Delivered at a ceremony marking the 100th anniversary of the birth of Harry S. Truman in a joint meeting of the House and Senate in the chamber of the Untied States House of Representatives beginning 9 A.M. and concluding at 11:40 A.M. on May 8, 1984.

[2]For biographical notes, see Appendix.

vorites of Truman, who also played the piano. Several speakers noted that although Truman was widely considered ill-equipped to assume the duties of the presidency, history has treated him kindly, and historians now rank him as among the great presidents. Representative Alan Wheat, a black Democrat congressman who represented Truman's hometown of Independence, Missouri, praised Truman's call for sweeping civil rights changes during the 1948 election campaign in the speech reprinted below.

While most of the remembrances focused on the feisty man and his often controversial policies, the most poignant came from Margaret Truman Daniel, the only child of Harry and Bess Truman. Mrs. Daniel, who received a standing ovation, stepped to the dais where her father had once delivered his State of the Union speeches and told the crowded chamber:

> When as a child you walk beside a good man, a warm-hearted man, and find comfort, love, and protection in his embrace, you never think of him as a great man. He is just your dad, and you love him.

Congressman Wheat's speech: Mr. Speaker, members of the other body, distinguished guests, members of the Truman family: Today marks the 100th anniversary of the birth date of Harry S. Truman. I am proud to represent in the Congress of the United States the hometown of Harry Truman, Independence, Missouri. This week I will be in Independence as we dedicate the Truman home to the national park system and honor Margaret Truman Daniel with the Harry S. Truman Public Service Award.

This last weekend I was in Independence for a parade honoring Harry Truman and in Grandview, Missouri, for another parade honoring Mr. Truman, as well as the dedication of the Truman farm home. All of Independence, Grandview, and Kansas City turned out to honor Mr. Truman, but I am most proud to be here today on this historical occasion as our nation honors the memory of Harry S. Truman, one of America's greatest presidents. But we do honor him because he was a man of the people, a working man, a bank bookkeeper, a railroad timekeeper, a soldier, a haberdasher, a farmer, a county judge, and a U.S. senator, and nowhere during his entire public nor private life did he ever lose his ability to stay in touch with the common man.

Harry Truman is remembered for many great attributes, but perhaps common people remember him more for his courage, his integrity, and his compassion than any other reason.

The year 1948 was an election year for Harry Truman. It was a very difficult election year and he had many advisers who told him that to push the Civil Rights Commission was an act of political suicide, but Harry Truman looked beyond political expediency to the greater goals that he had set for himself and for the nation. He demanded of the Congress new civil rights laws protecting fair housing in this country, guaranteeing an end to the discrimination in transportation, and protecting America's greatest liberty, the right to vote, and then to prove that he himself would do what he had asked the Congress to do, he desegregated the Armed Forces by executive order.

In 1984 we take these actions for granted, but in 1948 they created an uproar. Called upon to defend his actions at the Democratic convention, he responded this way to a delegate from Alabama: "The Bill of Rights applies to everyone in this country and don't you ever forget it," and he went on to say that, "It would be a good idea to read those 10 amendments every once in a while; not enough people do and that is one reason we are in the trouble we are in."

His courage was amplified by his integrity. In 1940, as today, it would be easy to give the Defense department a blank check, but Harry Truman saw things differently in 1940. He said,

It was an amazing thing. Every ten cents spent on a work relief project like the WPA or the PWA, every dime is looked into and somebody is always against spending a nickel to help the poor or to give a man a job who doesn't have any, but when it comes to the Defense department, the sky is the limit and no questions asked and the economy boys never open their mouths about that.

That was the integrity of Harry Truman. He did not believe in wasting government money for any program, not even when it came to himself, because when he retired from the presidency he did not retire with a great personal staff. He did not go back to a resort. He went to a modest home in Independence, a return to the private life he knew so well.

His courage, his integrity were tempered by his compassion; his love of all men, rich and poor, black and white, friend, and foe, was well known in Independence, Missouri, and perhaps can be described best by the situation that he faced after World War II.

There were many that urged Truman to take action to keep the Soviet Union from taking advantage of a war-ravaged Europe and, in fact, he did not recommend it for political expediency. This is the way he put it to Sam Rayburn, one of the toughest Speakers of the House Representatives ever to serve:

Sam, if we don't do it, Europe is going to have its greatest depression ever and I don't know how many hundreds of thousands of people are going to starve to death, and that is not something that we want to have on our conscience, not if we can help it, we don't.

That was Harry Truman. Perhaps today as we look at our foreign policy we should ask not only what Harry Truman would have done, but why he would have done it.

Ladies and gentlemen, he was one of the most powerful men of his century and yet at the same time remained firmly rooted in humble Missouri soil. Courage, integrity, and a compassion, those were all his, but perhaps his humility was his greatest gift. He put it best when he said:

I have tried my best to give the nation everything I have. There are probably one million people who could have done the job better than I did it, but I had the job.

And then he quoted an epitaph that he had read on a tombstone in a cemetery that said, "here lies Jack Williams. He done his damndest."

Well, Harry Truman said he wanted to be remembered that way and, ladies and gentlemen, Harry Truman done his damndest, too. Thank you.

Margaret Truman Daniel's speech: Mr. Speaker, Mr. President, ladies and gentlemen, first I would like to say that dad would have loved all of the music, as I am sure we all did.

You cannot imagine what a delight and honor it is for me to find myself once again in this place. It is both exhilirating and humbling to be standing in the same spot where my father stood when he delivered his annual State of the Union message.

This monumental building and its majestic site, towering over the capital of our republic, was once my playground. I skipped through its long corridors with my schoolbooks, I became familiar with the great men and great events memorialized here, I wandered casually into the family gallery of the Senate and listened to the nation's business being transacted.

It was a simpler, easier time, with no passes required for a daughter of the Senate, the guards all knew me and no electronic surveillance of visitors.

Most delightful of all, I rode the subway back and forth between the Senate Office Building and the Capitol to my heart's content.

And while my father labored in room 240 of the Old Senate Office Building, I did my homework until it was time for him to drive me home in his spiffy Chrysler.

When as a child you walk beside a good man, a warmhearted man, and find comfort, love and protection in his embrace, you never think of him as a great man. He is just your dad and you love him. It is only when you grow up and step back from him or leave him for your own career and your own home, it is only then that you can measure his greatness and fully appreciate it. Pride reenforces love.

My father was a great man and his greatness grows with time. I am given evidence of that in some way every day. Wherever I go, even in the hinterlands of China, where I was last fall, people came up to me and said, "I just want to tell you how much I admired your father." That is all, but they had a compulsion to say it.

Now on his 100th birthday the attention of the whole nation and much of the world beyond is focused on his accomplishments and his character. Without the character there would have been no accomplishments.

What was his character as it was revealed to his daughter, his only child? First of all, there was never a man more devoted to his family. You can see that in the letters he wrote to his wife, his mother, his sister, and to me. Even though with youthful carelessness I rarely replied, his letters kept coming.

It is extraordinary in this electronic age, an age of instant contact and communications, to recall that he wrote every word laboriously by hand. And even when he was President, he licked a three-cent stamp and pasted it on my personal letter. Actually, for those of you who are so young here, there really was once a three-cent stamp.

How in the midst of one of the most difficult and dangerous periods of American history did he as President and Commander in Chief, find time to write those letters every day? They were expressed in the homely idiom of Missouri and with the affection and longing of a man often separated from his family by his compelling sense of duty. They reflected his simplicity, directness, wisdom, and resolve, qualities that he had demonstrated in his public behavior, as well as his private life.

There was at the core of the man a gentleness that was often obscured by the brusqueness he sometimes displayed as a partisan politician and the firmness he showed as a statesman. Giving them hell was a rhetoric device, permissible in a politician context, but he really loved people. He was supremely confident of the people's ability to govern themselves, if properly led.

Above all, he loved the United States of America next to his family and he served it devotedly in war and peace.

His forthrightness was not an expression of irritation, but a sign of strong will and high purpose. And he was a great teaser. He liked to get your goat and then grin about it. His grin was as wide as his hat brim and as quick as his temper. Of course, he was capable of occasional expressions of anger. That is to say he could get fighting mad. But if you were the beloved beneficiary of his anger, as I was, and not its target, you kind of enjoyed it.

Every girl has a white knight in her dreams and he was mine. Now I have five white knights. My husband, Clifton Daniel, my sons, Clifton Truman Daniel, William Wallace Daniel, Harrison Gates Daniel, and Thomas Washington Daniel. At least I hope they are my white knights.

So it is with great pride that I have sat here today and seen dad honored, revered and eulogized. This august convocation would have delighted him. He would have felt right at home in the mist of it. He jokingly called the presidential mansion the Great White Jail, but he felt a sense of liberation, a certain expansiveness in the halls of Congress.

He loved the work and reveled in the comradeship he found here. Being one of the boys was his greatest pleasure. And he took pride in belonging to the world's most exclusive club, the U.S. Senate.

He was prouder still to be a member of that even more restricted group, Uncle Sam Rayburn's board of education, the bourbon and branch water college of congressional knowledge.

He loved politicians, even Republicans. True.

I hope that somewhere, somehow, he is watching these impressive proceedings and listening in. If he is, he probably thinks we are makig too much of the occasion, but he is nevertheless enjoying it.

He was a modest man, but not fanatically so.

On his behalf, I conclude with heartfelt thanks to all those who have made possible this great celebration and are contributing to all the other events marking the Truman centennial. You have worked long, hard, and successfully. My father would be grateful. My family, every branch of it, is honored. And we thank all of you.

ELEANOR ROOSEVELT[1]
ARTHUR SCHLESINGER, JR.[2]

Whether they came to celebrate her life, explore her times, or lay claim to her legacy, she remained just Eleanor. For four days in October, 1984, "a disparate assemblage of scholars, biographers, activists, and governmental officials gathered . . . at Vassar College on the centennial of Eleanor Roosevelt's birth, as much to recall her vision of America as to try to rejuvenate the liberalism she so vigorously embraced." (Edwin A. Gargan, *New York Times*, October 17, 1984, p. 19)

The interdisciplinary conference on "The Vision of Eleanor Roosevelt: Past, Present, and Future" encouraged the presentation of scholarly papers on the Roosevelt era, ranging from one examining Mrs. Roosevelt's role in drafting the Universal Declaration of Human Rights in 1948 to a paper describing her efforts to gain minimum labor standards for women and children. The conference of over 100 participants explored

---

[1] Delivered to the Interdisciplinary Conference on Eleanor Roosevelt: Past, Present, and Future, at Vassar College Chapel, Poughkeepsie, New York, at 2:00 P.M., October 13, 1984.

[2] For biographical note, see Appendix.

issues in five major panels, five working sessions, and 17 paper sessions. Before adjourning, conference participants drafted elements of "an agenda for the future" dealing with five areas of concern to Mrs. Roosevelt: peace, economic and social policy, women's opportunities, civil rights, and international human rights.

The conference, sponsored by Vassar College and the Eleanor Roosevelt Institute, was only one of many events observing the centennial of Eleanor Roosevelt's birth. Others included a symposium on civil rights at the Kennedy Library in Boston, ceremonies at the Roosevelt summer home at Campobello Island in New Brunswick, Canada; the Four Freedoms awards at the Franklin and Eleanor Roosevelt Study Center in the Netherlands; an observance at the United Nations where Mrs. Roosevelt had served as a member of the United States delegation; an exhibition at the Smithsonian Institute; seminars at various colleges and universities throughout the country, issuance of a commemorative stamp in her honor, and ceremonies at Val-Kill, the Roosevelt home in Hyde Park, New York, attended by surviving Roosevelt family members.

Keynote speaker at the Vassar meeting was Arthur Schlesinger, Jr., Pulitzer Prize-winning author, Roosevelt aide, Albert Schweitzer Professor of the Humanities at the City University of New York, and the major historian of the Roosevelt era. Schlesinger addressed the opening session of the conference in the Vassar College Chapel beginning his remarks at approximately 2:30 P.M. on Saturday, October 13. The session began with welcoming remarks by President Virginia B. Smith of Vassar and Trude W. Lash, Chairman of The Eleanor Roosevelt Institute. Franklin D. Roosevelt, Jr., then introduced Professor Schlesinger.

All events of the conference were open to the public. Schlesinger's audience of approximately 500 included academics, students, government officials, Mrs. Roosevelt's family and friends, and most of the 100 presenters at the conference.

"The long arc of her life provides a radiant example of what a woman can do and can be in the 20th century," said Schlesinger. "Eleanor Roosevelt was a supreme liberator—a liberator first of herself; then of her sex, of her country, of the abused and injured around the planet." After his speech, the historian, standing in the sun-dappled yard outside the chapel, wondered aloud, "Who is there in the world today remotely like her?" No one had the answer. (Richard Higgins, *Boston Globe,* October 14, '84)

Professor Schlesinger's speech: It is altogether fitting that this conference commemorating the centennial of Eleanor Roosevelt should be held here at Vassar College. For Vassar, as the leading institution of higher learning within easy reach of Hyde Park, has had a long Roosevelt connection. Franklin and Eleanor Roosevelt enjoyed friendly relations with Henry Noble MacCracken, Vassar's president throughout FDR's governorship and presidency, at least until MacCracken's support of the America First Committee in the great debate of 1940–41 divided them; and nothing ever divided them from Mildred Thompson, Vassar's famous dean. Eleanor Roosevelt, it might be additionally noted, was always envious of her great friend Elinor Fatman Morgenthau, Vassar '13, for her Vassar education and her Vassar degree. And it is appropriate that this college, which has sent so many brilliant women into American life, should now celebrate the most influential American woman in the 20th century.

In so describing Eleanor Roosevelt, one acknowledges not only what Eleanor Roosevelt did for America and the world but what she did for herself. The abiding fascination of her life resides in her personal triumph over vicissitude and adversity. Like her uncle Theodore and her cousin Franklin, she was born into the old Dutch aristocracy of New York. But the solidity of her circumstances was an illusion. She was brought up by an adoring but alcoholic and irresponsible father, a beautiful but cold and sometimes cruel mother, a stern grandmother, a couple of warm-hearted but wayward aunts. Her childood wounds afflicted her till the end of her days. The means by which she transcended them formed her character and defined her life.

She never felt that her mother loved her—the mother who called her "Granny" because of her old-fashioned ways and once remarked in company, "Eleanor, I hardly knows what's to happen to you. You're so plain that you really have nothing to do except *be good.*" When she was eight years old, her mother died; the ultimate betrayal. Her father's behavior had meanwhile become so disordered that her grandmother, now her guardian, refused to entrust the little girl to him. He kept in touch with his daughter by intermittent visits and loving letters; then, two years after her mother, he died too. His image haunted her for the rest of her life. "Everything I did with my father remains in my memory today," she wrote seventy years after his death. "Like most unhappy children, I lived a dream life in which everything was orderd to my liking. . . . My father was always the hero. . . . For years and years, I lived in that dream world with my father. I was lonely, and he was the person I loved best and I felt that he loved me."

An orphan at the age of 10, she was not at all a happy child. She had, she recalled, a "terror of displeasing the people I lived with. . . . My childhood and my early youth were one long battle against fear." The careless betrayals of a chaotic upbringing left her with a consuming hunger for affection and launched her on a lifelong search for an unattainable emotional security. Never achieving that security, she found the answer in mastering her frustrations and her anxieties. "I had such an intense longing for approval and love," she wrote, "that it forced me to acquire self-discipline. . . . I learned self-discipline as a kind of defense. I learned to protect myself from disappointment by not asking for what I wanted. . . . The discipline one imposes on oneself is the only sure bulwark against fear."

The struggle for self-mastery was helped immeasurably when she went at the age of 15 to boarding school at Allenswood in England and encountered the extraordinary headmistress Marie Souvestre. Mlle. Souvestre was the first person after her father to make Eleanor Roosevelt feel loved. She gave the tremulous girl a new sense of competence and of worth. A political radical, Mlle. Souvestre also encouraged in her the idea of social responsibility. These were, young Eleanor Roosevelt thought, "the happiest years of my life," and she returned to the United States in 1902 with more confidence than ever before. Marriage to Franklin Roosevelt three years later was both gratifying and unnerving. Nor could her affectionate and admiring but self-sufficient, often oblivious, sometimes impenetrable and, in a crucial episode, inconstant husband provide her the total emotional security for which she longed. Throughout her life she needed people who needed her, and she responded gratefully to need.

This psychological background, one might suppose, would produce a sad, defeated and ineffectual woman. It did not. Eleanor Roosevelt triumphed over her own vulnerabilities through an almost terrifying exertion of self-discipline. Because convictions of her own inadequacy had been so effectively instilled in childhood, because her adult life had its share of disappointment and shock, it took incomparable self-control to win maturity and serenity. Her life was both ordeal and fulfillment—as Joseph P. Lash recounts so beautifully in his great biography.

So in her private life Eleanor Roosevelt serves as a model in the everlasting human struggle for personal autonomy. Her example must strenghten us all when we are tempted by those demeaning feelings of self-pity and martyrdom that Eleanor Roosevelt recognized in herself and called "Patient Griseldaism." But her quest for selfhood did not stop there. The quest soon led her beyond self into territory that all too few women of her class and generation were disposed to enter.

Years later, asked to name the "most interesting and unforgettable" persons she had ever met, she responded chronologically: first her father, next Mlle. Souvestre, then her uncle, Theodore Roosevelt. She was his favorite niece, and she had been well prepared by Mlle. Souvestre to respond to the progressive concerns that Uncle Ted was now trumpeting from the White House. Perhaps also she unconsciously remembered her mother's injunction that, being so plain, she really had nothing to do except to be good. In fact, she was no longer plain, this willowy, appealing girl, but her capacity to do good was as yet untapped.

Soon she joned the Junior League, the organization founded in 1901 by Mary Harriman (whose younger brother Averell was a friend of Eleanor Roosevelt's younger brother) to enlist society girls in programs of welfare service for the poor. This was the great age of social work, and Eleanor Roosevlet, working in the Rivington Street Settlement House, began to understand how the other half lived. The Consumers League sent her to investigate conditions in sweatshops where little children made artificial flowers and feathers. One day Franklin Roosevelt accompanied her to visit a sick child who was a member of Eleanor Roosevelt's class at Rivington Street. When they left the tenement, Franklin Roosevelt said, "My God, I didn't know people lived like that."

Such experiences were a beginning but for her, at least, not much more. After their marriage, while Franklin Roosevelt entered politics and became a reform legislator in Albany, Eleanor Roosevelt retired dutifully and perhaps with initial relief to motherhood and domesticity. Then changes took place. The First World War, like all world wars, was a time of upheaval. The Lucy Mercer revelation strained and transformed her marriage. In 1921 Franklin Roosevelt was stricken by polio. Soon her children were away in school. She renewed her interest in the larger world outside.

She did this at first to affirm her own identity. Back in New York after eight years in Washington, she was already active in the League of Women Voters before her husband fell ill. His convalescence provided further stimulus. Determined to save Franklin Roosevelt from the valetudinarian life of a country gentleman, she became, as he liked to say, his eyes, ears and legs, his point of contact with people and with politics. "That I became, as the years went by, a better and better reporter and a better and better observer," she later wrote, "was largely owing to the fact that Franklin's questions covered such a wide range. I found myself obliged to notice everything." She learned much too from Louis Howe, who understood both her value and her vulnerability and devotedly built her wavering confidence in herself.

Women aspiring to a public role in those remote times generally went into nonpartisan, good-government organizations. After all, women did not even vote in the United States till 1920, and politics remained for a long time thereafter a rigidly segregated game. Eleanor Roosevelt was active in the good-government groups. She became a leader in the Women's City Club and in the Women's Trade Union League. But—and this was much bolder—she also invaded the masculine preserve of party politics. In 1922 she helped reorganize the Women's Division of the Democratic State Committee. In 1924 she was commissioned to present planks of interest to women to the Resolutions Committee at the Democratic presidential convention. This was an instructive experience. "I was to see for the first time where the women stood when it came to a national convention. . . . They stood outside the door of all important meetings and waited."

The new life was not always easy for this shy and awkward lady. Public speaking was a particular problem. When she was nervous, her voice became high and shrill and sometimes broke into a distraught giggle. Reassured by her husband, coached by Louis Howe, she suffered, persevered, conquered. In finding a role for women in the political process, as in her struggle for personal autonomy, she served as a model for her sex.

In spite of her interest in politics, she watched Franklin Roosevelt's rise to the Presidency with foreboding. "I did not want my husband to be President," she once confessed. " . . . It was pure selfishness on my part, and I never mentioned my feelings on the subject to him." She feared she would end as a captive in the White House, condemned to the innocuous domestic existence traditional for wives of Presidents. She wondered how she could help and tentatively suggested to her husband that he might like her to do a real job and handle some of his mail. He looked at her quizzically and said that he did not think it would work. "I knew he was right," Eleanor Roosevelt wrote, "and that it would not work, but it was a last effort to keep in close touch."

Instead she resolved to escape White House captivity and to preserve her own identity. Soon she was writing for the North American Newspaper Alliance and for the Hearst syndicate, editing a magazine infelicitously titled *Babies—Just Babies* and appearing on a commerical radio show. Later she began her newspaper column "My Day," much parodied at the time but also widely and gratefully read. This determination to pursue her own course after her husband became President struck many of her fellow citizens as unseemly. Then and later she was much derided and denounced. She bore criticism stoically and went on about her life.

Far from helping handle the President's mail, she found more than enough mail of her own to be handled. A nation sunk in depression, psychological as well as economic, discovered sudden hope in the Roosevelts. FDR was of course the superbly buoyant leader, but Eleanor Roosevelt played her distinctive part in the revivial of national morale. The unemployed and despairing turned to her as well as to the President. From inauguration day on 4 March to the end of 1933 she received 301,000 pieces of mail. Forlorn letters, sometimes scrawled in pencil on scraps of wrapping paper, even called her "Mother Roosevelt." "We do not hesitate to address you as Mother," one correspondent explained, "for such you are in the truest sense. Your national children have cried unto you, and you have heard and answered their cry."

Her own actions left no doubt that she had indeed heard the cry. She travelled back and forth across the country, visiting depressed areas, relief projects, experimental communities, mines and factories, and reporting back to her husband on conditions and needs. Her presence was visible demonstrations of the government's concern, and on her return she was steady and very often stern in reminding New Deal officials of the human dimensions of economic distress. And she reached out beyond the administration to three constituencies in particular—constituencies that, in her view, deserved more attention than the New Deal was giving them.

One constituency was black America. The New Deal policies created significant new economic opportunties for the black population. But the dependence of New Deal legislation on southern votes in Congress discouraged any direct challenge to discrimination and segregation. Eleanor Roosevelt moved out ahead. She attacked racial intolerance, promoted the appointment of blacks like Mary McLeod Bethune to government posts, invited blacks to the White House and served as black America's friend in court. And of course she famously resigned from the Daughers of the American Revolution when the DAR denied Marian Anderson permission to sing in Constitution Hall.

Walter White of the NAACP became a particular friend, and she worked with him in the vain effort to pass bills removing the poll tax and making lynching a federal crime. FDR privately favored these bills but declined to back them publicly. When his wife protested, he would reply, "First things come first, and I can't alienate certain votes I need for measures that are more important at the moment by pushing any measure that would entail a fight." But he never asked her to cease and desist, despite recurrent storms of vehement and sometimes unprintable criticism. As Roy Wilkins of the NAACP shrewdly observed, FDR was prepared to let his wife "run interference" on the Negro question. "Her enemies and critics used every device of criticism and slander to stop her," Walter White wrote in his last book, "but, undaunted, she continued to speak and act as her conscience dictated. She gave to many Americans, particularly Negroes, hope and faith which enabled them to continue the struggle for full citizenship." In making herself the tribune of civil rights, Eleanor Roosevelt anticipated the great moral struggle of the next generation.

Another special constituency was young America. Her maternal heart went out to the depression generation, deprived of jobs, of education, of hope for the future. "I have moments of real terror," she said in 1934, "when I think we may be losing this generation. We have got to bring these young people into the active life of the community and make them feel that they are necessary." She played a crucial role in the initiation of the National Youth Administration and thereafter served Aubrey Williams as not-too-silent partner in NYA planning and operations, helping shape the movement from relief to vocational training in NYA projects.

At the same time, she encouraged young people to develop their own organizations and formulate their own demands. Her particular concern was the American Youth Congress. Without endorsing the Youth Congress's platform, she respected what she regarded as the earnestness of purpose animating its leaders, and she believed that young people had a right to learn from their own mistakes.

After the Nazi-Soviet pact of August 1939, the Communist hand in the AYC was hardly concealed. But she persuaded her husband to address the Youth Congress in Washington in February 1940 and, even after delegates booed the President for his anti-Soviet remarks, she continued to defend the organization. "I do not condone bad manners," she wrote in April, "but I am experienced enough to understand them sometimes in both old and young. . . . All of the attacks upon the congress have only consolidated the feeling of 'youth against the world.' . . . Whatever else this meeting did, it awakened a great many more young people to the fact that they were being attacked as young people, and that is not a good spirit to foster." She asked Youth Congress leaders whether they were indeed members of the Communist Party and accepted their denials. Soon she knew that they had lied to her. When the party line changed again in 1941 after the Nazi attack on the Soviet Union, they came back, pleading for reinstatement. She refused to renew relations. "For years, in this country," she later said of the Communists, "they taught the philosophy of the lie. . . . Because I have experienced the deception of the American Communists, I will not trust them." Eleanor Roosevelt too had the capacity to learn from mistakes.

A third constituency, toward which her attitude was less fo-
cussed and on which her influence was less purposeful, was female
America. I am not rash enough to try and settle and argument
whether or not Eleanor Roosevelt was a feminist. Certainly she
was not a professional feminist in the sense of exclusive commitment to women's issues. Nor was she given to the sensational tactics feminists sometimes used to advance the cause. She was not
what her husband and Louis Howe called, without affection, a
"she-male." Her affiliations were rather with those social reformers who sought gains for all but retained a special interest in protecting women and enlarging their opportunities. Thus she
opposed the Equal Rights Amendment, as did Frances Perkins,
Helen Gahagan Douglas and most liberal women of the time, on
the ground that, until female workers were better organized, they
needed the protective legislation for which a generation of social
reformers had worked so hard. Only toward the end of her life,
when President Kennedy made her chairman of the Commission
on the Status of Women, was she much identified with a feminist
agenda.

Her thoughts on the problem were, by contemporary standards, rather old-fashioned. She did not doubt that men and wom-
en had different needs and roles. "While I am afraid I shall have
to admit that we women may be selfish, and we may do what we
want in some things, and we may like our apparent
independence," she wrote in 1941, "in the long run, I think, way
down deep inside of us, there is one thing that cannot be eradicat-
ed—we like to please the gentlemen."

When it came to politics, men and women, she wrote in 1932,
differ along very definite lines. "Men tend to look at things from
a legalistic point of view; women from a practical one. Women
will ask, 'What result will this bring?' Men will question, rather,
'How can this be done?'" She added, in capital letters for emphasis, "IT IS IMPOSSIBLE FOR HUSBAND AND WIFE
BOTH TO HAVE POLITICAL CAREERS. It requires all the
energy and united effort of an entire household to support one."

As late as 1941, she wrote that men ran the world because
women cared more about running their homes. "It isn't, she added, "that women haven't the brains or the ability or the physical

strength to dominate. It is that they want the world the way it is and for the most part are content. . . . I have a firm belief in the ability and power of women to achieve the things they want to achieve. It is a man's world now, however, and will be just as long as the women want it to be!" Though such sentiments might be read as a vote of confidence in the ultimate power of women, they amount to something considerably less than a feminist manifesto.

Yet, if Eleanor Roosevelt was not a professional feminist by creed, she was a great emancipator of women by example. She proved the effectiveness of women in the public square and provided a model for women bored by the trivialities of domestic existence and eager to help their community or nation. As she was President Roosevelt's special ambassador to the blacks, so she became his special ambassador to youth and to women. Her record of activity in the White House transformed popular expectations about the role of what has come to be known, in a distasteful term, as the First Lady. Here too Eleanor Roosevelt served as a model for future generations.

Thus Eleanor Roosevelt made her own distinctive contributions to the New Deal. That contribution must be carefully defined. Her areas of interest were limited. She operated on the margins. She had no great knowledge of economic problems and policies, for example, and did not altogether comprehend much of what the New Deal was about. In 1960, reading a book about FDR's first term, she commented, "I find it deeply interesting for it explains much that I only half understood at the time."

Where the New Dealers were a breezy, tough-minded, irreverent, skeptical lot, on fire with ideas, filled with jokes and zestful for combat, Eleanor Roosevelt expressed a gentler and simpler faith, innocent, guileless, idealistic, humorless, deeply informed by religious conviction. Where they drew on Holmes, Brandeis, Veblen, Keynes for inspiration, she drew on the life of Christ. She had known despair, and religious belief gave her a conviction of meaning and purpose running through the melancholy of life and dissolving the contradictions of quotidian existence. Churches she regarded with suspicion; "we have almost forgotten that religion was once preached by men who had no churches and no salaries and yet whose influence has kept alive the germ of spirituality down through the centuries in a materialistic world." Christianity, in her view, was "the greatest of all the underground revolutions but we've allowed churches & doctrines & priests to separate us from the reality which is as real today as it ever was." She wrote this as she sent a copy of Lloyd Douglas's *The Robe* to Joseph Lash in Guadalcanal. "Real religion," she believed, "when all is said and done, lies in the belief that the power of Christ is greater than that of Caesar!"

Christianity was for her a way of life, and the way of life was in her words "true democracy." American democracy, she believed, "had its roots in religious belief," and "the citizens of a Democracy must model themselves on the best and most unselfish life we have known in history. They may not all believe in Christ's divinity, though many will; but His life is important simply because it becomes a shining beacon of what success means. If we once establish this human standard as a measure of success, the future of Democracy is secure." If only we could found politics on "the Christian way of life as lived by the Christ," the torments of the world would vanish.

She was a genuinely good woman, and her faith was in the ultimate hope of goodness and love. "We can establish no real trust between nations until we acknowledge the power of love above all other power," she wrote in 1938. " . . . If we hope to see the preservation of our civilization, if we believe that there is anything worthy of perpetuation in what we have built thus far, then our people must turn to brotherly love, not as a doctrine but as a way of living."

William Allen White once called Calvin Coolidge a Puritan in Babylon. Eleanor Roosevelt against the kinetic backdrop of the New Deal can perhaps be accounted a Puritan in Rome. "I'm an idiotic puritan," she once confessed to her daugher Anna, "and I wish I had the right kind of sense of humor and could enjoy certain things." She was indeed a Puritan in her personal habits—in her disdain for good food, stylish women, worldly values, in her predilection for taking cold baths and carrying her own overnight bag, in her self-reliance, her lack of pretense and her frugality. "History would seem to show," she once said, "that with the advent of luxury there is an inevitable softening of the race, and the civilization which reaches the point of great physical comfort is shortly going to die." Character, she thought, is built *"by constant striving to overcome physical, mental, and material difficulties. . . .* Hardships of one kind or another are a necessity to the building of character." She was a Puritan too in her existential insistence that *"we make our own history."* We make our history "by the choices that shape our course." Democracy requires above all "a sense of personal involvement, of personal responsibility, of personal courage."

A Puritan in Rome, she became the conscience of the New Deal, the President's hairshirt. Before she went to Washington, she had written that there should be "no place for conflict where a husband's political career is concerned. The wife's opinions must be subordinated. . . . A wife, I have always held, has a perfect right to her own opinion, but she should *never* nag her husband." It cannot be said that she observed this injunction with perfect fidelity. She nagged her husband on many occasions. If she lacked analytical understanding of the New Deal, she had intense and careful human concerns, and she rarely hesitated to force these concerns on the sometimes weary and preoccupied President. FDR, she explained to Joseph Lash, was the "politician" while she was the "agitator."

Franklin Roosevelt endured the nagging with admirable patience and equanimity. He valued her private testimony, and he valued her public performance too, for it helped mollify groups his New Deal could not satisfy. The White House, Lash reflected after a conversation with Mrs. Roosevelt, was really divided into two households—the President's and Mrs. R.'s. "The predominant feeling was one of warmth, mutual consideration, and good spirits." But on another level "there were frequent clashes, generally good-humored but occasionally tense. It was the collision between what is and what ought to be; between politics and ethics."

Members of the President's household resented Mrs. Roosevelt's interventions more than the President did. They felt that her importunings were unfair to an overworked and hard-pressed executive, an unnecessary drain on precious time and energy. "She had none of the give and take," wrote Samuel I. Rosenman, " . . . that is one of the great essentials of a successful political leader.

It was hard for her to compromise, and she frequently disagreed with the President when he was willing to. She advocated the direct, unrelenting approach. If she had had her way, there would have been fewer compromises by Roosevelt, but also, I am afraid, fewer concrete accomplishments."

Yet she was more complicated than her pieties about the Christian way of life and brotherly love suggested. If her heart lay with what Max Weber called the "ethic of ultimate ends," her head moved her toward the "ethic of responsibility," which requires the taking into account of the foreseeable results of any decision. Even her nagging was a realistic contribution to the process by which her husband made up his mind, for her representations reminded him of other pressures and needs in the society and usefully counterbalanced the unending barrage from the right. Her marriage to that master political realist, her long experience in party politics, her concrete and practical intelligence kept her from capitulating to do-good simplicities. Even the bosses were slowly impressed. The woman who waited outside the door of the resolutions committee at the Democratic convention in New York in 1924 was summoned sixteen years later to quiet down a noisy and rebellious Democratic convention in Chicago—and did so with signal success.

While an indestructible faith in human possibility was the center of her life, it was accompanied by salty realism and, on occasion, by a sort of benign mercilessness. Artlessness was for her a deadly weapon. No one sliced off a head with more lovely ingenuousness. People scrapped with her at their peril, as in later years such rough hombres as Harry S. Truman, Cardinal Spellman, Andre Vishinsky and Carmine de Sapio learned. (I could add myself to the list.) She might forgive, but she did not forget. Under the facade of guilelessness and gentleness, she was, in fact, a tough old bird.

The approach of the Second World War nourished her latent realism. Her early associations and inclinations had been pacifists. She had many friends in the Women's International League for Peace and Freedom, and she had supported the League's campaign in the early 1930s to save the human race by denying toy soldiers to small children. She believed that another world war might destroy civilization. But she was not an isolationist. She subscribed to the Wilsonian faith in collective security. She did not delude herself about the threat the fascist states posed to civilization. When Mussolini's Italy attacked Ethiopia, she warned her pacifist friends, "Disarmament for one nation won't accomplish anything." She ardently favored the democratic government during the Spanish Civil War and opposed the administration's embargo on aid to Loyalist Spain. Afterward, talking in her husband's presence to Leon Henderson, another New Deal champion of the Loyalists, she said, "You and I, Mr. Henderson will some day learn a lesson from this tragic error over Spain. We were morally right, but too weak." Then, motioning toward FDR, "We should have pushed *him* harder."

The alternative to non-resistance was resistance. She hated militarism but had come to doubt the efficacy of pacifism. "Being a pacifist," she wrote in June 1937, "means that you do not seek a fight. . . . But if war comes to your own country, then even pacifists, it seems to me, must stand up and fight for their beliefs." Nor did she see virtue in isolationism. "Have we decided to hide behind neutrality?" she asked the conference on the Cause and Cure of War. "It's safe to be neutral," but I'm not sure it's always right to be safe."

In 1938 many pacifists and isolationists rallied behind the Ludlow Amendment, which provided that, exept in the event of invasion, "the authority of Congress to declare war shall not become effective until confirmed by a majority of all votes cast in a nationwide referendum." On the face it seemed plausible enough that the people as a whole should decide directly on questions of peace and war. But Eleanor Roosevelt publicly opposed the amendment. Not only was it, in her view, a threat in principle to representative government, but it was a threat in practice to prudent policy. There was peril, she wrote, in "a hasty vote by the people influenced by propaganda and not in full possession of the facts. . . . Responsible government officials know certain facts in a crisis that they cannot divulge to the nation at large." Moreover, she added, "one of the things which keep us free and clear of war is that back of our diplomacy lies a strong national defense ready for immediate use at the behest of the Congress and the President. . . . Would not the immediate availability of our military defense act as a deterrent on a foreign Power?"

Someone wrote her saying that, if "you and your kind" had to do the fighting, she might think differently about the Ludlow Amendment. "I would be entirely willing," she replied, "if we ever had to go to war to be in the front line trenches, and I think unquestionably that every one of my family would be there too." She was not a Roosevelt for nothing. When war came, all her sons were indeed in the front line trenches, or rather in the maritime and aerial equivalents thereof.

Eleanor Roosevelt thus combined idealism with growing realism in her world outlook. After the Second World War, the realistic side came even more to the forefront. This was partly because Hitler had divested her of illusions about pacifism, as the American Youth Congress had divested her of illusions about communism. Most of all, I think, it was because her husband's death in April 1945 subtly altered her own sense of herself and of her responsibility to the nation. As long as FDR was alive, she could freely act as the advocate of unbridled idealism in the court of the idealist who was also a master realist. Once she no longer had FDR to play off against, she began to incorporate within herself the things she had learned from him. The balance once produced by argument in partnership had now to be produced by the surviving partner alone. She had herself to be "politician" as well as "agitator." After FDR's death the mix of idealism and realism in Eleanor Roosevelt increasingly resembled the old mix in FDR. She became in the postwar years less and less of a visionary, more and more and old pro; a tough old bird indeed. With Adlai Steventon and others, she now found herself playing the realist, assuming with them the cautionary role that FDR had so oftern assumed with her.

One remembers the early days of Americans for Democratic Action. The united-front enthusiasm rising in the wake of the wartime alliance with the Soviet Union surged on for a season in the postwar years. Many goodhearted liberals had worked with Communists during FDR's last presidential campaign in organizations like the Independent Citizens Committee of the Arts, Sciences and Professions and the National Citizens Political Action

Committee. In 1945 Sidney Hillman asked Eleanor Roosevelt to head the NCPAC. She investigated, was repelled by the Communist role and declined. "I did not feel I could control the committee's policies," she explained.

But one small liberal organization, the Union for Democratic Action, had resisted the united-front embrace. Conceived while the Soviet Union was allied with Nazi Germany, it had refused to open its ranks to Communists after Hitler thrust Russia into war. In 1946 it was proposed that the UDA merge with NCPAC and ICCASP to form an umbrella liberal grouping. James Loeb, Jr., the UDA's director, sought Mrs. Roosevelt's counsel. She told him that she considered it of prime importance for liberals to maintain an organization divorced from Communist influence.

UDA became ADA in 1947. Mrs. Roosevelt was active from the start and later accepted the honorary chairmanship. Her intervention was crucial first in getting the blessing of Philip Murray, the president of the CIO, for the new organization and then in asking Murray to rescind a directive forbidding union officials to join either ADA or the Progressive Citizens of America, the product of the merger that the UDA declined to join. When Max Lerner complained to her that ADA was anti-Communist, Mrs. Roosevelt replied briskly, "The American Communists seem to have succeeded very well in jeopardizing whatever the liberals work for. Therefore to keep them out of policy-making and staff positions seems to be very essential, even at the price of being called red-baiters." Lingering personal fondness for Henry Wallace did not prevent her from identifying with clarity the Communist hand in his Progressive party of 1948. "I could not vote for Henry Wallace," she soon wrote. "I have completely lost faith in him."

Her experience with the American Communists helped prepare her for her entry onto the international stage after the war. Appointed by President Truman to the United States delegation to the United Nations, she made human rights her personal crusade. This involed her in endless wrangles with Vishinsky and other Soviet delegates, first over forced repatriation of refugees, later over the Universal Declaration of Human Rights. Once she defined the "usual USSR idea of compromise. You give up everything on your side and agree with the USSR on all points and then the compromise is accepted." For his part, Vishinsky called her a meddling old woman, and the Soviet press denounced her as a "hypocritical servant of capitalism . . . a fly darkening the Soviet sun."

The Declaration of Human Rights, as finally adopted in 1948, may well be Eleanor Roosevelt's most enduring bequest to the world. Declarations do not abolish evils, but they prescribe standards and set goals. Franklin Roosevelt's Four Freedoms and Eleanor Roosevelt's Declaration have given the fight for human rights the priority it holds—or should hold—today on the world's agenda and the world's conscience. Once more Eleanor Roosevelt serves as a model, this time for all humanity. President Truman called her the First Lady of the World.

The United Nations was the great cause of her last years. She saw the organization with hope but without illusion. The people who begged that she take a lead in converting the UN into world government, ignored, as she dryly commented, "the stark reality that Russia would be out at once and our Congress would never have let us go in. . . . We will have to crawl together, running will be out of the question until all of us have gained far more confidence in each other than we now have." She was in broad sympathy with the evolution of United States policy in the Truman years but was often critical of detail, especially when, as in the case of the Truman Doctrine, American initiatives bypassed the UN. Thereafter, in private life under Eisenhower and a delegate once more to the UN General Assembly under Kennedy, she remained an astute and inspiring leader, a now widely respected elder stateswoman, pressing liberal issues, striving for world peace and never abandoning hope in human decency.

How to define Eleanor Roosevelt's vision of America and the world? It was a moral rather than a political or intellectual vision. Its essence was spirit rather than program. Its foundation was religious faith. Through hard experience she had learned to temper idealism by the reality principle and to mediate between dream and necessity. She believed in hard work, self-discipline, civility, decency and goodness. She believed above all in individual responsibility. She feared what she described in her posthumous book as "the growing tendency among Americans today . . . to evade personal responsibility, to skirt the necessity of making a choice, to hesitate at expressing an opinion, to take comfort in being part of the herd." She concluded that, "in the final analysis, a democratic government represents the sum total of the courage and the integrity of its individuals. It cannot be better than they are."

The long arc of her life provides a radiant example of what a woman can *do* and can *be* in the 20th century. Eleanor Roosevelt was a supreme liberator—a liberator first of herself; then of her sex, of her country, of the abused and injured around the planet. One hundred years after her birth, her star still shines, strong, clear and incandescent. Its rays will light our paths for years to come.

NATIONAL CHALLENGES AND PRIORITIES

THE FACT OF POVERTY TODAY: A CHALLENGE
FOR THE CHURCH[1]
JOSEPH CARDINAL BERNARDIN[2]

In November 1984 for the second time in two years, the National Conference of Catholic Bishops confronted a controversial national issue at its annual meeting. In 1983 the bishops had approved a pastoral letter condemning nuclear war and criticizing the Reagan administration's nuclear weapons policy. The focus of their four-day 1984 meeting was another pastoral letter, this one sharply critical of the American economy. Although the 120-page letter technically was only a first draft that was to be discussed for a year before a final decision on its adoption, the 280 bishops seemed to be solidly in support of its main contentions, which proposed sweeping economic changes to help the poor.

While acknowledging the achievements of the country in many areas, the bishops argued strongly that the inequality in income and wealth in the United States was morally unacceptable. "We find it a disgrace that 35 million Americans live below the poverty level and millions more just above it," said Archbishop Rembert G. Weakland, chairman of the bishops' committee. "We are appalled at the sad sight of extreme poverty elsewhere on this globe." (Kenneth Briggs, *New York Times,* November 12, 1984, p. 1) Because the letter was highly critical of the Reagan administration's policies toward the poor, the bishops had delayed its release until after the election lest it be regarded as an attempt to influence the outcome.

The proposed letter predictably created a storm of controversy. The Reagan adminstration understandably was distressed. Anticipating the report, a group of prominent Catholic laymen, including former cabinet members, congressmen, and business executives issued a statement extolling capitalism and free enterprise. Fundamentalist Reverend Jerry Falwell, leader of Moral Majority, described the bishops' letter as an endorsement of socialism. Others argued that the bishops should stick to traditional religious matters. On the other hand Governor Mario Cuomo, of New York, a leading Catholic lay spokesman, endorsed the report and criticized politically conservative Catholics who had attacked the bishops'

---

[1]Delivered as the annual Cardinal John Dearden lecture at the Hartke Theatre on the campus of Catholic University of America in Washington, D. C., at 8 P.M., January 17, 1985

[2]For biographical note, see Appendix.

173

statement as an assault on basic American values.

Three months after the release of the draft of the pastoral letter Joseph Cardinal Bernardin, Archbishop of Chicago, delivered an address at Catholic University designed to clarify and defend the bishops' letter. A former president of the National Conference of Catholic Bishops, Cardinal Bernardin is liberal on some issues and orthodox on others, but above all a man who "knows his own mind. He knows the bishops, he knows the church and he is very compassionate." *Current Biography* described his as:

> . . . a stocky, balding man of swarthy complexion with a hint of reticence and self-effacement in his casual manner, putting even opponents at ease. Cool in controversy, he is warm and affable in his personal contacts, and his saving grace in all situations is his sense of humor. (*Current Biography*, October 1982, p. 30)

Cardinal Bernardin carefully plans his speeches, "almost never giving a speech or sermon without a text that he has carefully honed, probably in those late-night hours that devotes to writing." (*Current Biography*, October 1982 p. 30) Cardinal Bernardin delivered the speech at 8 P.M., January 17, 1985, to a capacity crowd of approximately 575 at the Hartke Theatre on the Catholic University of America campus in Washington, D. C. The speech, the second annual Cardinal John Dearden lecture, was free and open to the public.

Cardinal Bernardin's speech: Let me begin by expressing my appreciation to Father Byron, President of Catholic University, for the invitation to deliver this address on the fact of poverty and the challenge it poses for the church. Both the topic and the place of the lecture have special relevance.

The bishops of the United States are engaged in a major effort to help the church in the U.S. in its analysis and response to the fact of poverty. The first draft of the pastoral letter, "Catholic Social Teaching and the U.S. Economy," is merely an initial step in an extended process. Its goal is to engage every level of the church in study, discussion, and decisions about how the church can and must respond to the cry of the poor.

The opportunity for me to address an audience at Catholic University as part of this process has both symbolic and substantive significance. The church always acts with a sense of its history and its tradition. The tradition of the U.S. church's social teaching on poverty has been profoundly influenced by this university. To come to the intellectual home of Monsignor John A. Ryan and

Bishop Francis Haas, of Father Paul Hanley Furfey and Monsignor George Higgins is to acknowledge the U.S. church's debt to this university. It also recognizes that the social tradition continues here, symbolized by Father Byron's own ministry and by the work of so many of your faculty.

My purpose this evening is to analyze the relationship of the church to the fact of poverty in our time. I will examine where we stand as a church, what we can bring to the struggle against poverty, and how we should proceed in this struggle precisely as the church.

More specifically, I will address three questions: the nature of the problem we face, the role of the Church, and one aspect of the policy debate on poverty.

Let me begin with two assertions: (1) much of the poverty in the world is hidden from us; (2) the poor usually live at the margin of society and too often at the margin of awareness of those who are not poor. Yet, in the world of the 1980s, although many of the poor are hidden, it is also impossible for the rest of us to hide from the poor.

The faces of poverty are all around us. Chicago and Washington are different cities, but I have lived in both of them long enough to know that the only way to hide from the poor is to stay in one's room or home. We cannot walk to work or to the bus stop, we cannot run a noontime errand without seeing the faces of poverty—on the heating grates, in the doorways, near the bus terminal and huddled in the winter around the places which serve the cheapest cup of coffee.

After walking through the poverty of the city during the day, we are confronted with the faces of poverty on a wider scale in the nightly news. Ethiopia is an extreme case, but not as extreme as we might first think. The fact of poverty is the dominant social reality for over 100 countries of the world. Numbers can be numbing in their effect, but they can also crystallize a challenge.

The fact of global poverty means: 800 million people live in conditions of "absolute poverty," that is, "a condition of life so limited by malnutrition, illiteracy, disease, high infant mortality, and low life expectancy as to be beneath any rational definition of human decency" (Robert McNamara, Speech to Board of Governors

of the World Bank); 2.26 billion people—half of the world's population—live in countries with a per capita income of less than
$400 per year; and 450 million people are malnourished.

Statistics illustrating the global reality of poverty could be giv-
en in much greater detail, of course. But statistics do not tell us
all we need to know. The Gospel points out that these poor people
are our brothers and sisters. The first draft of the pastoral letter
wisely devotes a substantial section to the U.S. relationship with
the rest of the world because the resources of this nation and its
role in the world constitute a serious responsibility in responding
to the absolute poverty of our 800 million brohters and sisters.

My specific concern this evening, however, is not the faces and
figures of global poverty, but poverty in the United States. The
fact of poverty in the United States is a part of our national life,
but it is not recognized as a dominant fact of our existence. It can
easily blend into a larger picture which stresses—not poverty—
but the power and productivity of the nation.

Poverty is surely present but, in the dominant national perspective—provided by magazines, media and movies—it is not a
significant feature. Poverty is present, but in the policy debates of
the nation, the poor exercise little leverage.

The drafting of the pastoral letter on the economy is still in
its early stages. However, it has already accomplished something
which commentators have quickly noticed: the letter makes space
in the policy debate for the fate of the poor in a way which has
not been evident for some years now.

We need to make space for the faces of the poor in our personal
consciences and in the public agenda because the facts tell us that
poverty is not so marginal in this nation as we might think. At the
end of 1983, by official government estimates, 35 million Americans were poor. That meant 15% of the nation was defined as
poor. The hidden poor were another 20 to 30 million who lived
just above the poverty line.

Who are the poor? They represent every race and religion in
the nation. They are both men and women, and, so very often,
they are children. The poor are a fluid population. People move
in and out of poverty. With unemployment still affecting at least
7 to 8 million people, the condition of poverty touches millions for
some part of their lives.

No group is immune from poverty, but not all share it equally. Some of the statistics in the pastoral letter are striking: blacks are 12% of the American population but 62% of those persistently poor; women who head households constitute 19% of the family population, but 61% of persistently poor families. The very old and the very young know the reality of poverty in disproportionate numbers.

The causes of poverty are a subject of honest disagreement, but the fact of poverty, even in a nation of our resources, cannot be disputed. It is the church's response to this fact which is my major concern this evening.

The role of the church in this question or any other must be shaped by the perspective of the Scriptures as these are read in the Catholic tradition. The draft of the pastoral letter develops the scriptural case in detail. Here I will simply indicate the lines of an argument which is self-evident to anyone who examines the biblical basis of our faith. The argument is quite simple: The poor have a special place in the care of God, and they place specific demands on the consciences of believers.

The biblical argument runs through both Testaments, as the draft of the pastoral letter has shown. The prophets, in particular, specify the theme. In spite of their different styles and personalities, the prophets converge on a single message: the quality of Israel's faith will be tested by the character of justice in Israel's life. For the prophets, the test cases for Israel are specific: the way widows, orphans and resident aliens are treated measures the link between faith and justice.

Jesus himself continues the prophetic tradition. He clearly identifies his ministry with the preaching of the prophets as, for example, in the fourth chapter of St. Luke's gospel. He consciously finds those on the edge of society—the "widows, orphans and resident aliens" of his time—and lifts up their plight even as he responds to their needs. He identifies himself so concretely with the poor that the first letter of St. John can say that love of God is measured by love of neighbor.

The biblical mandate about the poor is richer and more powerful than I can convey in this address. I recommend further study of the pastoral letter because it concisely gathers these biblical themes in its first chapter. However, I can synthesize the lesson the church is trying to learn from the biblical perspective. It is found in a phrase which runs throughout the letter: the church must have a "preferential option for the poor." This concept, rooted in the scriptures, developed with originality by the church in Latin America and now becoming a guide for ministry in the universal church under the leadership of Pope John Paul II, illustrates how the church learns anew from the Scriptures in every age.

The power of the phrase, "preferential option for the poor," is that it summarizes several biblical themes. As the pastoral letter states, it calls the church to speak for the poor, to see the world from their perspective, and to empty itself so it may experience the power of God in the midst of poverty and powerlessness.

This, in all honesty, is an extraordinarily demanding view of what we should be as a church. It is clear we have a distance to go in implementing this view of the church's mission and ministry. Nevertheless, we have begun by taking the imperative seriously.

The option for the poor, I would suggest, will be realized in different ways according to the situation of the church in different societies and cultures. Now we need to ask what the phrase means for the ministry of the church in the United States.

I do not have a blueprint for determining the specific meaning of the "option for the poor" or integrating the concept into our ministry in this country. However, one dimension of the task especially interests me—the role of the church as a social institution in our society. The church as a social institution has made two distinct responses to the fact of poverty. The first has been to organize itself to carry out works of mercy. The fulfillment of the command to feed the hungry, clothe the naked and care for the sick has found direct and immediate expression in the church from the apostolic age until today. The methods of doing this work have varied, but all can be classified as direct, social service to the poor.

The manifestations of this dimension of ministry are well known in the United States. They include Catholic Charities and social services in every diocese, St. Vincent de Paul Societies in every parish, and institutions—such as, orphanages, hospitals and shelters for the homeless—established by communites of men and women religious and others throughout the country.

This form of social ministry is well known, but it is not the only way the church addresses the fact of poverty. The second and complementary witness to the option for the poor is the church's role as advocate and actor in the public life of society. The roots of this dimension of social ministry are found in the prophets who teach us to ask questions about how we organize our life as a society. The prophets asked questions in Israel about patterns of land ownership and wages, about the rules and customs used to design the social life of the nation. The prophets did not stop formulating the norm that the quality of faith is tested by the character of social justice. They pressed specific questions about the social patterns in the life of Israel.

The conditions of twentieth-century industrial society are radically different from eighth-century B.C. Israelite society. Nevertheless, the prophets' style of social questioning has been taken up in the church's social teaching of this century. The purpose of this social teaching is to measure the social and economic life of society by the standards of social justice and social charity.

The leadership of the popes in this century has, in turn produced a body of social teaching from the bishops. The best known example was probably drafted in some faculty residence on this campus by John A. Ryan when he authored the 1919 pastoral letter on the economy stands in this tradition of social teaching.

These two dimensions of the church's life—its ministry of direct social service and its role as an advocate for the poor in society—remain the principal channels for the church's response to poverty. The challenge we face in making an effective option for the poor is how these two aspects of social ministry are integrated into the full life of the church today.

In a large, complex, bureaucratic, secular society like the Unites States, the church's social service role is more needed than ever. We should not try to duplicate what society does well in supplying social services, but, in particular, we should bring two dimensions to the system of social care. First, the delivery of some social services is best done in a decentralized local mode. For many social services today, only the taxing power of the state can raise sufficient funds to meet human needs. But the state is often not the best agency to minister services to people in need. The church and other voluntary agencies can often deliver, in a humane and compassionate way, services that only the state can fund.

Second, the church's agencies of direct social service should be a source not only of compassion but also creativity. Public bureaucracy is not known for creative innovation. Its size and complexity often prevent it from acting in anything but routine patterns. In every field from housing to health care to hospices, there is room for new creative methods of public-private cooperation to feed the hungry, shelter the homeless and heal the sick. We can do better what we are already doing. With 35 million poor in our midst, we can reach beyond what we are doing!

In saying this, I want to be correctly understood. I am aware that Catholic Charities, the Catholic health care system and other diocesan and national networks are already involved in significant efforts of creative and direct services. It is the very success of these efforts which will give us courage to extend our efforts.

There is another sense in which I want to be clearly understood. We cannot be consistent with Catholic tradition unless we accept the principle of subsidiarity. I fully support a pluralist social system in which the state is not the center of everything. Nevertheless, I do not want the principle of subsidiarity used in a way which subverts Catholic teaching on the collective responsibility of society for its poor. I am not endorsing a concept of decentralization or federalism which absolves the government from fulfilling its social responsibilities.

Both the Catholic and American traditions urge a pattern of public-private cooperation. This means the state has a positive social role, and we have social responsibility as religious organizations. The churches alone cannot meet the social needs of this nation, and we should not try to do so. We should be prepared to play a major role, but part of our role is to enter the public debate and work for a compassionate, just, social policy.

This is the second challenge which confronts the church today: how to fulfill the role of advocate in the public debate. This is the role which the Bishop's Conference is seeking to fulfill in its pastoral letters, first on peace and now on social justice. It is the role Bishop Malone stressed in his presidential address to the bishops last November. He argued that, on issues as diverse as abortion,

Central America, nuclear war and poverty, failure of the bishops to speak would be a dereliction of civic responsibility and religious duty.

It is this role which puts the bishops in the midst of public controversy. Controversy is the companion of participation in public policy debate. That is why it should not be surprising that contributions of the scope and range of our two pastoral letters cause controversies.

At the same time, it is important to understand the purpose of the bishops' interventions. In the pastoral letters—and in many other documents, such as congessional testimonies, speeches and letters of individual bishops—we speak at the level of both moral principles and the application of these principles to particular policies. We regularly assert that we understand and want others to understand the moral principles we present have a different authority than our particular conclusions. We invite debate and discussion of our policy conclusions. We know they must be tested in the public arena, in the academic community and in the professional community. We have been using the process of successive drafts to stimulate this discussion.

Since I was so directly involved in the pastoral letter on war and peace, I believe there is specific merit in joining principles and policy proposals in the same document. Its purpose is not to forclose debate, but to foster it. The policy conclusions give a sense of how the moral principles take shape in the concrete situations our society faces. I think we would be mistaken as bishops if we did not distinguish principles from policy judgments. But I think we would fail to stimulate the public argument if we withdrew from the arena of policy choices.

Our role is not to design or legislate programs but to help shape the questions our society asks and to help set the right terms of debate on public policy.

We have an excellent example in the issue confronting the Administration, the Congress, and the general public as we begin 1985—the deficit debate. It is the kind of highly technical and complex question which a modern state must face. The way the question is decided will shape the life of our society. The fact is that the deficit must be cut. The choices facing the Administration and the Congress are how to cut spending to reduce the deficit.

The technical details are admittedly immense, but the general policy question is not purely technical. At the core of the deficit debate is the trade-off between military spending and social spending. How that trade-off is adjudicated requires moral discernment as well as economic competence.

In the 1980s virtually every program for the poor has been cut: more than 2 million poor children lost health care benefits; half a million disabled adults lost cash and medical assistance; and one million poor families lost food stamp benefits. In general, spending for the poor is less than 10% of the federal budget, but it has sustained 33% of all budget cuts.

These cuts in social spending have been accompanied by significant, steady increases in military spending. It is the responsibility of the federal government to provide for common defense and to promote the general welfare. Military spending will justifiably be a part of the budget. But the deficit forces us as a nation to ask who will bear the burden of the deficit. Military spending should not be insulated when plans for reducing the deficit are formulated.

I have no misconceptions about bishops being competent to write a national budget. But it is not beyond our competence or role to say that the burden of reducing the deficit should not be borne by the most vulnerable among us. Programs for the poor have been cut enough! The burden must be shared by all sectors of the eonomy. The specifics of how to do it fall beyond my responsibility, but shaping the question of how we face the deficit is clearly part of what the church should do as advocate in the social system.

In the deficit debate, the fate of many of the poor is at stake. This evening I would like to focus attrention on a particular group by addressing a specifc dimension of poverty: the feminization of poverty. This phrase has been coined by Dr. Diana Pierce, a Catholic University faculty member who has made a signifcant contribution to the study of poverty. She has focused her research on the plight of women who are divorced, widowed or unmarried. She has surfaced data which have special relevance for the church in the policy debate about poverty.

Dr. Pierce's pioneering work has helped many begin to under-stand the severe economic consequences of motherhood and sex discrimination in our country. Of course, men—especially minori-ties and youths—also suffer from unemployment and poverty, and millions of intact families have inadequate income. However, pov-erty is growing fastest among women and children.

As we look at this issue, it will be helpful to remember that nearly all (94%) women marry and nearly all of them (95%) have children. Reducing the economic price of motherhood should be a priority for our society. This disproportionate burden of poverty on women and children is appalling. Current statistics reflect some of this grim picture: two out of three poor adults are women; three out of four poor elderly are women; almost half of all poor families are headed by women, and half of the women raising chil-dren alone are poor; one in four children under six is poor; one in three black children under six is poor.

Even if poverty did not weigh so disproportionately on women, the growth of both the number and percentage of the poor would be cause for alarm and action. For those of us in the church, this situation is profoundly disturbing. The fact that poverty is so con-centrated among women and children should galvanize our ener-gies and focus our attention on the conditions that create the situation.

A closer look at poverty among women reveals that it strongly linked to two sets of factors: job and wage discrimination leave women concentrated in the lowest paying jobs, with more prob-lems finding full-time year-round work. But, even when women overcome these obstacles they still earn substantially less than male high school dropouts! Of course, most women workers are not college graduates, and so the disparity in incomes is even greater for those in the lowest paying jobs.

While this discrimination affects most women, those whose husbands are employed are partially insulated, at least temporari-ly, from its worst effects. For women raising children alone, of course, the situation is much worse because they are often finan-cially responsible for most or all of their children's support. De-spite some well-reported exceptions, child care and support fall mainly on women. The increased rates of divorce and out-ofwedlock births have left more women than ever solely responsible for the support of their children.

Increasingly, it appears that it now takes the earnings of two adults to support a family in the United States. A single parent— widowed, divorced or unmarried—finds it difficult to stay above the poverty line. When that parent faces additional obstacles, such as the cost of day care (which can easily take more than a fourth of an average woman's salary) and sex discrimination in employment, the cards are overwhelmingly stacked against her.

The job market often offers little hope to a single mother trying to escape poverty. Unfortunately, other potential sources of supplemental income are also very limited. Child support is paid regularly to only a very small portion of eligible mothers. Welfare benefits are so low that, in most states, the combined value of Aid to Families with Dependent Children (AFDC) and food stamps doesn't even approach the poverty line. For the fifty States and the District of Columbia, the median benefit is 74% of the poverty threshold.

I cite these statistics and the case of women in poverty not because it is the only issue we must face as a church in the policy debate but because it is one we should face with special emphasis. I have argued the case for a consistent ethic of life as the specific contribution which the church can and should make in this nation's public debate. Central to a consistent ethic is the imperative that the church stand for the protection and promotion of life from conception to death—that it stands against the drift toward nuclear war which has been so evident in recent years—and that it stands against the trend to have the most vulnerable among us carry the costs of our national indebtedness.

To stand for life is to stand for the needs of women and children who epitomize the sacredness of life. Standing for their rights is not merely a rhetorical task! The church has its own specifically designed social services to protect and promote life. Through them we must counsel, support and sustain women seeking to raise families alone and to provide their children with the basic necessities—necessities which the most well endowed society in history surely should be able to muster.

But the church can not simply address the problem of the feminization of poverty through its own resources. It must also stand in the public debate for such programs as child care, food stamps, and aid to families with children. I do not contend that existing programs are without fault or should be immune from review. My point is that something like them is a fundamental requirement of a just society.

Whenever I speak about the consistent ethic, I am always forced by time limitations to omit or neglect crucial themes. In the past, I have stressed that our concern for life cannot stop at birth, that it cannot consist of a single issue—war or abortion or anything else. I have always considered that substantial commitment to the poor is part of a consistent ethic and a concern for women in poverty a particularly pertinent aspect of this "seamless argument." This evening I am grateful for the opportunity to spell out why and how the church should stand on these issues.

Ultimately, the pastoral letter on peace and the letter on the economy should help us as a church develop the specific features of a consistent ethic. In the end, every social institution is known by what it stands for. I hope the Catholic Church in this country will be known as a community which committed itself to the protection and promotion of life—that it helped this society fulfill these two tasks more adequately.

THE NEW MIGRATION[1]
Franklin A. Thomas[2]

Both the date and place were historically significant when Franklin A. Thomas addressed the Cooper Union on May 23, 1984.

The date was important because it was the 125th commencement exercises of an unusual institution of higher education, which was founded in 1859 as the Cooper Union for the Advancement of Science and Art by Peter Cooper, a 19th-century inventor and industrialist. With a mission

[1]Delivered at the commencement exercisees of the Cooper Union for the Advancement of Science and Art in New York City in the Great Hall at 1:30 P.M., May 23, 1984.
[2]For biographical note, see Appendix.

to provide free instruction in science and art at the college level to the working classes, the private school still charges no tuition. Cooper, who never received a formal education, believed that education "should be as free as air and water." Today, the school has an enrollment of over 1,000 students and offers degrees in architecture, art, and engineering.

The place was also historically significant because it was the Great Hall of Cooper Union where Abraham Lincoln had given his famous "Right Makes Might" speech in 1860. Prior to his address at Cooper Union, Lincoln was known in the East mainly through newspaper reports of his debates with Stephen Douglas. The invitation to deliver a political lecture before a New York audience was precisely what Lincoln needed to attain national recognition. The speech, a masterful effort, elevated Lincoln to a leading challenger for the Republican presidential nomination. Years later, a second important historic event took place in the Great Hall when the National Association for the Advancement of Colored People held its organization meeting in 1909.

Franklin Thomas, the 1984 commencement speaker, had been president of the Ford Foundation since 1979. With some $3.4 billion in assets, the Ford Foundation is the largest private foundation in the world, with assets double that of the nearest United States foundation. Thomas, who has a Columbia Law School degree, grew up in the largely black Bedford-Stuyvesant neighborhood of Brooklyn and for ten years was a community development director for that area. Thomas delivered his speech at 1:30 P.M. on May 23, 1984, to an audience of 900 which included 224 graduating seniors, parents, faculty, administrators, and trustees. In addition to Thomas' speech, to celebrate its 125th anniversary for the first time in history Cooper Union awarded honorary degrees.

Franklin A. Thomas's speech: The chronicles of this unique institution give three explanations of why it came to be called Cooper Union. According to one source, the word "union" describes the fusion of the arts and sciences into a single curriculum. A second explanation, noting Peter Cooper's deepening fears of the approaching Civil War, speaks of his hope that the school would be a bridge of peace between North and South. The third, recalling Peter Cooper's lifetime commitment to philanthropy, tells us that the word "union" symbolizes a merger of the private and the public interest.

Today I would like to offer a fourth explanation. I suggest that the word "union" also describes the organic linkage that exists between this exceptional school and its exceptional graduates, an attachment that will last for the rest of your lives. Through Cooper Union each of you shares a remarkable heritage that enriched you during your years of study here, and it is one that will be further nourished by what you will accomplish in the decades ahead. Wherever your careers and your destinies take you, each of you will wear a badge of honor linking you to generations of Cooper Union graduates.

Cooper Union represented a sharp turning in the evolution of higher education in America. It was among the first—and for much of its history one of the very few—private institutions to provide pathways of opportunity to the underprivileged. Doors of learning were unlocked to admit people determined to improve their own life chances and that of their children.

Cooper Union's reputation for excellence and accessibility to those confined by barriers not of their own making is well earned. It is not altogether surprising that 75 years ago Cooper Union became the birthplace of the National Association for the Advancement of Colored People. The NAACP's first organizational meeting was held here in the Great Hall in 1909, the year after a series of tragic race riots occurred in Springfield, Illinois, Abraham Lincoln's hometown and the site of his burial.

Among the ambitious students who enrolled here were the sons and daughters of some of the new immigrants who poured into America during the years following Cooper Union's beginning. These new arrivals sought to move from the factory floor and sewing machine to the architect's or designer's drawing board. Cooper Union was there to receive them.

To help these newcomers adapt, new institutions arose in our cities—nighttime classes, neighborhood libraries, settlement houses, and mutual aid societies. It is against that horizon—a cityscape of institutions that promoted adjustment and assimilation for America's newest arrivals—that one best understands the unique place of Cooper Union. It has always been an entry point to those motivated to win their way into America's mainstream.

Today similar institutions for adjustment and assimilation are as urgently needed as they were a century ago, for once again America is experiencing a huge wave of immigration, equal in magnitude to the past and greater in its diversity. Beginning in 1965 and accelerating through the 1970's, the inflow of migrants to the U.S. approached levels not seen since the turn of the century. By 1978, immigration hit the million-per-year mark.

Today's new migration is not an isolated event. It is the by-product of convulsive upheavals all over the globe. A vast movement of people is taking place on a vast geographical scale. The flood of refugees from Afghanistan to Pakistan, from Indochina to Thailand, and from Ethiopia to Somalia reflects the same forces that have brought Cambodians to Los Angeles and Cubans to Miami.

America is the primary receiver of migrants who seek a permanent home. From every point on the immigration compass, the United States is Magnetic North. And, for every one that makes it here, there are hundreds who are desperately eager to follow. Given the state of the world, the pressures will be toward larger rather than smaller pools of potential migrants.

Today's immigration rate in the United States matches the record levels of the early twentieth century, when, from 1900 to 1910, nine million settlers arrived. A second resemblance is its diversity, drawing from even more countries than before 1914. Then, more than 80% of the newcomers were from Europe; now 80% of the current wave are predominantly of Latin America, Caribbean, and Asian origin. Migration, once the mirror of one continent, is now the mirror of all the world.

History is not repeating itself in the most important respect of all. The new migration has not kindled the hatred of the pre-1914 era. The reaction to the migration at that time was one of the darker chapters of our history, a series of exclusionary laws that were nakedly discriminatory toward the Asians and other non-Nordics. That is not to say there isn't hostility today, but on the whole, there has been a calmer response. Our generation, the offspring of immigrants, seems to be more tolerant of other cultures and creeds. Perhaps pluralism begets pluralism.

If the new migration has not provoked hysteria, it has provoked uneasiness. There is a foreboding that we are losing control of our borders and that the problem has become not only the size of the inflow but also its unpredictability and unmanageability. That foreboding resulted, in 1978, in the establishment by Congress of a Select Commission on Immigration. Over a three year period, the commission sponsored studies and conducted hearings to provide the background for a national immigration policy.

The commission invited to its deliberations every major interest group concerned with immigration issues. From the arguments presented, two notable lessons emerged. One is that today's conflict over immigration is not between those who would slam the immigration gates shut and those who would open them up completely. Rather, it is a controversy about relative numbers, between what may be called the "restrictionist" and the "expansionist" approaches.

A second lesson was that the immigration debate has spawned some unusual political combinations. Employers' groups have joined with Hispanic groups and the American Civil Liberties Union in supporting an expansionist policy. On the restrictionist side is an implausible grouping of the AFL-CIO, extreme rightists, and, with respect to certain of the issues, some minority civil rights organizations. Because political forces have split into such unfamiliar coalitions, it has become more difficult to find an effective consensus.

Behind these coalitions lie some specific interests and concerns. First, the restrictionists. From organized labor there is fear about an overburden on public services, especially welfare and schools. The environmentalists voice alarm about an overburden of population on natural resources. And, heightened tolerance notwithstanding, there is apprehension about an overburden of new influences on our mainstream cultural traditions. Some worry that in paying attention to newcomers we may forget those native-born Americans who are suffering.

The most pervasive anxiety of the restrictionists centers on the perceived threat to America's mainstream culture—on the limits of the nation's capacity to assimilate new religions, values, and lifestyles. Cross-cutting all political lines is an uneasiness about an irresistible drift toward a bilingual America. There looms the image of our nation divided by language-based cleavages.

The arguments of the expansionists are the precise opposite of those of the restrictionists. Some employers argue that American workers reject millions of distasteful yet indispensable jobs, that without a continuous flow of immigrants many needed goods and services would be undersupplied or higherpriced or lost to foreign competition.

The most eloquent advocates for a liberal policy, however, are those who hold before us the ideals of our origins, of America as example and haven. They remind us that we became an independent nation not just to assert our autonomy, but to provide the world with a new model of democracy, one that, we hoped, would be emulated by other nations. If not, their people were free to come here and share ours. The sentiments expressed in that poem on the Statue of Liberty are true at the core. The American Dream is the immigrants' dream.

And they add one more argument: in our time immigration policy is an extension of foreign policy. In America's struggle for influence in the world, our most potent tool is not the ideological pamphlet or the shipment of arms or even economic aid. It is the example of a free, tolerant, and prosperous America. And there is force to the argument that other countries may triumph at global conferences where world representatives vote with their hands, but America seems to win every contest whenever the world's people have an opportunity to vote with their feet.

Even so, lofty ideals alone would not be persuasive were they not reinforced by the successful outcome of two centuries of relatively free migration. Free migration represented a gamble with destiny that America has decisively won.

No one doubts that our progress depended heavily upon almost unlimited land and bountiful resources. Yet that is far from the whole story. Other resource-rich nations have not done nearly as well, and many countries have advanced without any natural endowment. What seems to make the difference is the presence of motivated, striving, family-centered people. The immigrants to America were all of those things. They were tireless in the struggle to enlarge their own lives and obsessive in the compulsion to build springboards for their children. They and their descendants have climbed high on every scale and have captured their share of every prize. In enlarging themselves they have enlarged the nation.

If America has won a previous gamble with destiny, why, ask the expansionists, will it not win another? One can already observe many hopeful signs. Census and other data show that after ten to fifteen years of residence legal immigrants have income and civic participation at least equal to that of the native-born. Deteriorating neighborhoods have been reborn by the entry of immigrants. They have transformed Astoria, northern and middle Queens, and Brighton Beach. One immigrant is busy levating the quality of Park Avenue.

As with jobs and neighborhoods, so with schools. Each year's list of academic awards is thickly sprinkled with the names of immigrant youth, and tomorrow the valedictorian at City College, who has a 3.9 average in electrical engineering, will be a young man who five years ago arrived from Vietnam unable to speak English.

Still even the most buoyant expansionists realize that immigration cannot be unlimited. There are simply too many people in the world who want to become Americans. And the restrictionists realize that they must reconcile themselves to inflows much larger than they would like. The resolution of these two forces is what we must find. Some believe the Simpson-Mazzoli Bill is a reasonable compromise between compassion for those who are already here and stricter rules for those who are not. Others disagree. For the present, America's national policy with respect to immigration seems to be not to have a policy, other than spasmodic and often inequitable enforcement of existing rules.

The fact is the new migrants and their children will constitute an ever-increasing portion of the U.S. population growth in the decades ahead. Our economy, our cities, and our culture will be dramatically affected by their presence. That is an outcome more to be welcomed than feared.

I believe that the new migration will in the long run be a positive force. America, formed by immigrants, has continually been transformed by immigrants. Each wave has been a source of national renewal.

But if new Americans are to adapt and advance, every institution must help in that effort—our schools and local governments, our employment services, and our social agencies and nonprofit organizations, including private foundations. We at the Ford Foundation have expanded our work on urban poverty to include a series of initiatives aimed at these newcomers. Many of the initiatives involve self-help programs in cities where the new immigrants are concentrated. We have learned that the key to progress is to motivate individuals in a nurturing context of family and community. We have programs to help them start businesses and to bring them into the electoral process and to protect their civil rights. And we have research programs to find out more about them and their rates of progress.

The task of assimilation will challenge all of our capacities as a nation—especially our inventiveness. Late nineteenth-century America treated the newcomers with more anger and less humanity than is now the case. Yet it was extraordinarily imaginative in creating effective means to absorb the shock of entry and to advance the entrant. Will we in the last years of the twentieth century be as inventive?

It is a task that must engage all of us for decades to come. Given the heritage of Cooper Union, its graduates, who will share in the process of renewal and change in the coming decades, have more than an ordinary obligation to be part of the solution. The Cooper Union badge of honor you receive today is also a memento of responsibility.

DOES TV HAVE THE COURAGE TO PIONEER A NEW COMMERCIAL ETHIC?[1]
NORMAN LEAR[2]

Where is the conscience of television? Does television, indeed, have a conscience? These questions were raised at a conference entitled, "TV and Ethics: Who's Responsible?," held in Boston, Massachusetts, on December 6 and 7, 1984. The meeting was cosponsored by the Academy of Television Arts and Sciences and Emerson College. The academy, an organization 12,000 persons actively involved in all aspects of television performing and production, has as its purpose the advancement of the arts and sciences of television and the fostering of creative leadership in the television industry for artistic, cultural, educational, and technological

[1]Delivered at the conferences on "TV and Ethics: Who's Responsible?" sponsored by the Academy of Television Arts and Sciences and Emerson College in the main meeting room of the Sheraton-Boston Hotel at 10:00 A.M., December 6, 1984.

[2]For biographical note, see Appendix.

progress.

Setting the tone for the conference was Norman Lear, creator of the highly successful "All in the Family" television series and producer of several other popular situation comedies. In his keynote speech, he charged that those responsible for television entertainment, news, and public affairs proceed with very little consideration for the ethics involved. Ratings—"How do we win Tuesday night at 8?"—seemed to be the main concern of television industry executives, who, Lear said, displayed an almost total disregard for the medium's potential to teach, illuminate, and inspire.

Other prominent speakers at the conference, most of whom reinforced Lear's criticism of the industry, included the Reverend William Sloan Coffin, senior minister of the Riverside Church in Manhattan; Chester F. Collier, vice president of Metromedia productions; Henry Rivera; Federal Communications Commission member; Len Mathews, president of the American Association of Advertising Agencies; and Public Citizen president Joan Claybrook.

Lear delivered the keynote address at 10:00 A.M., December 6, 1984, in the main meeting room of the Sheraton-Boston Hotel to an audience of more than 300 advertising and television people, academics, and special interest ethnic, political, and religious group representatives.

Lear's speech and the conference were widely reported by the national press and were the subject of special features by Peter Kaplan in the *New York Times* (December 10, 1984, p. 23) and Christopher Swan in the *Christian Science Monitor* (December 20, 1984, p. 27).

Norman Lear's speech: It is very good to be here this morning and I am grateful to the New England Chapter of the Television Academy of Arts and Sciences and Emerson College for convening this conference.

I attended Emerson College, class of 1944, so I take special pleasure in being here. Today, Emerson students studying communications work in a complex of TV studios and other facilities that were, in 1942, the Emerson Theatre, just off the Esplanade behind 130 Beacon Street. It was in that little theatre that I made my first appearance as an actor, playing "Uncle Stanley" in the Emerson production of "George Washington Slept Here." And, thanks to that experience and the specific advice of our director, Gertrude Binley Kay, it was my last appearance as an actor.

I have many memories of Boston, too, dating back long before I attended Emerson. As a child, we lived in Chelsea, Winthrop, Everett, and my father, who was my prototype for the character of Archie Bunker, wasn't paid by Everett to live in Chelsea, by Chelsea to live in Winthrop, and by Winthrop to live in Brookline.

Our subject for this conference is "Television and Ethics: Who's Responsible?" As I thought about this, preparing for these remarks, the very linkage of those two notions, television and ethics, struck me as some kind of bizarre juxtaposition of terms. Like "supermarket music" or "airline food." For almost fifty years, the companies introducing new communications technologies have promised that their new inventions would lead to a cultural renaissance. General David Sarnoff, the founder of the Radio Corporation of America and one of the founders of the television industry itself, predicted that "television drama of high caliber and produced by first rate artists will materially raise the level of dramatic taste of the nation." That was in 1939. In 1951, another pioneer, Edward R. Murrow, said of television: "This instrument can teach. It can illuminate. Yes, it can even inspire. But it can do so only to the extent that humans are determined to use it to those ends. Otherwise it is merely lights and wires in a box."

In Sarnoff's words, have we been seeing television drama of high caliber that raises the level of dramatic taste of the nation? And in Mr. Murrow's words, is the instrument of television being used to teach, to illuminate, to inspire?

May I state quickly and remove from doubt that I understand that television is not entirely a wasteland. I am well aware of the many fine Movies-of-the-Week and miniseries that appear on all three networks. I applaud with you "The Dollmaker" and "A Streetcar Named Desire" and "Live From Lincoln Center" and "Nova" and "The MacNeil-Lehrer Report" and "Brideshead Revisited" and the Shakespeare plays and the distinguished "Dance in America" series; and I stand behind no one in my appreciation for "Hill Street Blues" and "Cheers" and "Family Ties" and "St. Elsewhere," and that latest gift of laughter, "The Bill Cosby Show," which also illuminates the nuances of familial interpersonal relations and inspires.

But average American viewers are currently watching 7 hours and 34 minutes of television every day of their lives. Children between the ages of 6 and 11 are watching an average of 27 hours a week, 1400 hours a year. By the time a youngster graduates from high school, he or she will spend more time in front of the tube than in the classroom—and I ask you, how much of what is available for them to view do you believe can materially raise the level of their taste? How much of it do you believe serves to teach, illuminate, and inspire?

My references thus far have only been to entertainment on television. Think about news and public affairs. How much of the news and public affairs available to the average American, seven days a week, meets the challenge? To my mind, the answer is simple: precious little.

I believe that the manufacturer of television entertainment, news, and public affairs, and those responsible for preparing and broadcasting it, proceed with very little consideration of the ethics involved. I believe that there is too little consideration for the ethics involved in most American businesses today.

Why are we reading so much about new toxic waste sites; about the increasing hazards of old toxic waste sites; and the continued do-nothing attitude of local, state and federal government?

Why are we reading so much about the further pollution of the air we breathe and the water we drink; of the do-nothing attitude toward acid rain and the contamination of our lakes and streams?

Why are the breakfast cereals sold on supermarket shelves that scientists tell us should be labelled candy?

Why are so many unsafe automobiles sold to American consumers by companies fully aware of their products' defects, only to be recalled later?

Why are drugs that could cost the consumer pennies, sold and advertised under multitudinous brand names at many hundreds times their costs?

Why is American business so consumed with short-term thinking—so obsessed with the need for a profit statement this quarter larger than the last—that it is losing its position of world leadership in industry after industry?

Business forever condemns people like me—writers for the stage, theater, television or books—for portraying business and business people too often in an unflattering light. Well, this writer believes that American business earns every bit of that. And if I am wrong and we writers do overdo it, America won't die of our sins. I believe America is dying, slowly, of theirs.

I feel better for having said that because I don't think television should ever be considered out of context with the rest of American business. As a matter of fact, I am pertetually angered by the way television is lashed at and berated and heaped on by the print media—raked over the coals daily for its sins—while the rest of American business goes relatively scot-free. Now, having said that—where its ethics are concerned—I would like to lash at, berate, and heap on television, too!

And let me confess, sadly, that I do not exclude myself or my company, Embassy Communications, from the problem. Despite all the awareness herein expressed, Embassy, too, must plead guilty.

Commercial television's moral north star, from which nearly all bearings are set, is quite simply: "How do I win Tuesday night at 8 o'clock?" That is the name of the game, the only thing that matters.

When television producers and/or production companies decide what ideas should be developed, their sole criterion is, too often, "What will the networks buy?" And, when deciding what programs are worthy of air time, network television program executives, locked in an overwhelming competitive race that is reported by the print media day in and day out across the nation, have no charter from management to take risks. They have no character to nurture innovation, to seek the kind of quality that might teach some, illuminate some, and inspire. The need to win quickly is too great. Winning in the short-term, beating your competitor's brains out, half-hour by half-hour, that is the ethic that prevails in TV today.

It is an ethic I call the "binary imagination." By "binary" I am using a computer metaphor, the computer habit of reducing everything down to binary codes, either one or zero. If something cannot be captured in that code, it doesn't exist as far as the computer is concerned. Television has come to a place where it, like any other business, insists upon reducing everything down to its own binary code of numbers. Television, in fact, is a cult of numbers: Nielsen ratings, market share percentages, viewer demographics, audience research demographics—did you know that television has now taken to researching program *ideas* for new series before a script is even written?

This reduction of everything to numbers results in a stunted, number-based mentality that impoverishes our understanding of the world by screening out the non-quantifiable facts of life. If something cannot be distilled into a number—or a sliding scale of numbers—the subtler value-laden facts that also constitute reality are disenfranchised, and the wondrous resources of the human mind and soul and spirit are replaced with the binary imagination.

Now I submit that it is one thing to apply the binary imagination to pork bellies, toothpaste, and tires, and quite another to apply it to television, the nation's largest-by-far marketplace of ideas and values, whose product springs largely from the creative impulse of the writers and other artists who serve it.

Asking a writer to conceive to please the machines and tests and graphs that measure audience response to his ideas, is like imagining Michelangelo and a hundred other painters painting the Sistine Chapel from their Sistine Chapel Paint-by-Numbers Kits.

And so, television shows, which have the potential to teach, illuminate, and inspire—shows that have the potential for raising the dramatic and general level of taste of the nation—are too often forfeited to the vagrant, highly imperfect whims of the marketplace, as measured by some highly deceptive numbers. If a show cannot make a 20% market share with the 18–34 year-olds or jump though some other set of arbitrary numerical hoops, it is dropped within a matter of weeks. No opportunity exists for something innovative and different to become an acquired taste. Of course there are exceptions, but we are dealing with the rule. It is the rule, not the exception, that defines ethical behavior.

Television's rationale for this is, of course, that its obligation is to give the viewer what it wants. So if television is serving up a diet that is largely junk and the viewer is watching that junk, television is off the hook, it is the viewer's fault. Let's stop and examine the ethics of that proposition.

When television insists it is merely responding to public taste, it effectively renounces any obligation to lead and places the viewer in charge. Now does that really make sense? Does the television executive who asserts that really believe it? Are we to assume that these highly educated men and women, people who attended major universities and received their masters in communication, then made their way slowly up the television industry ladder to positions where they are the ones who decide what will play on television in American homes—are we to assume that they came that distance, just to take a seat on the back of the bus and let the viewer do the driving? No, I believe that they adopted that attitude when they arrived at their positions of power, because it goes with the territory.

Now, let's look at it from the angle of the average American viewer. The average viewer is the average American, and we know that he or she is leading an emotionally embattled life somewhere in the country, harassed by the economy, by concerns for the future, struggling just to get from Monday to Friday—somewhat under-educated, and probably underpaid and overtaxed. Do you really believe that that individual—who uses television as a means of escape from an otherwise cruel day—could even imagine himself in the job of a television programmer, making such sophisticated determination as what America will see on TV? Uh-uh.

The average TV viewer doesn't run for mayor, doesn't seek a seat in the Congress and isn't looking to program television. He or she is looking, however, in all those places, for leadership. Life and fate and circumstance place leaders in positions of overview, which means that they are able to see things that others can't, and in those positions of overview, responsible leaders will suggest a direction that may not be popular in the short-term, but will benefit *everyone* long-term. Politicians fail this ethical question in leadership when they sacrifice that long-term interest of the electorate, for the immediate gratification of casting a more popular vote now. And, similarly, television programmers ignore the opportunity, if not the obligation, to select programming that will, in the long-term, teach, illuminate and inspire as it entertains, for the sake of yet another instant carbon copy ratings success, short-term.

Grant Tinker, Chairman of the Board at NBC, told the *New York Times* recently, "I think it's criminal of people to stare at television so uncritically." The man who created NBC, General Sarnoff, said that "television drama of high caliber . . . will materially raise the level of dramatic taste of the nation." What has happened to us in 50 years? General Sarnoff wasn't satisfied to blame the consumer for the product. He obviously believed that the proper role of leadership was to continually improve upon the product and help the consumer reach for it.

It is only television executives who insist that television merely responds to public taste. Educators, sociologists, and other observers of the media tell us it is shaping public taste. Both positions are right, but this is one situation where the chicken comes squarely before the egg.

Yes, three networks will respond to the success of MTV by creating their own music video shows. But it was all those years of sharply edited, highly expensive, musically sophisticated TV commercials that paved the way and weaned the viewer to an appetite for what became MTV. Yes, they were responding to the success of the prime-time soap opera, "Dallas," when the competition created "Dynasty" and "Hotel" and "Falcon Crest" and "Knots Landing" and "Glitter"—but it was all those years of daytime soap operas that weaned a major portion of the viewing public toward the acceptance of a glossier kind of soap opera in prime time.

If television will accept the responsibility for weaning generations of Americans to programs that most television executives will tell you privately shame them—or as they put it, are "not my personal cup of tea"—television might at last be ready to fulfill the promise held for it by the men who created the medium.

But television has weaned several generations of Americans to accept more than just the style and content of its programming. America's esthetic sense, its sensibilities and much of its behavior has been shaped by television, too.

How many adult family members can we watch on game shows—jumping up and down like little children, under instruction from the producers—clapping their hands and shrieking wildly at the sound of a bell that tells them they have guessed right and won $80—before we begin to believe that it is proper and normal to explode in front of millions of your peers, in a kind of foolish and herd-like ritual of childish abandon?

How many people will we have to see on the evening news—in a moment of consummate grief, just having learned of the death of a loved one—responding politely to the voyeuristic questions of an aggressive TV newsperson, before we begin to believe that it is our obligation, even in moments of unspeakable pain, to stand still and answer the media's questions?

And how many little white lies do we have to hear—such as "We'll talk to so-and-so when we come back after this message"—only to sit through not only one commercial message, but two or three before "so-and-so" appears—how many of these little white lies do we have to hear before we become so deadened by them that we are ready to accept larger ones?

If these examples stretch your belief, remember that there are many examples of TV influencing behavior that have been documented. When the Fonz on "Happy Days" got his first library card, thousands of youngsters everywhere visited libraries the next day for theirs. When the father on "Good Times" was diagnosed as suffering from hypertension, thousands of black males across America sought similar help after the broadcast. Of course, television influences behavior—and of course, that should be a matter of ethical concern for every individual in a leadership role in the medium.

Most television programming executives will not buy this. And yet, ironically, they have been victims of the weaning process themselves. A young writer of the situation comedy that I had mentored sent me this note not too long ago:

I don't think the networks understand the real people. Most of the programming executives are only 32 or 33, like me—and we all grew up watching a lot of television—I mean, *really* a lot of television. Then we all went to college and studied communications. I don't know how I escaped this, Norman—maybe it's because I always knew I wanted to write—but I swear, most of those guys at the network are all confused about what real human behavior is. They ask us to write stupid things for people because the only thing they know about how people talk and behave is what they've seen all their lives on television.
Sometimes I think TV is not so much a reflection of society as a reflection of other TV shows. *And they don't know that.*

It is arrogant of television to accept so little responsibility for the nature of its programming and for its effect on society. And if that attitude isn't certifiably lacking in ethical considerations, it's awfully close. Especially when you consider that the binary imagination and the obsession with ratings applies as much to news and information as it does to entertainment.

Don't believe for a minute that the top priority of Dan Rather, Tom Brokaw, and Peter Jennings and their staffs is to present the news in a way that helps the American viewer understand the world and events around him. These are earnest and talented people and they would hope to achieve that end, but their broadcasts are in a life-or-death struggle with the competition, and the name of the game for them is to win Monday through Friday at 7:00 P.M. This is as true in every city with more than one local independent station as it is at the networks.

We all know that violence has a very special place in the evening news. Murder, rape, fire, a highway accident—especially those that provide terrific photo opportunities—are premium items on America's newscasts. The people responsible will tell you that that's what the viewers want. As a matter of fact, a recent piece of research conducted on behalf of the Radio Television News Directors Association, revealed that when viewers were asked what they remembered most on news, "Murders and murderers totally outdistanced foreign wars . . . homicidal maniacs as a class proved seven times as memorable as the brutal war between Iran and Iraq."

The research concluded, in part, with: "Violet crimes are more memorable as news events than all but the most dramatic political occurrences." I am not shocked by that report. Why wouldn't a hot local murder or a major traffic accident—especially as photographed with the zeal and zoom lens of one of our macho, staccato, late-breaking news teams—be more memorable than the same two minutes or less allotted to the coverage of a war between Iran and Iraq?

The problem with the research conducted for the News Directors Association, among television viewers nationwide, was: one-quarter of the respondents said that they had never heard of presidential advisor Ed Meese; 64% replied that they never knew that Gary Hartpence had changed his name to Gary Hart. Of this the Radio Television News Directors Newsletter said smugly: " . . . The public enthusiastically exhibited the right not to know."

Okay, so the average viewer doesn't remember some of the more important stories covered by TV news as well as he does the lesser reports of local violence. The same Gary Hart, in a television interview during the primary campaign, didn't know who Louis Farrakhan was, or the news reporter he had threatened with death just that week. During the recent campaign, your own very able Congressman, Ed Markley, was asked to name the Prime Minister of Israel on a Boston show, admitted he didn't know, and then guessed wrong.

If the truth be known, your keynote speaker—this Talmudic-looking fellow who stands here working hard to impress you with his depth of knowledge—is sadly lacking in information on many of the more pressing domestic and international problems that confront us today. If I had to state a quick opinion on aspects of the situation in Nicaragua and El Salvador or participate in a discussion on some of the more sophisticated problems concerning the Middle East, I would turn privately to people I consider experts in the field to get the information needed before I could perform.

Now, I think you will grant that Gary Hart and Ed Markey and Norman Lear, by virtue of fate, fortune, and circumstance, lead less emotionally-embattled lives than the average American I described earlier. We are better educated, have more time and better opportunity to learn about the issues, and we suffer less *angst* than that citizen who is simply struggling to get from Monday to Friday. And yet, often enough, *we* don't know. The wonder is we don't get caught at it more often.

Why then are the self-appointed arbiters of taste and judgment so quick to put down the average television viewer? How dare television interpret his confusion at the complexity of the issues that confront him—and his inability to recall the myriad of names and events with which he is constantly bombarded—as evidence that it has no responsibility to them? Ethically, those in positions to lead must accept that obligation or, ethically, it is a case of the blind leading the blind.

Television has, of course, had an effect on the political scene, too, and I am again sorry for the viewer. I am not sorry for the politicians. In the 1984 election, they were co-conspirators in a ten-month television extravaganza that sacrificed everything to the binary imagination. The issues, the ideas and the candidates themselves were largely sacrificed to an obsession with numbers and percentages, statistics and polls. Here was the binary imagination run amok.

TV coverage of the 1984 presidential campaign was a triumph of images over substance. It was the horse race and hoopla of the campaign, not the ideas and merits of the issues, which received the most attention. From the primaries through to November 6th, the big story most evenings was the result of the latest poll. Again and again, the candidates were seen on the evening news, responding to the same tired questions: "The polls show you so many points behind, Mr. Mondale. How are you going to catch up?" "The polls show you slipping a little among this or that constituency, Mr. President. What are you going to do about it?"

And talk about being *weaned* by the media: convention delegates no longer complain if their view is obstructed by TV cameras and crews. The real floor manager at political conventions is the man who points the camera. "Spontaneous" demonstrations are scheduled to last twelve minutes, *precisely,* to satisfy the needs of the convention floor, Olympus-like, and senators of great reknown scurry like beggars from booth to booth hoping that Dan Rather or Tom Brokaw will think them worthy of an interview.

I had the privilege of travelling with a presidential candidate in the 1980 primary campaign, and I was fascinated to observe the minuet for news coverage that was danced by the politician and the TV journalist. It took place each afternoon, when everyone paused, the TV lights were on, the cameras pointed, and every Sam Donaldson on the tour sought to ask that provocative fifteen-second question which would elicit a sharp twenty-second response that would assure *him* a place on the evening-news along with the candidate.

Television news, like television entertainment, is a business. And business today, all businesses, perform for the bottom line. Is there anything ethically wrong with this? Not on the surface, I suppose. But I believe our society is threatened by an unhealthy emphasis on success in the short-term, as measured by The Numbers. Much has been written to indicate that the American motor car ceased to be the standard of the world when Detroit, all those years ago, thought it could not and should not diminish a current profit statement to meet the challenge of the smaller, less expensive, foreign imports. In recent years, we have witnessed the same phenomenon in consumer electronics, steel, and many other industries.

Americans have been shaken by these losses. Across the country, in city after city that were once known as "company towns", the compact between the family and the company—a compact that had been carried forward from generation to generation, where fathers and uncles and brothers and nephews all worked in the same plant—has been broken. When we talk about the breakdown of the American family and try to list its probable causes, how much should we attribute to this overwhelming loss of continuity and stability?

Was there an ethical responsibility to attempt to prevent this from occurring? And if so, whose responsibility? Certainly the union chieftains, responsible for the long-term interests of the work force, saw the handwriting on the wall at some point, but they never blew the whistle. On the other hand, they were only representing their workers, who were interested only in increased wages and a larger package of benefits. Then what about management? Certainly they could see trouble down the road if they didn't diminish a current profit statement to modernize, or otherwise meet the threat of foreign competition. Yes, but they were tied to contracts that demanded they produce in the short-term, so they couldn't blow the whistle either.

Those who run television are in the same boat. It is no secret that the networks have been losing their share of audience steadily for years; the largest of the capable enterprises, HBO, is losing share precipitously now, and all of the broadcast television is beginning to lose to the videocassette. They are in a trap, not of their own devising.

And so it is very hard to pin down where ethical responsibility lies. We have created a kind of climate in our country, a climate in which leadership everywhere—in the Congress, federal agencies, business, labor, the universities, television—leadership everywhere glorifies instant success—whether in profit margins, ratings, or polls—and refuses through indifference or myopia to make adequate provisions for the future. All the while, committing suicide in the long term.

Because television probably affects us more profoundly than any other of America's businesses, and because its profile is certainly higher than any other American business, it would be helpful to see it lead in accepting its ethical responsibilities. It would be helpful to see those television executives, who have been content to let the viewers do the driving, finally take the wheel. General Sarnoff was driving when he said that what he envisioned for television drama would raise the taste of the American viewer, and Edward R. Murrow was driving when he told us that television had the capacity to teach, illuminate and inspire.

We can't let that kind of leadership end with the pioneers. Television needs some new pioneers: men and women in every area of the industry who will resist the inexorable commercial logic of the present day television which tends to trivialize everything that comes in its path; men and women who will strive for more than seeking to win Tuesday night at 8 o'clock; writers, directors, producers, actors, and executives who will not forfeit their moral judgment to the Bottom Line.

When I grow up, I hope to be just such a writer and executive myself.

REKINDLING THE COMMITMENT TO CIVIC RESPONSIBILITY[1]
CHARLES S. ROBB[2]

Citing what he perceived to be a greater national need for commitment to civic involvement than ever before in order to cope with increasingly complex national and international issues, Governor Charles S. Robb of Virginia told the 40th National Conference on Higher Education that he was "disturbed by evidence that even as we face a rising need for

---

[1] Delivered at the closing plenary session of the American Association for Higher Education's National Conference in the Grand Ballroom of the Palmer House Hotel, Chicago, Illinois, at 10:20 A.M. on March 20, 1985.

[2] For biographical note, see Appendix.

citizens with the capacity and motivation to participate and assume leadership, the will and confidence to do so seem to be declining."

The conference was sponsored by the American Association of Higher Education, an organization of administrators, trustees, faculty, students, public officials, and interested individuals which seeks to clarify and help resolve critical issues in post-secondary education. Governor Robb delivered his speech at the closing plenary session of the conference. Preceding his address, more than 250 prominent educators and others concerned with higher education had spoken at 80 sessions and several workshops.

Robb delivered his speech at 10:30 A.M. on March 20, 1985, to an audience of 500 conference attendees in the Grand Ballroom of the Palmer House Hotel in Chicago, Illinois. Robb's address was followed by extended remarks in reaction by President Howard Swearer of Brown University and then a question and answer period.

Governor Robb's speech: Let me say in response to your kind introduction that I take special pleasure and pride in this opportunity to talk about several matters of mutual concern. Incidentally, it has been my pleasure as Chairman of the Education Commission of the States [ECS] to learn much about your Chairman, Frank Newman, in the months during which ECS conducted the search that led to Frank's appointment as both President and Executive Director of the Commission, and to work closely with Frank since he officially joined ECS on the first of January. Both of our organizations are the better for Frank's leadership.

I'd like to talk today about an issue that has been on my mind for several years, as I have attempted in my own state to improve both the climate in which our colleges and universities, private and public, conduct their work, and the condition of higher education itself. And that issue is what I have come to see as our national retreat from efforts to foster sound civic values in young people, and particularly our apparent unwillingness to make the cultivation of character and civic commitment a central purpose of education at all levels, and especially at the level of the undergraduate college.

I must warn you that my perspective is one that has not always been popular inside higher education, for I believe deeply in the interdependence of all of the many functions of state government in our common pursuit of the public good. In my state, all of education accounts for about 57% of our general fund expenditures, and the public and private colleges and universities receive about a third of this money. Higher educaton, then, matters to our people and to our leaders for reasons that go far beyond our conviction that the colleges are our great equalizer as a free people, and far beyond our conviction that the life of the mind is, in and of itself, an essential object of public support. For me, and for most of my fellow governors, higher education is an essential, productive, and uncommonly expensive public commitment. As I know many of you do, we struggle constantly to define the middle ground between the public's interest in accountability, efficiency, and effectiveness, and the academy's interest in the intellectual or academic freedom, and all of the values that the term conveys.

As we address this queston of how state leaders and institutional leaders can work together to achieve our common goals, I am brought more than once to recognize that certain cornerstones of our system of education are at stake in the discussion. Our future as a nation is as closely tied today as it has ever been to our capacity to open our society and our economy to all of our people, regardless of their wealth, or race, or geographical origins, or family history. Almost since the very beginning, education in this land has had the uncommon charge to equip every citizen not only to think independently, to contribute economically, and to be self-sufficient, but also to assume responsibility for the common good. The conditions in which education meets this charge change from one era to another. Much of what I have to say today obviously relates to the climate of our times as that climate serves to define the conditions in which colleges conduct their vital work.

From my point of view, our national need for commitment to civic involvement is probably greater today than ever before. National issues grow more complex daily. So, too, does our dependence on higher education for both the skills and the knowledge necessary to our individual success in this new climate. Moreover, our evolving experience with new conditions of international cooperation and competition tells us that the nation as it will be tomorrow requires citizens with the will to tackle seemingly intractable problems, to accept and indeed thrive on the absence of obvious and simple solutions, to tolerate diverse values and perspectives, to change as our tools and methods change, and to be aware many individual problems yield only to common or even global solutions.

Let me confess to you that I am disturbed by evidence that even as we face a rising need for citizens with the capacity and motivation to participate and assume leadership, the will and confidence to do so seem to be declining. Consider if you will some indications of which we have all read. (1) Responding, perhaps, to a prolonged period in which we were buffeted by what seemed to be almost routine evidence of the abuse of public trust in national affairs, the polls are showing significant declines in trust in government and a related decline in confidence that our common problems can be solved through traditional political processes. (2) Almost all sectors of society report declines in confidence in other institutions: in organized labor, the press, medicine, the military, organized religions, and even in education itself. (3) Many Americans, and especially young people, report doubt that an individual can make a difference. Our young people seem somehow to have moved from the almost frantic activism of the 1960s through a period of something like disengagement with public life to a condition that now approaches lethargy.

These changes are reflected in the decline in the number of people voting in presidential and other elections, in increased participations in narrowly focused interest groups, and in the growing influence of such groups at all levels of the political process. Indeed, the nationwide trend actually shows a scarcity of candidates for school boards and similar bodies and a marked decline in the number of volunteers for major public service. You know, as I do, that leadership of this kind has been from the beginning one of the predictable outcomes of collegiate study.

Freshmen coming to higher education, reflecting broader trends in society, know less now about the American political system than their predecessors knew. And they show a decided shift toward self-interest as opposed to civic responsiblity. The annual results of the American Council of Education–UCLA surveys of college freshmen show a fifteen-year decline in expectations of participation in the political life of the country, in any form of altruism, or in concern for the interests of others. Over the same time, student interest in values associated with money, status, and power has risen steadily.

Most of us would agree, I think, that the college years ought to be a period of personal growth, including growth in responsibility toward and awareness of the interests of others. Yet the recent evidence suggests that these influences may not be as strong as in the past.

The challenge of rekindling the commitment of civic responsibility is one that we all face: government, the private sector, education, and leaders from all segments of society. Clearly, the colleges and universities cannot solve all these problems by themselves. Indeed, many of them may not yield to solutions other than those that occur slowly and incrementally over time as humanity itself changes. Yet there are actions that college and university leaders can take in cooperation with others in positions of responsibility to foster the capacity and motivation to reach beyond self and to play an active part in addressing the nation's problems.

Let me describe an approach that appeals to me and to several others who took part in a national forum two weeks ago under the sponsorship of ECS's Business Advisory Commission. I have felt for a long time that we give up something as a nation and take away something from young adults when we omit service to the community, state, or nation from the list of normal experiences shared by virtually all. In fact, my own personal bias is that we made a fundamental tactical error in moving away fron the concept of universal military service, a concept as old and as deeply entrenched in our body of national tradition as the first gatherings of local militias on village greens in towns like Williamsburg and Boston. But I did not come today to argue this issue *per se*, and I know as you do the many obstacles to reinstituting this particular kind of service as a component of the experience of growing up in this country.

Considering youth service in another sense, however, I am increasingly persuaded that a broadly-framed program of national service may be one excellent way to cultivate the sense of citizenship—of responsibility—to give of one's self to the larger community. It may have the effect also of building understanding, tolerance, and maturity, and other traits essential for effective performance in business, government, or other activity later in life.

I do not intend today to advance a specific proposal, but I think that most of us might agree, in the absence of a hard proposal, that certain principles ought to be observed if we ever move toward some system of youth service. First, the program should make a minimal interruption of people's careers; yet it should make a life-long impact on our understanding of the concept of community itself. Second, the emphasis should be on incentives to motivate young people to serve and the service itself should be designed in such a way as to benefit each young person who participates. Third, youth service should involve a range of options rather than a single monolithic system. Most who have looked at this issue believe, as I do, that the primary force behind any successful program of youth service must be the federal government, if only because no other entity is comprehensive enough to administer a system. But the service need not be federal service. The federal government, the states, the localities, and the private sector could provide alternatives for young people to meet their service obligations, and without incurring substantial additional expense to the public. Many programs already exist. What is missing is the scale necessary to accommodate large numbers of young people and the general commitment in public policy to service as a component of growth and maturation. Fourth, in terms of basic principles, fulfillment of the service obligation ought to bring educational benefits, perhaps not unlike those that worked so well under the G.I. Bill. Several educational leaders, including David Saxon of M.I.T., have advanced this notion as a possible response to the brooding national crisis in funding for student financial aid. And, fifth, youth service should not be primarily an employment program. Rather, it should be a means of fostering commitment to civic responsibility and engagement with the mainstream of our national society and economy for all of our young people—rich, poor; privileged and not privileged; black, white, hispanic, and Asian; male and female; and so on. Indeed, to make such a program a make-work program or a welfare effort would be, to my mind, a serious mistake.

Many arguments can be posed for and against youth service, whether voluntary or compulsory. Fortunately, many programs do in fact exist and we can study their impact in terms other than the theoretical. Many programs exist in colleges and universities, and they have received notice in the recent calls for reform of undergraduate education. I am sure that these will be addressed, if they have not been already, in President Swearer's remarks and in the discussion period.

All of us know about such federal efforts as the Peace Corps and the Job Corps. What many may not know is that some thirty states and localities now support their own youth service programs. These tend to be projects that benefit the community, such as resource conservation, emergency relief, care for the elderly or work rebuilding roads, bridges, or inner-city neighborhoods. Young people 18 years old and older work under close supervision and on tight schedules that teach them good work habits, job-related skills, and civic values. Examples include the California Conservation Corps, the San Francisco Conservation Corps, and the City Volunteer Service in New York City.

At least three proposals before Congress this year would address youth service, and at least two of the three include overt links between service and student financial aid. Senator Gary Hart of Colorado and Congressman Robert Torricelli of New Jersey have jointly called for creation of a national commission to determine the feasibility of a "national youth service" to which all young people would belong for periods of 12 to 24 months. Congressman Leon Panetta of California has called for the federal government to give grants to state and local voluntary youth service programs on a 50/50 matching basis. Under the terms of the federal grants, states may provide post-service benefits including education grants or loans in addition to in-service remuneration. Senator John Glenn of Ohio has proposed having student volunteers contribute one-quarter of their salary to an education trust fund, which would be augmented by federal matching funds equivalent to double their personal contribution upon completion of their service.

And, of course, there are also proposals to restore the traditional G.I. Bill for military service to replace the current version and to establish a new program that would provide federal student aid in return for community service on the part of young men and women.

With specific regard to the colleges and universities, several options are possible. The College Work Study Program could be expanded both in funding and in the options available for use of the funds to provide meaningful work opportunities for students while enrolled in college. As an alternative to virtually all of the current proposals about Guaranteed Student Loans, this option seems to me to make excellent sense. It can enable needy students to attend college, yet curb the potentially disastrous impact of interest obligations on the large sums that some students now need to borrow. Loans should continue to play a role in the financing of student opportunities, but we need to be cautious about the negative consequences of an over-reliance on loans, in terms of the attitudes and opportunities of the nation's youth.

I believe that the future of this nation in an increasingly complex and competitive world depends greatly on the capacity and the motivation of its citizens to participate actively in service to and leadership of their communities and the nation as a whole. One basic purpose of higher education in this nation is to provide education for citizenship. I know that you share my concerns and are at work in many ways within your own institutions to address the problem. I realize that you cannot do this alone, and, as chairman of the Education Commission of the States, I am committed to working with you, and with the leaders from the federal government, the states, local communities, business, industry, labor and other segments of society, to ensure that our youth are equipped for responsible service to the nation.

Thank you.

APPENDIX

Biographical Notes

Bernardin, Joseph Louis Cardinal (1928-   ). Born, Columbia, South Carolina; A.B. in Philosophy, St. Mary's Seminary, Baltimore, Maryland, 1948; M.Ed., Catholic University of America, 1952; Ordained priest, Roman Catholic Church, 1952; assistant pastor, Diocese of Charleston (S.C.), 1952–54, vice chancellor, 1954–56, chancellor, 1955–56, vicar general, 1962–66, diocesan consultor, 1962–66, administrator, 1964–65; auxilliary bishop, Atlanta, 1966–68; pastor, Christ the King Cathedral, 1966–68; secretary, member of the executive committee, National Conference of Catholic Bishops–U.S. Catholic Conference, general secretary, 1968–72, president, 1974–77; archbishop of Cincinatti, 1972–82; archbishop of Chicago, 1982–   ; elevated to Sacred College of Cardinals, 1983; member of Sacred Congregation of Bishops, 1973–78; delegated member, permanent council; World Synod of Bishops, 1974,77–   ; member Pontifical Commission, Social Communications, Rome, 1970–72; member, advisory council, American Revolution Bicentennial, 1975; President's Advisory Committee on Refugees, 1975; member of National Catholic Education Association (chairman, board of directors, 1978–79). (See also *Current Biography,* October 1982.)

Boyer, Ernest Leroy (1928-   ). Born, Dayton, Ohio; A.B., Greenville College, 1950; M.A., University of Southern California, 1955; Ph.D., 1957; postdoctoral, University of Iowa Hospital, 1959; LL.E., Seattle Pacific University, 1980; Litt.D., Chapman College, 1971, University of Maryland, 1978, Rider College, 1979, Western New England College, 1979; L.H.D., Dowling College, 1971, Pace University, 1972, Fairleigh Dickinson University, 1977, City University of New York, 1978, Canisius College, 1979, American University, 1980; LL.D., University of Southern California, 1971, Fordham University, 1973, University of Akron, 1973, Roberts Wesleyan College, 1973, University of Rochester, 1975, College of William and Mary, 1978, Wilmington College, 1979, Union College, 1979, University of Missouri, 1979, Drake University, 1979, Virginia Union University, 1980, Temple University, 1980, Earlham College, 1980; P.S.D., Greenville College, 1971, University of Maryland, Baltimore County, 1980; D.Sc., Alfred University, 1973; D.F.A., Wheeling College, 1978; D. Paed., Yeshiva University, 1978, Eastern Michigan University, 1979, Doane College, 1980; member of faculty, Upland (California) College, academic dean, professor, speech pathology, 1956–60; teaching assistant, University of Southern California, 1950–55; assistant professor, speech, director of forensics, Loyola University, Los Angeles, 1955–56; director commn. to improve education teachers, Western College Association, 1960–62; director, Center Coordinated Education, University of California at Santa Barbara, 1962–65; executive dean, university wide activities, State University of New York, 1965–68; vice-chancellor, 1968–70, chancellor, 1970–77; U.S. commissioner of education, 1977–79; president, Carnegie Foundation for Advancement of Teaching, 1979– ; fellow, Battelle Research Center, Seattle, 1969, Wolfson College Cambridge (Eng.) University, 1976; member advisory panel, Institute of Higher Education, University of New England (Australia), 1980; member executive committee, National Advisory Board of the Center for the Book, Library of Congress, 1980– ; member, National Commission Financing of Postsecondary Education, 1972–73, Commission on Critical Choices for Americans, 1973–74, Carnegie Council on Policy Studies in Higher Education for Women, 1975; President's Advisory Council on Women's Educational Programs, 1975–77; New York State Health Planning Commission, Research Foundation; State University of New York (chairman of the board), State University Construction Fund (chairman, board of trustees); board of directors Arts, Education, and Americans, Inc., 1980– ; recipient, President's medal, Tel Aviv University, 1971; Governor's Award, State of Ohio, 1978; Presidential fellow, Aspen Institute of Humanistic Studies, 1978; Achievement in Life award, Encyclopaedia Brittannica, 1978; New York Academy Public Education Award, 1979; award Council Advancement and Support of Education, 1979.

CUOMO, MARIO MATTHEW (1932–). born, Queens County, New York; B.A., St. John's College, 1953; L.L.B., St. John's University, 1956; admitted to New York bar, 1956, U.S. Supreme Court bar, 1960; confidential legal assistant to judge New York State Court of Appeals, 1956–58; associate firm Corner, Wiesbrod, Froeb and Charles, Brooklyn, 1958–63, partner 1963–75; secretary of state State of New York, 1975–79; lieutenant governor, 1979–82, governor, 1983– ; faculty, St. John's University School of law, 1963–73; counsel to community groups including Corona Homeowners, 1966–72; charter member 1st Ecumenical Community of Christians and Jews for Brooklyn and Queens, 1965; member, ABA, New York State, Brooklyn, Nassau and Queens County bar associations, Association Bar City New York, American Judicature Society, St. John's University Alumni Federation (chairman, board, 1970–72), Catholic Lawyers Guild of Queens County (president, 1966–67), Skull and Circle; recipient Rapalla award Columbia Lawyers Association, 1976; Dante medal Italian Government–American Association of Teachers of Italian, 1975; silver medallion Columbia Coalition, 1976; Public Administrator award C. W. Post College, 1977; author, *Forest Hills Diary: The Crisis of Low-Income Housing*, 1974, *Diaries of Mario M. Cuomo: The Campaign for Governor*, 1984; contributor of articles to legal publications. (See also *Current Biography*, August 1983.)

DANIEL, MARGARET TRUMAN (1924–). Born, Independence, Missouri; A.B., George Washington University, 1946, Litt.D., 1975; L.H.D., Wake Forest University, 1972; H.H.D., Rockhurst College, 1976; concert singer, 1947–54; actress, broadcaster, author, 1954– ; author, *Souvenir,* 1956, *White House Pets,* 1969, *Harry S. Truman,* 1973, *Women of Courage,* 1976, *Murder in the White House,* 1980, *Murder on Capitol Hill,* 1981, *Letters from Father,* 1981, *Murder in the Supreme Court,* 1982, *Murder in the Smithsonian,* 1983.

GOLDENSON, LEONARD HARRY (1905–). Born, Scottdale, Pennsylvania; Grad., Harvard College, 1927, Harvard Law School, 1930; L.L.D., Emerson College (Boston), 1981; admitted to New York bar, Pennsylvania bar, 1930; practice in New York City, from 1933, vice president in charge of theatre operations, 1938, vice president Paramount Pictures, New York City, 1942–50, director, Paramount Pictures, Inc., 1944–50; chairman, president, and director, United Paramount Theatres, Inc., 1950–52; president, director, American Broadcasting–Paramount Theatres, Inc., (name changed to ABC, Inc., 1965), from 1953, chief executive officer, now chairman and chief executive officer, director Allied Stores Corporation; co-founder, past president, director, United Cerebral Palsy Association, Inc., 1949–53, chairman of the board, 1954– ; vice chairman, board of directors, United Cerebral Palsy Research and Education Foundation; board of directors, Daughters of Jacob Geriatric Center, New York City, World Rehabilitation Fund; founding member, Hollywood Museum; member, National Citizens Advisory Committee on Vocational Rehabilitation; advisory council, White House Conference on Handicapped Individuals; member, Motion Picture Pioneers, National Academy of Television Arts and Sciences, International Radio and TV Society.

HAIMAN, FRANKLYN SAUL (1921–). Born, Cleveland, Ohio; B.A., Case Western Reserve University, 1948; M.A., Northwestern University, Evanston, Illinois, 1948, Ph.D., 1948; served with USAAF, 1942–45; member, faculty of Northwestern University, Evanston, Illinois, 1948– , chairman, department of communication studies, 1964–75, professor, communication studies and urban affairs, 1970– ; president Illinois division ACLU, 1964–75; member, Speech Communication Association, American Psychological Association, AAUP, Phi Beta Kappa; author, *Group Leadership and Democratic Action,* 1951, *Freedom of Speech: Issues and Cases,* 1965, *Freedom of Speech,* 1976, *Speech and Law in a Free Society,* 1981; co-author, *The Dynamics of Discussion,* 1960, 2nd edition, 1980; editor, (series) *Protect These Rights,* 1976–77; contributor of articles to professional journals.

HOLLAND, JEFFREY R. (1940–). Born, St. George, Utah; A.S., Dixie College, 1963; B.S., Brigham Young University, 1965, M.A., 1966; M.Phil., Yale University, 1972, Ph.D., 1973; dean, religious instruction,

Brigham Young University, 1974–76, president, 1980–   ; teacher, Latter-day Saints Church Educational System, 1965–74; commissioner of education, Church of Jesus Christ of Latter-day Saints, 1976–80; board of governors, Latter-day Saints Hospital, Salt Lake City; board of directors, Polynesian Cultural Center, Laie, Hawaii; member, advisory board, National Multiple Sclerosis Read-a-Thon Commission; contributer of numerous articles to professional journals.

HOOK, SIDNEY (1902–   ). Born, New York City, New York; M.A., Columbia University (New York), 1926, Ph.D. 1927; L.H.D., Columbia University, 1960; L.L.D., University of Maine, University of California, University of Florida, Hebrew Union, University of Utah, University of Vermont, Rockford College; D.H.L., University of Maine, University of Utah; fellow, Center for Advanced Study in the Behavioral Sciences, Stanford, California; fellow, American Academy of Arts and Sciences; fellow, National Academy of Education; public school teacher in New York City, 1923–28; New York University, Washington Square College, New York, New York, instructor, 1927–32, assistant professor, 1932–34, associate professor and chairman of department, 1934–39, professor of philosophy, 1939–72, head of department of philosophy of graduate school, 1948–67, chairman of division of philosophy and psychology of the graduate school, 1949–55, head of all-university department, 1957–72; lecturer at New School for Social Research, New York, New York, 1931–   ; Internal Committee for Academic Freedom, International Committee for the Rights of Man, American Philosophical Association (Eastern Division, vice president, 1958, president, 1959–60), American Association of University Professors (former Council member), John Dewey Society, New York Philosophy Club; awards, Guggenheim fellowships, 1928–29, 1953; Nicholas Murray Butler Silver Medal of Columbia University, 1945 for *The Hero in History*; Ford Foundation traveling fellowship, 1958. (See also *Current Biography* October 1952.)

LEAR, NORMAN MILTON (1922–   ). Born, New Haven, Connecticut; student, Emerson College (Boston), 1940–42; H.H.D., 1968; served with USAAF, 1942–45; Decorated Air medal with four oak leaf clusters; engaged in public relations, 1945–49; comedy writer for TV, 1950–54; writer, director for television and films, 1954–59; writer, director, producer, 1959–   ; writer, producer: films, *Come Blow Your Horn*, 1963, *Divorce American Style*, 1967, *The Night They Raided Minsky's*, 1968; writer, producer, director: film, *Cold Turkey*, 1971; creator, producer: TV shows, "TV Guide Awards Show," 1962, "Henry Fonda and the Family," 1963, "Andy Williams Special," also Andy Williams Series, 1965, "Robert Young and the Family," 1970; developer, "All in the Family," 1971–1980; creator: TV show, "Maude," 1972; co-developer: "Sanford and Son," 1972; developer: "Good Times," 1974, "The Jeffersons," 1975, "Hot L Baltimore," 1975, "Mary Hartman, Mary Hartman," 1976, "One Day at a Time," 1975, "All's Fair," 1976, "A

Year at the Top," 1977; co-creator: "All That Glitters," 1977; creator: "Fernwood 2 night," 1977; developer: "The Baxters'", 1979, "Palmerstown," 1980; creator, developer, writer: "I Love Liberty," 1982; president, American Civil Liberties Foundation, Southern California, 1973– ; board of directors, People for the American Way, Constitutional Rights Foundation; member, advisory board, National Women's Political Caucus; member, Writers Guild of America (Valentine Davies Award, 1977), Directors Guild of America, AFTRA; emmy awards for "All in the Family," 1970–73; Peabody award for "All in the Family," 1977; named one of the Top Ten Motion Picture Producers, Motion Picture Exhibitors, 1963, 67, 68; Showman of the Year Publicists Guild, 1971–77; Association of Business Managers, 1972, Broadcaster of Year, International Radio and TV Society, 1973; Man of the Year, Hollywood Chapter of the National Academy of Television Arts and Sciences, 1973; Humanitarian award, NCCJ, 1976; Mark Twain award, Pub. Counsel, 1981; 1st Amendment Lecturer, Ford Hall Forum, 1981; Gold medal International Radio and TV Society, 1981. (See also *Current Biography,* February, 1974.)

LORD, MILES WELTON (1919–). Born, Pine Knoll, Minnesota; B.S.L., University of Minnesota, L.L.B., 1948; admitted to Minnesota bar, 1948; practiced law, Minneapolis, 1948–51; assistant United States district attorney, District of Minnesota, 1951–52; attorney general, State of Minnesota, 1955–60; United States attorney, St. Paul, 1961–66; United States district judge, District of Minnesota, 1966– ; member of Minnesota Society for the Prevention of Cruelty to Animals; member, National Association for Attorneys General (chairman, Midwestern Conference, 1957), American, Minnesota and Hennepin County bar associations, Citizens League, Greater Minneapolis, Minnesota Historical Society.

MOYNIHAN, DANIEL P. (1927–). Born, Tulsa, Oklahoma; B.A., Tufts University, *cum laude,* 1948, M.A., 1949; Ph.D., Fletcher School of Law and Diplomacy, 1961; LL.D., St. Louis University, and Political Science, 1950–51; M.A. (honorary) Harvard University, 1966; recipient, more than twenty-three other honorary degrees, 1966–72; special assistant to U.S. secretary of labor, 1961–62, executive assistant, 1962–63; assistant secretary of labor, 1963–65; director, Joint Center Urban Studies, Massachusetts Institute of Technology and Harvard University, 1966–69; professor, education and urban politics, senior member, Kennedy School of Government, Harvard University, 1966–73; assistant for urban affairs to president of United States, 1969–70; counselor to President Nixon, member of Cabinet, 1971–73; U.S. ambassador to India, 1973–74; U.S. ambassador to United Nations, 1975–76; United States Senator from New York, 1977– ; U.S. Navy Reserve, 1944–47; member, American Academy of Arts and Sciences, numerous committees, including New York State Democratic Convention, 1958–60, New York state delegation, Democratic National Convention, 1960; vice chairman, Woodrow Wilson International Center for Scholars, 1971– ; author (with Nathan Glazer) *Beyond the Melting Pot,* 1963; editor, *The Defenses of Freedom,* 1966, *On Understanding Poverty,* 1969, *Toward a National Urban Policy,* 1970; joint editor, *On Equality of Educational Opportunity,* 1972, *Ethnicity: Theory and Experience,* 1975, author, *Maximum Feasible Misunderstanding,* 1969, *The Politics of a Guaranteed Income,* 1973, *Coping: On the Practice of Government,* 1974, *A Dangerous Place,* 1979, *Counting our Blessings,* 1980, *Loyalties,* 1984. (See also *Current Biography,* February 1968.)

REAGAN, RONALD WILSON (1911–). Born, Tampico, Illinois, B.A., Eureka College (Illinois), 1932; sports announcer, radio station WHO, Des Moines, Iowa, 1932–37, motion picture and television actor, 1937–1966; program supervisor, General Electric Theater; president, Screen Actors Guild, 1947–52, 1959; captain, US Air Force, 1942–45; governor, California, 1967–74; unsuccessful candidate for Republican presidential nomination, 1976; US President, 1980– ; author, *Where's the Rest of Me,* 1965 (reprint 1981 as *My Early Life*), *Abortion and the Conscience of the Nation,* 1984. (See also *Current Biography,* February 1967 and November 1982.)

REHNQUIST, WILLIAM HUBBS (1924–). Born, Milwaukee, Wisconsin; B.A., M.A., Stanford University, 1948, LL.B., 1952; M.A., Harvard University, 1949; admitted to Arizona bar; law clerk to Supreme Court Justice Robert H. Jackson, 1952–53; with Phoenix law firms of Evans, Kitchel, and Jenckes, 1953–55, Ragan and Rehnquist, 1956–57, Cunningham, Carson, and Messenger, 1957–60, and Powers and Rehnquist, 1960–69; assistant attorney-general, office of legal counsel, Department of Justice, Washington, 1969–71; associate justice, United States Supreme Court, 1971– ; member, National Conference of Commissioners for Uniform State Laws, 1963–69; member of United States Army Air Force, 1943–46; member of Federation of American County Bar Associations, Arizona State Bar Association, National Conference of Lawyers and Realtors, Phi Beta Kappa. Contributor to law journals and national magazines. (See also *Current Biography* April 1972.)

ROBB, CHARLES SPITTAL (1939–). Born, Phoenix Arizona; student, Cornell University, 1957–58; B.B.A., University of Wisconsin, 1961; J.D., University of Virginia, 1973; served with United States Marine Corps, 1961–70; co-comdr., aide to cmdg. general Second Marine Division; information co comdr; Vietnam; Decorated Bronze Star, Vietnam Service medal with four stars; Vietnamese Cross of Gallantry with Silver Star; recipient Raven award, 1973; Bar: Virginia, 1973, U.S. Supreme Court, 1976; law clerk to John D. Butzner, Jr., U.S Court of Appeals, 1973–74; attorney, Williams Connolly and Califano, 1974–77; lieutenant governor, Virginia, 1978–81, governor, 1981– ; vice president, director,

LBJ Company, 1971–81, No. Virginia Radio Company, 1978–81; chairman, Virginia Forum on Education, 1978–81, Concerned Citizens of the Commonwealth, 1978–81; member, Southern Governors Association (chairman); Democratic Governors Association (chairman); Res. Officers Association; USMC Res. Officers Association; American Legion; Omicron Delta Kappa.

SCHLESINGER, ARTHUR JR. (1917–   ). Born, Columbus, Ohio; A.B., *summa cum laude,* Harvard University, 1938; member, Society of Fellows, 1939–42; Doctor of Letters, Muhlenberg College, 1950; associate professor, Harvard University, 1946–54; professor, 1954–61; member, Adlai Stevenson campaign staff, 1952, 1956; special assistant to President of the United States, 1961–64; Albert Schweitzer Chair in the Humanities, City University of New York, 1967–   ; member, Board of Trustees, American Film Institute; trustee, Twentieth Century Fund; awards, Pulitzer Prize for history, 1945, Guggenheim fellowship, 1946, American Academy of Arts and Letters grant, 1946, Pulitzer Prize for biography, 1965, National Book Award, 1965; author, *The Age of Jackson,* 1945; *The Coming of the New Deal,* 1958, *Kennedy or Nixon,* 1960, *A Thousand Days: John F. Kennedy in the White House,* 1965, *The Bitter Heritage,* 1967, *The Crisis of Confidence,* 1969, *The Imperial Presidency,* 1973, *Robert F. Kennedy and His Times,* 1978, and other works. (See also *Current Biography,* January, 1976.)

SHULTZ, GEORGE PRATT (1920–   ). Born, New York City, New York; B.A., Princeton University, 1942; Ph.D., Massachusetts Institute of Technology, 1949; served to Captain United States Marine Corps Reserve, 1942–45; member of faculty, M.I.T., 1946–57, associate professor, industrial relations, 1955–57; professor, industrial relations, Graduate School of Business, University of Chicago, 1957–68, dean of school, 1962–68; fellow, Center for Advanced Studies in Behavioral Sciences, 1968–69; U.S. Secretary of Treasury, also assistant to the President, 1972–74; executive vice president, Bechtel Corporation, San Francisco, 1974–75, president, 1975–80; also director; president Bechtel Group, Inc., 1981–82; professor, management and public policy, Stanford University, 1974–82; United States Secretary of State, 1982–   ; former director, General Motors Corporation, Dillon, Read, and Co., Inc,; member, American Economics Association, Industrial Relations Research Association (president, 1968), National Academy of Arbitrators; author (with T. A. Whister) *Management Organization and the Computer,* 1960, (with Arnold R. Weber) *Strategies for the Displaced Worker,* 1966, (with A. Rees) *Workers and Wages in the Urban Labor Market,* 1970, (with Kenneth W. Dam) *Economic Policy Beyond the Headlines,* 1978; also articles, chapters in books, reports. (See also *Current Biography* May 1969.)

THOMAS, FRANKLIN AUGUSTINE (1934–   ). Born, Brooklyn, New York; B.A., Columbia College, 1956, LL.B., Columbia University, 1963; LL.D. (honorary), Yale University, 1970, Fordham University, 1972, Pratt Institute, 1974, Columbia University, 1979; member, United States Air Force, 1956–60; admitted to New York State bar, 1964; attorney, Federal Housing and Home Finance Agency, New York City, 1963–64; assistant United States attorney for South District, New York, 1964–65, deputy policy commissioner for legal matters, New York City, 1965–67; president, chief executive officer, Bedford Stuyvesant Restoration Corporation, Brooklyn, 1967–77; president, Ford Foundation, 1979–   ; director, Citicorp/Citibank, CBS Incorporated, Aluminum Company of America, Allied Stores Corporation, Cummins Engine Company; trustee J.H. Whitney Foundation, Columbia University, 1969–75; awards, L.B.J. Foundation award for contribution to betterment of urban life, 1974, Medal of Excellence, Columbia University, 1976.

WERTHEIMER, FREDRIC MICHAEL (1939–   ). Born, Brooklyn, New York; B.A., University of Michigan, 1959; L.L.B., Harvard University, 1962; fellow, Kennedy Institute of Politics, Harvard University, 1972; served with U.S. Army, 1962–63; Bar: New York bar, 1963; attorney, Security Exchange Commission, 1963–66; legislative counsel, Congressman Silvio Conte, 1967–68; counsel, House Small Business Committee, 1969–70; lobbyist, legislative director, vice president, Common Cause, Washington, 1971–81, president, 1981–

WHEAT, ALAN DUPREE (1951–   ). Born, San Antonio, Texas; B.A., Grinnell College (Iowa), 1972; Economist, Housing and Urban Development, Kansas City, Missouri, 1973–75; aide, County Executives Office, Kansas City, 1975–76; member, Missouri House of Representatives, 1977–82; member, 98th Congress from 5th District of Missouri, 1982–   ; member, executive committee, Democratic Study Group; member, Democratic Caucus Committee on Party Effectiveness; member, Women's Congressional Caucus, Environment and Energy Study Conference; member, NAACP; named Best Freshman Legislator, *St. Louisan Magazine,* 1978, One of Ten Best Legislators, *Jefferson City News Tribune,* 1980, *Missouri Times,* 1980.

WIESEL, ELIE(ZER) (1928–   ). Born, Sighet, Romania; attended Sorbonne, University of Paris, 1948–51; foreign correspondent at various times for *Yedioth Ahronoth,* Tel Aviv, Israel, *L'Arche,* Paris, France, and *Jewish Daily Forward,* New York City, 1949–   ; Distinguished Professor, City College of the City University of New York, New York City, beginning 1972; Andrew Mellon Professor in the Humanities, Boston University, Boston, Massachusetts, 1976–   ; chairman, U.S. Holocaust Memorial Council; member, Authors League; Foreign Correspondents Association; U.N. Correspondents Association; author of many books including *Night,* 1960, *Dawn,* 1961, *The Accident,* 1962, *A Begger in Jerusalem,* 1970, *Souls on Fire,* 1972, *The Fifth Son,* 1985.

CUMULATIVE SPEAKER INDEX

1980-1985

A cumulative author index to the volumes of *Representative American Speeches* for the years 1937–1938 through 1959–1960 appears in the 1959–1960 volume, for the years 1960–1961 through 1969–1970 in the 1969–1970 volume, and for 1970–1971 through 1979–1980, in the 1979–1980 volume.